ADVANCE PRAISE FOR

Grifting Depression: Psychiatry's Failure as a Medical Science

"*Grifting Depression* by Dr. Allan Leventhal smacks you in the face and tries to wake you up. The book systematically dismantles the 'con' that is promoted by the drug industry and organized psychiatry to push medications we call antidepressants. Reading the book is like someone telling you how a magic trick is done. Once you know how the trick is done you will never be able to see the trick in the same way. Your new amazement will be about how you could have been fooled for so long."

—David Antonuccio, Professor Emeritus of Psychiatry and Behavioral Sciences, University of Nevada, Reno School of Medicine

"In *Grifting Depression,* clinical psychologist Dr. Allan Leventhal has written an exceptionally clear and persuasive critique of the use of antidepressant drugs to treat depression, as well as a cogent exploration of psychological alternatives."

—Irving Kirsch, Author of *The Emperor's New Drugs* and Associate Director of the Program in Placebo Studies, Harvard Medical School

Grifting Depression

This book is part of the Peter Lang Education list.
Every volume is peer reviewed and meets
the highest quality standards for content and production.

PETER LANG
New York • Bern • Berlin
Brussels • Vienna • Oxford • Warsaw

Allan M. Leventhal
with Sharaine Ely

Grifting Depression

Psychiatry's Failure as a Medical Science

PETER LANG
New York • Bern • Berlin
Brussels • Vienna • Oxford • Warsaw

Library of Congress Cataloging-in-Publication Control Number: 2021055783

Bibliographic information published by **Die Deutsche Nationalbibliothek.**
Die Deutsche Nationalbibliothek lists this publication in the "Deutsche Nationalbibliografie"; detailed bibliographic data are available on the Internet at http://dnb.d-nb.de/.

ISBN 978-1-4331-9283-8 (hardcover)
ISBN 978-1-4331-9179-4 (paperback)
ISBN 978-1-4331-9180-0 (ebook pdf)
ISBN 978-1-4331-9181-7 (epub)
DOI 10.3726/b18829

Peter Lang Publishing, Inc., New York
80 Broad Street, 5th floor, New York, NY 10004
www.peterlang.com

To Carol

Who are you other than what you do.

—Deborah Eisenberg

Contents

Acknowledgments

I am grateful to many people for helping me to write and publish this book. Most importantly, I want to credit my wife, Carol. Absent her unswerving support during the years it took me to produce a publishable manuscript, this book would not now be before your eyes. I also want to recognize my son Scott's contribution for his legal expertise and advice in negotiating the contract with the Peter Lang Publishers, as well as for his help in steering me through the pre-publication requirements of the editing process. And I want to thank Dr. Dani Green, the Acquisitions Editor at Peter Lang Publishers, for her availability and help during the evaluation and production process. I also want to thank Robert Whitaker for writing a Forward for this book. There is no more authoritative voice on this subject.

I must thank as well the readers of this book who gave me helpful feedback during various stages of my writing. They include Dr. Peter Roemer, Dr. Susan Drumheller, Dr. Walter Schaffer, Dr. Irving Kirsch, Dr. David Antonuccio, Dr. J. R. Leibowitz, Dr. Karen Kuehl, Katharine and Tom Bethell, Gary Gleason, and Carlo de Joncaire Narten. These readers represent an array of perspectives: several psychologists, a psychiatrist, and a social worker from the field of mental health; a cardiologist who brought a medical perspective; representing the natural sciences are a physicist and a biochemist, the latter having worked as a science adviser at the NIH for many years; a teacher and a writer-editor from the field of education; and a banker, from the world of commerce. My expression of gratitude in no way implies that these readers endorsed all of what I have written. They gave me their views, and their training and perspective aided in the construction and narrative of the book.

Finally, I wish to thank Jamie Leventhal and Toby Levine for their great help in solving the myriad mysteries I faced (as someone with little computer knowledge) in preparing this book for publication.

Foreword
By Robert Whitaker

When I was writing *Anatomy of an Epidemic*, I struggled with making sense of the STAR*D study, which Allan Leventhal writes about in Chapter 5 of this book. I am detailing my own encounter with this study because it illuminates the challenge that Leventhal has undertaken in *Grifting Depression*, and the expertise he brings to the subject.

In *Anatomy of Epidemic*, I was focused on investigating the long-term effects of antidepressants and other psychiatric drugs. There is abundant evidence that these treatments worsen long-term outcomes, at least in the aggregate, and yet, at first glance, the STAR*D results contradicted that conclusion.

This NIMH study was the largest antidepressant trial ever conducted, with the NIMH stating at the outset that the results would be used to guide clinical care of depressed patients in the "real world." The results rolled in, and the NIMH announced that 70% of the 4,041 patients enrolled in the trial had remitted. The key to this success, the investigators concluded, was the clinical care that was provided: patients who didn't remit on the first antidepressant were switched to a second one, and if that one didn't work, to a third, and after four such attempts, 70% of patients had found a treatment that worked for them.

Not long after those positive results were published, I overheard a family physician in the locker-room of a local gym explain to a nearby person that finally, thanks to the STAR*D trial, there was solid evidence that antidepressants "worked." "You just have to keep on trying until you find the right one," he said happily.

When I first studied the various STAR*D reports that had been published, it was easy to see that the 70% success rate was, in fact, a finding woven from statistical sleight of hand. When patients dropped out after failing a first, second or third treatment, the investigators—rather than chalk them up as study failures—instead calculated what percentage of those dropouts might have remitted if they had stayed through all four treatments (a calculation based on remission rates for the handful of patients who continued through all four rounds.) That turned a significant number of them into study successes.

There were other statistical machinations that had been employed to inflate the remission rate, but the short-term remission rate wasn't my primary interest. I wanted to know the long-term outcomes of the patients. There were 4,041 patients who had enrolled in the trial, and of this number, 1,518 had remitted during one of the four treatment periods and been whisked into a one-year follow-up. How many in this group of 1,518 remitted patients had stayed well and in the trial to its 12-month end?

In one of the STAR*D reports there was a graphic that seemingly showed these numbers, but I couldn't make sense of it, and there was no explanation in the discussion section that could enable you to do so. The best I could make out was that at most 800 patients—from the initial group of 4,041—were still well and in the trial at the end of one year. This was a documented stay-well rate of less than 20%, which, in fact, was fairly consistent with other research showing that over the long-term relatively few patients treated with antidepressants stay well.

Shortly after *Anatomy of an Epidemic* was published, Allan Leventhal, Ed Pigott and John Boren published a paper that thoroughly deconstructed the STAR*D study and made sense of the very graphic that had left me befuddled. Of the 4,041 enrolled patients, there were only 108 patients who were still in remission and in the trial at the end of one year. That was a documented "long-term" stay-well rate of less than 3%. All the rest of the enrolled patients had either never remitted, relapsed after remission, or dropped out.

I have told this story for one reason: It illustrates the extraordinary gap between what is told to the public about psychiatry and its treatments, and what can be found through a careful study of the research literature. The public had been told of care that enabled 70% of patients to get well; the data told of a stay-well rate at one year that was the worst outcome I have ever seen in a study of depressed patients.

At the same time, the STAR*D story illustrates the challenge that Leventhal has undertaken in this book. Our society has organized itself around a narrative that tells of great advances in psychiatry. Researchers, we were told, had discovered that major psychiatric disorders are "illnesses" of the brain and that new drugs brought to market in the 1980s and 1990s fixed the chemical imbalances that cause such illnesses. If this were so, given the complexity of the brain, it could be seen as the greatest medical discovery of all time.

And we, as a society, believed it to be true.

What Leventhal does in the first two-thirds of this book is explain to readers, with a thorough review of the relevant science, that it was all a grift. A swindle. However, when readers first encounter a deconstruction of a conventional narrative, there is a natural reaction: could this possibly be true? And so Leventhal begins where he must, with the publication of *DSM* III in 1980.

This was the book that gave us the "disease model" and served as the foundation for the narrative of progress that was then told to our society. Once readers understand that there never was a scientific basis for this model, the narrative starts to crumble, and it fully collapses with the dismantling of the chemical imbalance myth.

From that point on, it's easy for readers to get on board with details of the swindle. The STAR*D study? That just elicits a knowing wag of the head. Of course the public was told of a 70% remission rate with antidepressants, because if the real results had been publicized, then the grift would have been revealed.

The final third of this fine book takes readers into an exploration of a fundamental question: what do we know about ourselves? As a species? The disease model sold to us by psychiatry told of how we were little more than dancing marionettes controlled by our neurotransmitters: these molecules determined our moods, our behaviors, and our thoughts.

Leventhal presents a much different picture. He explores how animal life evolved on this planet, and how we humans learned to shape our behaviors in response to our environments. He writes: "Far more effectively than any other animal, we learned what behaviors worked under different circumstances, we remembered those behaviors, and we communicated this information to others of our kind."

It is with this understanding, informed by behavioral science, that Leventhal argues for the merits of therapies that take advantage of this capacity of ours. We can learn new behaviors, which can help alleviate emotional pain, and we can seek out environments that are more supportive of our well-being. We are not prisoners of our neurotransmitters, but rather capable of learning new ways of being.

That is what makes *Grifting Depression* much more than a take-down of psychiatry and a detailing of the harm it is causing us with its false stories. Leventhal asks the vital question: what should replace that narrative that tells of people who have chemical imbalances and thus are powerless to remake their lives? The last third of his book offers an optimistic vision of what is possible.

Introduction

Health, and that includes mental health, is an essential aspect of human life, and it has preoccupied individuals from the earliest societies until the present. Thanks to science, we have made critical progress in the areas of physiological and public health during the last hundred plus years, a progress that has, for example, changed our expectation of life span drastically. From the Spanish flu in 1918 until the Covid-19 pandemic in 2020, life expectancy has doubled. Medical care for physical illnesses has advanced dramatically. "Apoplex" (stroke) and "Dropsie" (swelling) have been replaced by diagnoses and treatments that are informed by science, routinely reducing suffering and saving lives. Infant mortality rates have plummeted and diseases that we had little hope of conquering at the turn of the 20th century, like malaria, tuberculosis and even leprosy are now eminently treatable and, in many cases, even curable. These medical advances were driven by systematically tracking health data and subjecting these data to objective analyses. Good health care depends on science.

This means that, as a society, we are acutely aware of the need to base good health care on sound scientific principles, and we have established protocols—or rules—that healthcare scientists and providers know are crucial. Gone are the days when diagnoses and treatments depended on custom, intuition and anecdotal evidence. Scientific protocols apply to mental health just as they do to physical health.

Any good health care practitioner who sees scientific rules violated has a duty to examine the transgressions minutely and to make every effort to correct them. This happened, for example, in the practice of lobotomy, a draconian and dreadful "treatment" for mental disorder that gained great popularity in the 1930s, 1940s, and into the 1950s. When the procedure did not kill them, it turned patients into infants, destroying their sense of identity. This did not prevent lobotomy from being embraced with great enthusiasm by the medical profession of the day.

It is the contention of this book that mental health care has once again taken a dangerous turn. This time, by a mistaken reliance on psychiatric drugs that often are more harmful than helpful. Doctors have been misled about these drugs to the detriment of patients. Depression is the subject of this book because it is the best example of the problem, having become in just a few decades and without scientific justification, the #1 psychiatric diagnosis.

Explaining what has gone wrong with mental health care is a matter of science. So, this is ipso facto a book about science. If it is about science, it is therefore about data, since science is about data. This should not alarm the lay reader. Basic scientific principles are eminently accessible, and I have done my best to explain them clearly. The data analyses are very understandable. Concepts are explained and applied in everyday language. The only prerequisite is an open mind on the part of the reader as well as a willingness to reason logically and, when necessary, to apply good common sense to facts.

The critical question at this juncture then concerns the qualifications of the author of this book. It is essential to share with you an outline of the training, experience, and focus that I believe have provided me with the knowledge to write this book which challenges the currently established and accepted protocols for the diagnosis, explanation, and treatment of depression.

Let me be clear: I am not the first or alone in my critical examination of a subject that is significantly affecting the lives of so many millions of people. This book quotes many authorities, whose names are more recognizable than mine. That said, I am the author of this book and therefore, the reader must be concerned with my qualifications.

I am an academic and a practitioner, now retired. I earned a PhD in Clinical Psychology at the University of Iowa in 1958, where the PhD programs in Experimental and Clinical Psychology were chaired by Kenneth Spence. Dr. Spence was a leading authority in advocating and conducting psychological research on animal and human behavior, both normal and abnormal, insisting on this research meeting strict scientific standards. He was one of the pioneers of research on how learning experiences determine animal and human behavior. For many years, PhDs from the University of Iowa ranked first in the annual number of publications in scientific journals.

My first job was at the University of Maryland, where I became the Assistant Director of the University Counseling Center and was promoted from Assistant to Associate Professor in the Department of Psychology. The Director of the Counseling Center was Thomas Magoon. He, too, was a mentor. Dr. Magoon was legendary in his field for normalizing counseling services to college students, exerting great influence in this regard nationally.

In 1968, I was recruited by Dr. Donald Bowles, Dean of the College of Arts and Sciences at American University in Washington, DC (AU), to initiate the creation of a new behaviorally oriented PhD program in Clinical Psychology in the Department of Psychology at AU and to expand and improve the University Counseling Center. Dean Bowles also recruited Dr. Stanley Weiss, an experimental psychologist, to establish as well, a new behaviorally oriented PhD program in Experimental Psychology at AU. Nine years later, after the Counseling Center and these academic programs were well-established, I resigned from my position as Director of the Counseling Center, remaining a Professor in the Psychology Department. Together with three colleagues, we established the Washington Psychological Center (WPC) in Washington, DC, an outpatient psychological treatment facility. WPC also offered workshops to mental health professionals and we supervised interns from local PhD programs who provided low cost or no cost therapy to those who could not otherwise afford treatment.

In my practice as a psychologist, I made my orientation clear to patients in a written statement that I provided in our first meeting together. I stated that my practice reflected a behavioral orientation to mental health care that had a solid research basis. I made clear that I rejected widely endorsed and accepted mental health practices that had been medicalized in the absence of good science, and that often were detrimental to patients. Those who sought my help who were taking psychiatric drugs were advised they must first return to their doctors and get off medication under medical supervision.

My background as a teacher has been invaluable in helping me to express some of the more complex ideas in this book simply and clearly. I have been very ably assisted as well by Sharaine Ely whose background as an editor, translator, and writer has made her capable of demonstrating even more ways to write this story so that it will be accessible to an audience of regular readers and undergraduate students less acquainted with the basics of the scientific method. She has been a sounding board and she has helped me elucidate the order and priority of concepts.

That said, I must leave it up to you, the reader, to determine both the clarity and the persuasive quality of what I am presenting.

1 Sadness and Depression

> *The current "epidemic" (of depression) . . . has been made possible by a changed psychiatric definition of depressive disorder that often allows the classification of sadness as disease, even when it is not.*
>
> —*Allan Horwitz, PhD and Jerome Wakefield, PhD*

Our understanding of how to diagnose and treat mental disorders pales in comparison to our understanding of physical illness. The commonly accepted explanation for this disparity is the great complexity of the brain compared with other organs in our body. Although there is some truth to this explanation, it has much less merit than you may think.

There is a far more compelling explanation: *Whereas medical science and practice related to physical illness is sound, psychiatric claims and practices regarding mental disorder are not.* Beginning in the mid-1800s, medical scientists began applying the scientific method to studying various diseases, discovering the physiological cause of many illnesses. Since then, our knowledge of how to diagnose, explain, and treat physical illnesses has grown exponentially. Over the course of this same century and a half, researchers also sought to find a physiological basis for mental disorder. Contrary to what you have been told, with the exception of only a few mental disorders (for example, Down syndrome and Dementia), there have been no discoveries of a physiological (medical) cause for the great majority of the mental disorders.

Nevertheless, psychiatry has medicalized mental health care. Vigorous efforts over many, many decades to scientifically substantiate their medical claims and practices have failed. Psychiatric diagnoses do not fulfill basic requirements of medical diagnostic systems. Psychiatric brain theories of mental disorder are contradicted by scientific testing. With regard to treatment, research results show any benefit derived from antidepressant drugs *is psychological, not physiological.* Moreover, the chemicals in psychiatric drugs (medical treatments) can be harmful, contributing to rather than alleviating mental disorders. Thus, *scientific tests fail to support the most basic psychiatric claims and practices.* Instead, the record strongly suggests that psychiatric claims and practices are medical because medicalization serves the interests of psychiatry and the drug companies.

A summation of this kind is very likely to generate skepticism. Why wouldn't you be skeptical, given that 40 years and billions of dollars of marketing have been devoted to persuading you to believe in the medicalization of mental health care. However, in this book I will review, one by one, the false claims that are alleged to be the basis for medicalizing psychiatric practices.

As the facts are revealed, the unmistakable picture that emerges is of psychiatry's fidelity to economically advantageous principles of marketing, not the requirements of medical science. Very few people, including doctors, are aware of the array of research results related to psychiatric claims and practices that have been found to be mistaken or fabricated. I have collected and assembled them to reveal the truth about what has gone wrong. The evidence is damning. Fortunately, there is a better, scientifically validated *psychological* system available.

For those of us conditioned to accept the authority of medical professionals, I urge you to remember that the scientific method is based on rules. Researchers who abide by these rules in how they analyze the data they collect are applying the scientific method. Researchers who violate these rules are not applying the scientific method; they are not reporting what they are studying accurately.

The task of invalidating what has been accepted by so many and by what appears to be scientifically established medical methodology may seem daunting. So how do I make this case? The case is based on the conclusions of highly respected scientists who have studied this subject objectively and *who are without conflicts of interest.* It is based also on detailed and comprehensive evaluations of medical research by one of the founders of the Cochrane Collaboration and Public Citizen. Cochrane is an organization made up of thousands of scientists worldwide who volunteer to provide reviews of the effectiveness and safety of drugs. Public Citizen, formed by Ralph Nader, serves a very similar role. And I cite The National Institute for Health Care Excellence, which plays the same role in Great Britain as an arm of the Department of Health. I also cite evaluations of research by former editors-in-chief of our most prestigious medical journals, such as the New England Journal of Medicine, Lancet, and the British Medical Journal. And I cite reports by science journalists published in major newspapers that fact check their stories (New York Times, Washington Post, Boston Globe). In other words, while I may express my own views, I am relying critically on objective medical authorities with unimpeachable credentials for confirmation and validation.

The reviews of these objective, respected authorities provide us with the best–least biased–evaluations of research results available pertaining to the diagnosis, explanation, and treatment of mental disorders. Their conclusions are the most trustworthy statements of what we have reason to know. As you go through the chapters in this book, you will discover that the scientific findings about mental disorders diverge sharply from the expectations that the media, TV, the internet, doctors and even your own experience have led you to have.

****

Diagnosis, explanation, and *treatment* are the three pillars of the science of health care. To explain how our approach to mental disorder has gone wrong, I will focus on this triad with respect to one mental disorder: *depression*. This is because the diagnosis, explanation, and treatment of depression furnish such clear examples of the absence of medical science behind psychiatric mental health claims and practices.

I will begin by examining the absence of science behind how depression is *diagnosed*. Whereas depression previously was a rare diagnosis, it is now the #1 psychiatric diagnosis. Why? At the heart of the problem is a lost distinction between *sadness*, a normal response to losses in life, and *depression*, a mental disorder. It has become customary for our doctors to tell us quite easily that we are "depressed," that we are ill, when in reality most are suffering from a *normal psychological reaction* to stressful life experiences, not an illness.

It may be hard to imagine that so many doctors can be wrong, but the odds are that when someone feels down, listless, has difficulty concentrating, has feelings of inadequacy and lowered effectiveness, is irritable, and has sleep problems—alleged to be symptoms of depression—they are not suffering from a disease or a disorder. *They are in pain, but they are reacting as should be expected to a loss encountered in their lives*. They are sad.

During the past year or so, the association between sadness and loss has been made obvious by the social and economic losses associated with combating Covid-19. Referring to the response as "depression" rather than "sadness" confuses things. The point is: Loss leading to sadness is very common in life; it is not an illness.

At this point, some may shake their heads. If it walks like a duck and quacks like a duck, what's the difference? Who cares about the semantics? If it were a question of semantics there would be no need for a book like this, but it is not a question of semantics. Sadness and depression are two very different creatures—even if they manifest early on in many similar ways. For centuries, the distinction was clear. It is only since 1980 that doctors have erased the difference—to the detriment of millions of people.

Let's examine what we have reason to know: Sadness is a normal, natural response to big and small losses in life; for example, the loss of an important relationship, income, status, or self-esteem. It is not a mental disorder. *To be of help, the focus needs to be on improving the effectiveness of the person's response to the loss and on remedying the cause of the loss.*

To assume that someone is depressed when they are sad is a dangerous misdiagnosis because it leads to mistreatment. In today's era of taking pills, it often means a prescription to antidepressant drugs. What few lay people and too few doctors realize, but what more and more scientists are coming to understand, is that depending on these pills can and often do make matters worse. They can cause those taking them not only to *become* depressed but for the condition to be *permanent* and *debilitating*; that is, for *normality to become abnormal.*

If many people aren't really depressed and if taking pills can make matters worse, then why, you may well ask, doesn't everybody know it? Why do doctors think that antidepressant pills are the answer to your state of woe or the state of woe of someone you care about? I can only encourage you to keep reading. By the time you finish reading this book you will know the answer to these questions. And you will know about an alternative psychological system that has good science behind it and has proven to be more effective.

If you have been prescribed an antidepressant drug you have an especially important reason to read this book to learn about what is known about the effectiveness and safety of these drugs compared to an alternative treatment, behavior therapy.

****

Two historians of medical science, Dr. Allan Horwitz and Dr. Jerome Wakefield have described the sadness/depression issue in scholarly detail in their book, "The

Loss of Sadness: How Psychiatry Transformed Normal Sorrow into Depressive Disorder," which was published in 2007. Dr. Horwitz is a Professor of Sociology and Behavioral Sciences at Rutgers University and Dr. Wakefield is a University Professor and Professor of Social Work at New York University. They are authorities on medical history as it applies to mental health care.

Their book was reviewed in the New England Journal of Medicine, a prestigious medical journal, by Dr. Paul McHugh, Distinguished Professor of Psychiatry at Johns Hopkins University:

> This book identifies a central problem that cries out for correction . . .. (Horwitz and Wakefield) elucidate the naturalness of various forms of sadness(. . ..)Horwitz and Wakefield describe how practicing psychiatrists gradually came to think about and treat specific states of demoralization and discouragement that arose from life contexts in the same way they treated pathologic mood disorders. They document the way in which the "imparting of pathology" impaired the effectiveness of practice and research in the field of mental health(. . ..)The authors note that DSM-III(. . .)medicalized human suffering, diminished attention to human meaning in the field of psychiatry, and hampered communication between patients and physicians. With the DSM, psychiatrists not only lost sadness as a basic construct, but also lost touch with these different contexts as crucial for the planning of coherent therapeutic interventions and research programs.

For 2,500 years it was a commonplace understanding that sadness is a normal, temporary response to loss. Sadness is characterized by emotions and behaviors that I cited above. These reactions are commensurate with the problems a person faces. For centuries we viewed this as understandable and appropriate. Family and friends gave support to help the person recover from the loss. Doctors and the public considered medical attention to be unnecessary. With time and social support, *most people overcame their sadness by replacing their loss or finding ways to surmount it or accommodate it.*

Depression, on the other hand, was viewed by doctors as a mental disorder because the reaction to loss defied reasonable explanation. It wasn't that adverse experiences hadn't occurred. The response was out of keeping with the provocation. When a person who failed to receive a promotion refused to return to work and stayed in bed for weeks or even months, something beyond the ordinary seemed wrong. The reaction was out of proportion to the loss, and the distress did not resolve within a reasonable time period. When such unreasonable reactions did abate, they tended to recur with no further cause. Little or no effort was made to overcome the loss. This made the person's reaction difficult for family and friends to understand. At this point they might urge the person in question to seek the help of a doctor.

It is important to understand that it was not the intensity of the response to the loss that determined the distinction between sadness and depression. It was how well the reaction *fit the context* that distinguished the two. Sadness can be every bit as intense as depression, depending on the severity of the provocation. Grief is a well-recognized example of this. If your beloved spouse dies in a tragic accident and you take to your bed for a period of time, this is obviously very different from the person who does so because they have not received the aforementioned job promotion.

Because loss is such a common experience, the number of people who were viewed as experiencing a normal response of sadness far outnumbered those who were diagnosed as depressed. Before 1980 (not so long ago), only about *one out of fifteen* people over the course of their entire lifetime were ever diagnosed as depressed and considered to be in need of treatment.

In 1980 this changed drastically. This is when the American Psychiatric Association published the third edition of its Diagnostic and Statistical Manual for Mental Disorder (DSM), called DSM-III. Two editions of the DSM had preceded DSM-III, DSM-I in 1952 and DSM-II in 1968. DSM-III rejected the previous psychological determinants of depression in favor of making the diagnosis on the basis of a list of symptoms we now know were unverified. Sadness, a normal psychological response to loss, and depression, an abnormal response following loss, became one: depression. A distinction that made sense for hundreds of years was gone. As was sadness itself. And this new entity, depression, was defined as a mental disorder.

Since DSM-III became the model for all of the subsequent DSM manuals, the diagnostic system instituted with DSM-III has been in place for forty years. The DSM is *the* publication that establishes the criteria for diagnosing mental disorders. It is used by doctors in the United States and around the world to diagnose patients as having a mental disorder, and it is also used by insurance companies and governments to establish disbursements. Let's be clear before we continue that while it is widely used and wields great influence, this doesn't mean that the DSM has ever commanded much respect as a medical manual.

As I have indicated, prior to DSM-III only about 6% of the population (1 in 15) received a diagnosis of depression during a person's lifetime. Ten years later, by the early 1990s, that figure had risen to 15% and by the early 2000s, to 26%. Thirty years after publication of DSM-III, *five times* as many people were diagnosed as depressed and receiving medical/psychiatric attention. The figures have continued to rise to a level where one in three people will have been diagnosed by a doctor as clinically depressed at some point in their lifetime.

With the publication of DSM-III, a diagnosis of depression was predicated on the presence of some of a number of listed "symptoms." According to the new interpretation, depression was indicated by a lowered mood and accompanied by at least three of the following for two weeks or more: low energy, restriction in pleasurable activities, insomnia, irritability, tearfulness, social withdrawal, decreased productivity, decreased attention, feelings of inadequacy, loss of interest in sex, pessimism about the future, or thoughts of death or suicide.

Previously, the behaviors included on this list would have been viewed as true of sadness as well as depression. Now they were absolute "symptoms" of a *mental disorder*. Subsequent editions of the DSM follow the same system (DSM-V requires five of these "symptoms").

This change (and some others) represents a shift of tectonic plates that has produced a veritable earthquake in society, not only in the United States but in the world. It has transformed how millions of people view their lives. We are often told in the popular press that this or that discovery has led to this or that new theory. So surely, we say to ourselves, there must have been a scientific basis for such a momentous change, for this new theory. There must have been a discovery. Not at all. As you shall see, the astounding fact is that this change was not made on the basis of scientific evidence.

Although it is not widely known or was recognized at the time, the data collected in the construction of DSM-III did not back up or warrant the changes that were made to diagnosing depression and other disorders. Many assumed that they were there, in data not yet published. The psychiatrists who constructed the manual claimed they had a scientific basis for the changes. They declared unhesitatingly and repeatedly that their determinations were based on empirical evidence. The qualifications of those who created the new manual, and the strength and frequency of their assertions were such that what they said acquired a bogus veracity over time. Contrary to the claims made, you will see that ideological and economic interests drove the transformation they wrought, not science.

Those who understood how to evaluate classification systems did not regard DSM-III any more favorably than previous DSM manuals. Such as the case with me. My training as a clinical psychologist made it obvious that the DSM was a classification system of little merit. All of the DSM manuals fail to meet the most basic requirements expected of medical and psychological diagnoses. The criteria cited are arbitrary and overlapping, within and between diagnostic categories, a clear violation of scientific standards. In contrast to diagnoses of physical illnesses, there are no cause-and-effect references distinguishing the disorders.

These defects produce poor agreement among doctors making diagnoses of the same patient. Here is the problem with regard to depression: Doctors easily find a basis within the manual to apply very different diagnoses to a patient. Diagnoses of depression are listed under the Organic Disorders, Psychoses, Neuroses, Adjustment Disorders, and as a feature to several of the Personality Disorders. One doctor may diagnose a patient as depressed with a psychosis, another that the patient is depressed, not psychotic, another that it is an adjustment disorder or personality disorder—very different conceptualizations of the patient's condition. The fact that the criteria for depression appear so regularly in the manual should not be surprising since they are the criteria for sadness, and sadness is such a common experience in life. Other doctors may not diagnose this same patient as depressed at all and cite different criteria in making their diagnosis. Doctors easily find a basis within the manual to apply very different diagnoses to a patient. In addition, it is not unusual for doctors to prefer a particular diagnosis. Because the system is so unsubstantiated and arbitrary, they do not have a problem finding "criteria" within the DSM to support their bias.

When I was in practice, applying a DSM diagnosis to a patient added nothing to my understanding of what was wrong with that patient. Nor did it tell me how I could be of help. Being of help was what was important to me. It was why I became a psychologist, and it was why the patient had sought me out. A diagnosis is supposed to assist a practitioner in helping patients, but the DSM serves no such useful purpose. From my point of view, the DSM was good for only one thing: It enabled my patients to get insurance reimbursement.

Most of the professional colleagues that I respect have come to the same conclusion. We dutifully filled out the forms for our patients' insurance and that was it. Some practitioners delight in debating the value of one DSM diagnosis over the other, but from an informed perspective such discussions are useless and even silly—like debating the medieval obsession with the number of angels that can stand on the head of a pin. Doctors like this seem so caught up in their own arguments that they are oblivious to the DSM's flaws, and sometimes to their own patients' needs. In Chapter 3 I will go over the data related to the construction of DSM-III so you will see just how defective this system is and how fraudulently it was presented.

****

Nevertheless, at this point a reader still may ask why the distinction between sadness and depression is so basic in its importance. After all, you want to recover from both and, as I said earlier, they manifest with similar symptoms. Let's look at the issue and try to understand why this separation matters.

Positive and negative emotions are built-in potential responses. Their occurrence is associated with different satisfactions and challenges to our sense of well-being. The psychologist Dr. Paul Ekman's cross-cultural research on emotion disclosed a universality of emotional expression. *He identified sadness as one of six basic emotional expressions, the others being fear, anger, surprise, pleasure, and disgust.* Sadness is a normal emotion. Emotions are viewed as normal when they fit their context. Their presence and strength are influenced by how we interpret our experiences. Since human beings are highly social animals, these emotions often occur in a social context. Thus, emotions are regarded as related to our successful functioning as individual and social beings. Within this theoretical context, the emotion of sadness was "selected" in a Darwinian sense to occur when we lose valued attachments, whether to people, places, social status, economic security, or even personal meaning.

Max Tegmark is a professor of physics and Scientific Director of the Foundational Questions Institute at the Massachusetts Institute of Technology (MIT). He has applied Charles Darwin's theory of survival of the fittest to the basic function of feelings. Dr. Tegmark has written that feelings are primitive mental representations in the human brain that instigate person/environment interactions related to survival behaviors:

> A living organism is an agent of bounded rationality that doesn't pursue a single goal, but instead follows rules of thumb for what to pursue and avoid.
>
> Our human minds perceive these evolved rules of thumb as *feelings* which usually (and often without us being aware of it) guide our decision making toward the ultimate goal of replication. Feelings of hunger and thirst protect us from starvation and dehydration, feelings of pain protect us from damaging our bodies, feelings of lust make us procreate, feelings of love and compassion make us help other carriers of our genes(. . . .)

Let's look at the confusion created by the conflation of sadness and depression that began with DSM-III. I will do this by making some comparisons with some other universal emotions identified by Dr. Ekman. Suppose we conflated normal and abnormal *fears* by suddenly deciding that fear is abnormal no matter what the cause. We would take the position that all fears are phobias and that there is no such thing as a rational fear. Anyone who was afraid of falling off the edge of a rocky cliff would be regarded as abnormal. Or suppose we conflate *pleasure* and *mania* by deciding that all joyful enthusiasm is mania, an expression of a mental disorder, that there is no such thing as normal happy excitement. That all those who freely celebrated a joyous occasion are abnormal. Conflating such emotions would be absurd, and while such comparisons may seem extreme at first sight, they are as we shall see, apt.

The distinction between sadness and depression is akin to that which we make between *rational and irrational* behavior. Being afraid of falling when at the edge of a rocky cliff is not the same as being afraid of contracting a disease by touching a doorknob (even Covid-19 poses little or no risk in this regard). Some fears make sense–they fit their provocation; others do not. Understanding this distinction is basic to meaningful diagnoses and effective treatments.

This confusion of sadness and depression is central to what went very wrong in the construction of DSM-III. Psychiatric authorities likened DSM-III to medical manuals of physical illnesses because it, too, based diagnoses on *objective* criteria. But the strength of the diagnoses of physical illnesses lies in the *scientific meaningfulness and the actual objectiveness of the criteria* that identify the different conditions. Basing diagnoses on objective criteria does not guarantee value.

A simple analogy illustrates this point: Suppose we eliminate the distinction between apples and peaches and call them both peaches. We can do so on an apparently objective basis of comparison. After all, they both are fruit, and both are round. Both are juicy, sweet to the taste, and have skins. And they both grow on trees. We would call this comparison scientific because we have developed a check list of objective criteria, and I suppose that anyone who had never seen or eaten either fruit might even find it convincing.

Anyone who had tasted both fruits would laugh and point out the differences between the two are more important than the similarities. They taste and look different from each other. The trees they grow on are not the same. They have different nutritional values. In short, they are different fruits. We have used objective criteria (criteria that actually are objective), but we have created a system (peach = apple) that is misleading. It is a *reductio ad absurdum*, a logical fallacy. We have entered the domain of pseudoscience. This is what the psychiatric community has done by conflating sadness with depression, and it is only because we are so very used to it that we no longer recognize its absurdity.

If you think about it, the conflation of sadness and depression is not only absurd logically, it is also *detrimental to mental health*. As Dr. Tegmark has pointed out, sadness plays an important role in our lives. It helps us understand what we value and thus it assists us in our future choices. It is important also because overcoming sadness can increase our resilience, and it can lead to a more generous understanding of our fellow man as well as to a greater awareness of our own place in the world. Learning how to contend with loss is of vital importance in life. If we construe sadness as mental disorder, we are unable to learn the lessons that it can teach. Sadness is a transitory state by definition, but its lessons can be lasting.

****

Let's now look outside the psychiatric sphere, and take a look at what some literary thinkers have expressed on this subject:

For centuries, how losses in life relate to sadness and depression has been the subject of literature, both fiction and non-fiction. There has been a long-standing recognition that we all have problems. Simply put, as R.E.M., the American rock band, wrote, "Everybody hurts." Lives are full of disappointments and personal tragedies that are not confined to any particular time in life. A common theme is that *the way we respond to life's travails* often defines us and can be an important determinant of the quality of our life experience and be the difference between health and disorder.

The distinction between sadness and depression has a venerable past in literature. Story tellers and writers have expounded on the differences between these two states by telling stories of people who face up to circumstances of loss and of others who find it difficult to do so and who are ultimately swallowed up into a sea of misery and despair.

Homer was one of the earliest writers to ponder these differing human responses to loss. In the Iliad, Agamemnon, the leader of the Greeks, demands that Achilles give up his war prize, the slave girl, Briseis. Achilles inner state erupts, and he retires from the war in a fury to sulk in his tent. He spirals downward in grief and indecision, indifferent to the war raging around him. We see the disproportion in his response when a regretful Agamemnon, worried that the tide of war has turned against the Greeks, offers to return the war prize and with it, further compensation if only Achilles will fight again. Achilles refuses. His state has detached from its initial trigger and, untethered, it has taken on a life of its own. He is depressed.

The Trojan hero, Hector, is the counterpoint to Achilles. A loving husband and father, he recognizes the injustice of the Trojan cause—since it stems from the theft of the Greek queen, Helen. He defends his country with deep foreboding but whole-hearted commitment. He is profoundly sad in his recognition of the disaster he believes his people are courting, but it never stops him. His responses are measured and unlike Achilles he does not sink into dejected passivity. He is never overwhelmed by his sadness and fears, and his responses are rational and never disproportionate.

For an iconic example of depression, we can turn to Melville's character Bartleby (the Scrivener) whose retreat from life and eventual death is never fully understood, but clearly signaled by his ubiquitous reply to any request, the famous line: "I would prefer not to."

Sylvia Plath's protagonist in the novel, "The Bell Jar," although not as terse, is also deeply unhappy, and while she has reasons for this state of mind, she also has reasons for satisfaction, and her misery seems disproportionate to her circumstances. She compares her life to being trapped inside an airless jar, and as the author herself does later, she commits suicide. The protagonist in William Styron's "Lie Down in Darkness" comes from circumstances that are even less favorable, a dysfunctional family, for example, but her deep unhappiness extends far beyond any expected effect and ultimately leads to her suicide as well.

These authors have created characters who suffer from depression. Each one, in his or her sorrow, has left the 'land of the living' where cause and effect can be traced to float untethered in a misery that has taken on an all-consuming life of its own.

Drs. Horowitz and Wakefield make the distinction between sadness and depression in relation to Arthur Miller's play, "Death of a Salesman":

> Consider Willy Loman, the lead character in Arthur Miller's classic play Death of a Salesman and possibly the fictional character most representative of American life during the decades following World War II. As he enters his 60s, despite his fervent belief in the American dream that hard work will lead to success, Willy Loman never accomplished much. He has heavy debts, his health is failing, he is barely able to continue working at his job as a traveling salesman, and his sons despise him. When he is finally fired from his job, he is forced to admit to himself that he is a failure. He kills himself in an automobile accident in the hope of getting his family some money from an insurance settlement. The tremendous popularity of Death of a Salesman on its introduction on Broadway in 1949 stemmed from Willy Loman's embodiment of the Everyman in American life who embraced the goal of achieving great wealth but found himself destroyed by it.
>
> Death of a Salesman received a very different response during its revival 50 years later. According to a piece in the New York Times titled, "Get That Man Some Prozac," the director of the revived version sent the script to two psychiatrists who diagnosed Loman as having a depressive disorder. The playwright, Arthur Miller, objected to this characterization, protesting, "Willy Loman is not a depressive . . . He is weighed down by life. There are social reasons for why he is where he is."

In addition, Ernest Hemingway in "A Farewell to Arms," argues that the experience of sadness and the overcoming of adversity *can have a strengthening value.* He famously wrote, "The world breaks everyone and afterward many are strong at the broken places." Leonard Cohen puts this same idea poignantly in his song, "Anthem:"

Ring the bells that still can ring
Forget your perfect offering
There is a crack in everything
That's how the light gets in.

And, in a recent essay in the New York Times, Laren Stover wrote:

> Sadness has a bad reputation. But I soon came to feel that melancholy–the word itself is late Latin from the Greek melancholia–is a word with a romantic Old World ring, with a transient beauty like the ring around the moon . . .. In pre-Effexor eras melancholy was treasured.. . .melancholy has been celebrated by Tim Burton ("The Melancholy Death of Oyster Boy and Other Stories," Johnny Depp in Burton films), Batman ("The Dark Knight"), Heathcliff in "Wuthering Heights" and Anne Rice's wistful, brooding vampire Lestat. It was reassuring also to see in the recent animated film "Inside Out" that Sadness, the gloomy Eeyore of emotions, saves the day with perky persistence of overbearing Joy. The American commercial message is not so generously inclusive.

Writers of *non-fiction* also have recognized the distinction between sadness as normal and depression as a mental disorder. Doris Kearns Goodwin, in writing her biography of Abraham Lincoln, cites the difference:

> Before I began this book, aware of the sorrowful aspect of his features and the sadness attributed to him by his contemporaries, I had assumed Lincoln suffered from chronic depression. Yet(. . .)there is no evidence he was immobilized by depression(. . ..) To be sure, he had a melancholy temperament, most likely imprinted on him from birth. But melancholy differs from depression. It is not an illness(. . .)It has been recognized by artists and writers for centuries as a potential source of creativity and achievement.

Whether or not Goodwin is correct in her assumptions about a hereditary basis for Lincoln's melancholy (an issue I will examine later), she clearly recognizes the difference between sadness as normal, and potentially helpful, and depression as a mental disorder. In fact, Goodwin also makes the same point that sadness in contending with adversity can be formative.

Eric Wilson in his book, "Against Happiness," has provided an example of this positive effect of sadness in this biographical description:

> It is 1952. A polio epidemic has just spread through the cold towns of Canada. A young girl named Roberta Joan Anderson is unexpectedly laid low by the disease. She is only nine years old. She finds herself in a hospital. The season is winter, just around Christmastime. Her parents and others, worried sick, come to visit her regularly. She is told that she might not ever be able to walk again and that she definitely will not be able to go home for Christmas. Roberta is pained to the point of tears, terrified and despondent. But then, just when her despair is deepest, she decides to bring Christmas to her hospital room. Though confined to her bed, she begins to belt out carols, sending her vibrant Christmas ecstasy abroad. Her horror of being divorced from the evergreens and the dances makes her sing all the louder. She is pained into song. Some years later, when she was in her early twenties, after she had, by pure luck, regained her ability to walk and had developed into an accomplished guitar player and singer, Roberta—soon to go by her stage name, Joni Mitchell, and also soon to be world famous—became pregnant. She decided to have the child. In February 1965 she gave birth to Kelly Dale Anderson, a girl. Young and confused and ambitious, Roberta, now Joni, put her child up for adoption. This experience of choosing to be separated from her infant shattered her. Much of the melancholy of Mitchell's early songwriting was informed by a pervasive sense of loss. As she later confessed to the media. "Bad fortune changed the course of my destiny. I became a musician."

Drs. Horwitz and Wakefield sum up by stating, "What our culture once viewed as a reaction to failed hopes and aspirations, it now regards as a psychiatric illness."

****

It is clear from the above that the conflation of sadness and depression goes counter to the received wisdom of generations. Going counter to tradition and received wisdom is, of course, not necessarily bad. In modern times, we have relied on the weight of scientific proof to banish countless beliefs and superstitions that had no positive effect on our physical and mental health or that have proven to have a deleterious effect. The conflation of sadness with depression provides us with an interesting reversal, however. The wisdom of the ages turns out to have a genuine basis, both psychological and scientific while the new and iconoclastic theory turns out to have, as you will see more and more clearly, a dubious basis indeed.

Let's look now at the *scientific research basis* for the conclusion that sadness and depression are psychological consequences of *how we respond to losses in life.* The scientific evidence is substantial. A large number of studies, dating back to the 1960s and replicated over the course of the next half century, have shown that stressful events, most of which involve some kind of *loss*, may lead to sadness and depression. Death of a spouse, divorce or marital difficulties, job loss and unemployment, poverty, social isolation, surgery (loss of health), serious illness of a loved one, and assault (rape), have all been found to be predictive of sadness and depression. Critically important is the quality of the response to the loss.

The research psychiatrist and geneticist, Kenneth Kendler, has studied how sadness and depression are related to exposure to stressful events, events that are characterized by losses in life. Although he does not specify the distinction between sadness and depression, he discusses the methodological problems in this area of science, and he concludes that losses of one kind or another predict sadness/depression. His research findings are extensive, and they confirm that the strength of the relationship between severe life events and sadness/depression is greater than that found for any of the genetic factors he examined. He sums up the relative contributions of genetics and experience by concluding that any genetic factors are weak and nonspecific whereas environmental (psychological) factors have "been shown to have causal specificity." In Chapters 4, 10, 11, and 12, I will review research which aligns with the conclusion that stressful life events, and the response to them, not specific genes, are the cause of sadness and depression.

Dr. Ronald Kessler, a psychologist, has provided a comprehensive review of studies that identify experiences of loss as preceding sadness/depression: loss of self-esteem, failure to achieve an important aspiration, financial loss, retirement, loss of an important relationship through death or rejection, loss of personal health or the health of a loved one, etc.

There is an unusual concordance among theorists and researchers holding widely divergent viewpoints that loss is basic to both sadness and depression: Freud's psychoanalytic theory traces melancholia to the loss of a love object. Harlow studied the effects on monkeys of loss of contact with their mothers. Bowlby, following up on this research in his work with children, devised attachment theory, which focuses on the emotional effects of separation of children from their mother. Sadness/depression was attributed to loss of that attachment. Skinner's behavioral theory attributes sadness and depression to disruption (loss) of positive reinforcers. If a man is attracted to women but afraid of rejection and avoids them, the quality of his life is compromised. Despite the considerable differences among these psychological theorists, they all point to loss as causative.

One of the questions that needs to be asked is how this body of *genetic and psychological research* could be ignored in the DSM. How did the substitution of a *medical explanation*, which as you will continue to see is without scientific verification, replace this body of verified research that points so clearly to the importance of loss and the response to loss as determining depression? How was it that pronouncements about the medicalization of DSM-III and the medicalization of psychiatric care, put forward without scientific validation and with only a bold conviction of rightfulness, affect the beliefs and practices of the general public so profoundly?

I will have a great deal to say about the roles played by psychiatry and the pharmaceutical industry in creating and maintaining this unsupported medical theory. Psychiatry's medicalization of mental disorder, which conflated normal sadness with abnormal depression, is the causative factor for the huge increase in the number of people diagnosed with a mental disorder. And, so has the number of people diagnosed as depressed and treated medically with psychiatric drugs who then qualify as being mentally disabled increased exponentially as well.

As all good students of science know, when there is an epidemic, there is a Patient-Zero. In the case of an epidemic of falsely ascribed depression, that role is assigned to Dr. Robert Spitzer, the psychiatrist who headed up the construction of DSM-III, the manual that conflated sadness with depression. The plague of this conflation, depression, is the poster child of his efforts.

Dr. Spitzer chose to ignore the science that existed concerning loss. This body of knowledge provided a *psychological* explanation for depression (loss) and he was a member of a group of psychiatrists who were intent on *medicalizing* the diagnosis and treatment of mental disorders as a brain disease. His conflation of sadness and depression was the first and most significant error wrought by the medicalization of psychiatry. In the next chapter I will discuss in detail his reasons for doing so, but for the moment, let us look at the how rather than the why.

As I have indicated, he created a diagnostic system that appeared to have a medical framework, basing the diagnoses on check lists of symptoms that followed the structure of medical manuals. But there was a significant omission in his manual. Unlike those medical manuals, *he could cite no physiological basis for the symptoms that made up the check lists*. By this I mean that there was nothing equivalent to, for example, the blood tests that are the basis for medical diagnoses. No such empirical substantiation existed for the great bulk of the disorders listed in the DSM. He set the stage for the medicalization of mental disorder even though *he had no empirical data to justify it*, no scientific basis for doing so. It was brazen and it was spurious, but it was, unfortunately, very effective.

Why brazen and why spurious? It was brazen because he knew that there was no scientific evidence for it. It was spurious because specifying the physiological mechanisms responsible for an illness is a crucial fixture in medical diagnoses. Diagnoses pertain to what governs an illness. It is how we know how to treat that illness. This knowledge is what gives diagnoses meaning.

Dr. Marcia Angell, at Harvard Medical School and a former Editor-in-Chief of the New England Journal of Medicine, has commented on this failure of the DSM to meet the standards expected of medical manuals:

> Not only did the DSM become the bible of psychiatry, but like the real Bible, it depended a lot on something akin to revelation. There are no citations of scientific studies to support its decisions. That is an astonishing omission because in all medical publications, whether journal articles or textbooks, statements of fact are supposed to be supported by citations of published scientific studies.

As the astrophysicists and science writers Neil de Grasse Tyson and Donald Goldsmith have written, "We can hardly comprehend the essence of anything without knowing where it came from."

Dr. Spitzer became a revered figure in psychiatry because the rhetoric surrounding DSM-III so elevated psychiatry's reputation. Yet in 2007, in the book authored by Drs. Horwitz and Wakefield, Dr. Spitzer acknowledged DSM-III's fundamental error of conflating sadness with depression and how this error has determined how depression has been misdiagnosed ever since. He wrote:

> Horwitz and Wakefield persuasively argue, as the book's central thesis, that contemporary psychiatry confuses normal sadness with depressive disorder because it ignores the relationship of the symptoms to the context in which they emerge. The psychiatric diagnosis of Major Depression is based on the assumption that symptoms alone can indicate there is a disorder; this assumption allows normal responses to stressors to be mischaracterized as symptoms of disorder. The authors demonstrate that this confusion has important implications not only for psychiatry and its patients but also for society in general.

This is a remarkable admission by Dr. Spitzer, given the profoundly negative consequences his re-definition of depression has produced. In the quote above, Dr. Spitzer admits that the conflation of sadness and depression, which began with DSM-III and has continued in subsequent editions of the DSM, *was a conflation of normality with abnormality*. Psychiatry, as you will see, has refused to acknowledge the fundamental problem with these diagnoses and with the drug treatments that are yoked to them. Few doctors know about Dr. Spitzer's acknowledgment and how little justification there is for the DSM's method for diagnosing depression (and other disorders). And many doctors are unaware of what is wrong about the psychiatric theories of brain disease and the psychiatric drug treatments that have followed.

Drs. Horwitz and Wakefield summed up this over-diagnosis of depression as follows:

> . . . the recent explosion of putative depressive disorder, in fact, does not stem from a real rise in the condition. Instead, it is largely a product of conflating two conceptually distinct categories of normal sadness and depressive disorder and thus classifying many instances of normal sadness as mental disorders.
>
> The current "epidemic," although the result of many social factors, has been made possible by a changed psychiatric definition of depressive disorder that often allows the classification of sadness as disease, even when it is not.

Examination of the manuals that followed DSM-III reveals that when changes were made, they continued to be unsubstantiated inventions and even increased in magnitude. Take as an example what has qualified as grief (bereavement) in the DSM. DSM-III considered bereavement to be a depressive disorder if it lasted for more than a year. With DSM-IV, bereavement was diagnosed as a depressive disorder if it lasted for more than two months (17% as long as DSM-III). In DSM-V it's two weeks (4% as long). Let us be clear. There is no scientific basis for any of these periods. The obvious conclusion is that Dr. Spitzer and his successors succeeded in establishing a diagnostic manual that is *far more representative of a business model than a model based on medical science.* In the next chapter I will examine this economic motive in detail, but for now let's look at the effects of this conflation in business terms.

What the psychiatrists who transformed DSM-III did not anticipate was that their new conceptualization of depression and the antidepressant drug treatment they ushered in would interfere so drastically with the *healthy process of problem solving.*

The rampant growth in the number of people considered to be clinically depressed is documented in a report from the Centers for Disease Control (CDC). The CDC reported that from 1988–1994 and from 2005–2008, the rate of antidepressant drug use among people age 12 and over in the United States increased by 400%. According to The Journal of the American Medical

Association (JAMA), from 1999 to 2012 the percentage of American adults taking antidepressants increased from 7% of the population to 13%. That translates to 38 million adults in this country taking these drugs.

On this point, let me give you another analogy. Suppose while driving down the highway your brakes suddenly failed to work as they should. You would experience fear. Would you consider your fear to be abnormal? Would you think that it meant there was something wrong with your brain?

No, you would know that your fear got your attention, but that it was supposed to. You would know that the way to deal with that negative feeling would be to take action to remedy its cause, to get your car's brakes repaired.

In this book you will learn how well this analogy applies to the misguided faultiness of how psychiatrists diagnose, explain, and treat depression. In the next several chapters you will learn about the verified absence of medical science behind psychiatric care. It is a shocking story that you will find easily understandable and as compelling as a crime story. Fortunately, later on in this book, you also will learn about a psychological explanation and treatment of depression that is based on sound science and proven to be more effective.

2

The Medicalizing of Psychiatry

The good thing about science is that it is true whether or not you believe it.
—Neil deGrasse Tyson, PhD

In 1969, Dr. Rema Lapouse, a noted epidemiologist, wrote: "If all persons who cough are counted as cases of tuberculosis, both incidence and prevalence rates will skyrocket. Fortunately, the laboratory provides a safeguard against that kind of diagnostic extravagance. Psychiatric diagnosis has no such safeguards." In this chapter and the next I will continue to review the DSM, and you will see that not only is "diagnostic extravagance" still common today, the DSM fails to meet the most basic requirements expected of a diagnostic system in health care.

The lack of a laboratory safeguards is just one of the reasons why the diagnosis and treatment of physical illnesses has far outstripped that of mental and emotional problems. There was a time when doctors who were diagnosing physical illnesses also used unverified and unreliable checklists of symptoms. Misdiagnosis was frequent, especially when different conditions shared similar symptoms, just as psychiatrists now mistake sadness for depression and regularly diagnose normality as abnormality. *Importantly, misdiagnosis leads to mistreatment.*

For centuries physical illnesses and mental disorders were diagnosed, treated and explained with a strange mixture of anecdotal evidence, superstition, and mistaken assumptions about the nature of the body and the mind as related to disease. Doctors interpreted symptoms accordingly, sometimes with coincidental success and sometimes disastrously. To give one example, you have read about how doctors used to believe that many illnesses were due to an excess of bodily fluids. They recommended bleeding patients to cure them of their ills. Some patients even got better. People can heal despite being misdiagnosed and mistreated. In a very few cases, and quite by chance, it was even the correct procedure since that is how the rare condition of haemochromatosis—an excess of iron in the body—is treated successfully today.

However, countless others were not so lucky. Women who had lost a great deal of blood in childbirth often died as a result of losing still more blood to the doctor's scalpel. George Washington died after having been bled over the course of a day and a half of 5 to 7 pints of blood to treat a sore throat, in all likelihood directly contributing to his death.

In the mid-1800s, Louis Pasteur brought such practices to an end. His laboratory studies demonstrated the value of *the scientific method* as the means for understanding and treating physical illnesses. Instead of relying on tradition, anecdotal evidence or intuition, medicine adopted the procedure—long used in the study of natural science—of formulating hypotheses, gathering data, analyzing the data to test the hypotheses, and by these means arriving at conclusions that were demonstrated to be trustworthy.

Pasteur's research showed that the *physiological cause* of a physical illness could be identified *objectively*, and he introduced *the germ theory* of disease. Throughout the 1900s, the scientific method led to great advances in medical science enabling the successful treatment of a large number of physical illnesses. However, there were no discoveries of a physiological basis for the great majority of mental disorders, including depression. Prior to the application of the scientific method to health care, psychiatry had embraced explanations of mental disorders that encompassed spirituality, superstition, and wildly divergent ideas of what it meant to be troubled. Naturally, psychiatry sought to reproduce the success of science-based medicalization of physical illnesses in the care of mental disorders, but their efforts failed.

Faced with this failure, in the 20th century psychiatrists promoted a number of medical treatments that lacked scientific verification, claiming they were science-based. In short, they made stuff up—"medical" stuff. Two systems of psychiatric theory and treatment stand out: *eugenics* and *lobotomy*. Early in the 20th century, psychiatrists endorsed the "science" of eugenics. Their advocacy of eugenics originated with Emil Kraepelin, who is regarded as the father of psychiatry.

Dr. Kraepelin stated that the mental disorders resulted from genetic weaknesses and promoted eugenics as the solution. His views took hold at the beginning of the 20th century when they were echoed by G. Alder Blumer, a prominent psychiatrist and president of the forerunner of the American Psychiatric Association. Dr. Blumer advocated limiting the reproductive rights of those considered "unfit" because of "mental illness."

Over the course of several decades, twenty states banned marriage by persons with epilepsy and those with intellectual disability (low IQ). State laws prohibited racial mixing to prevent the neutralizing of "better genes." The Supreme Court legitimized forced sterilization of the mentally retarded (more than 18,000 were forcibly sterilized). Various luminaries supported eugenics, such as the inventor, Alexander Graham Bell; the founder of Planned Parenthood, Margaret Sanger; The African American intellectual, W. E. Du Bois; the author, George Bernard Shaw; and politicians, Theodore Roosevelt, Herbert Hoover, and Winston Churchill . . . Thus, there was no shortage of prominent authorities endorsing the theory. However, the beliefs and practices of another politician, Adolph Hitler, led to the demise of this theory after World War II.

Psychiatry also advocated psychosurgery to cure mental disorders. Lobotomies were the most popular of these brain damaging psychosurgeries. The connections between the prefrontal cortex–the part of the brain associated with our cognitive abilities-and the rest of the brain were severed. In topectomy, parts of the frontal cortex were removed and in talectomy the nerve tracts to the thalamus were severed. The thalamus relays motor and sensory signals to the cortex. These devastating surgeries were heralded by psychiatrists as being science based and verified to be the best treatments for a number of mental disorders as well as for homosexuality. Medical authorities endorsed the procedures. Their originator, Dr. Antonio Moniz, was awarded the Nobel Prize for Medicine in 1949. Over the course of thirty years, 40,000 lobotomies in this country killed 5% of those operated on and caused many more to be severely mentally impaired.

Both of these horrendous biological systems of thought and medical practice were solemnly regarded as scientifically sound by doctors and the public for several decades, even longer, until it was discovered that there was no good science behind the horrors they inflicted. Medical historians have explained this medicalization of mental health care as examples of an attempt by psychiatry to emulate the success of the care of physical illnesses as well as an effort by psychiatrists to gain the respect of their medical colleagues. The only lasting thing psychiatrists demonstrated was that *rhetoric could succeed where science did not.*

With the discrediting of these systems, after WWII the medicalization of psychiatry took a back seat. Psychoanalysis became dominant for the next thirty years or so. Psychoanalysis, being psychological, not medical, is a very different theoretical system and method of treatment. The theory and treatment were developed by Sigmund Freud and his followers. The theory was presented and "verified" by case histories. The psychoanalysts make similar false claims that their diagnoses, explanations, and treatments are based on a respectable form of science.

Freud's emphasis on the power and pervasiveness of psychological factors in human behavior has been enormously influential. Novelists, whose stories often include psychological accounting for people's behavior, have been enamored with Freud's theory and helped to popularize it.

From DH Lawrence in his poem "Snake" to TS Eliot in the "Wasteland" to Philip Roth in "Portnoy's Complaint," authors have accepted (sometimes with joy and often with despair) psychoanalytic theory about the primacy of the sexual instinct and the importance of the unconscious as the fundamental determinants of human behavior. Alfred Hitchcock made a career of enthralling audiences by playing on the fears and desires of both his audience and the characters he created.

Insights related to understanding the power of psychological processes contributed not only to literature but also to the development of advertising. Although the marketing success that ensued did not verify the specific contents of Freud's theory, the basic point that human behavior can be influenced and managed by psychological means is now well known to be true. Critically, Freud demonstrated how important *emotion* and *storytelling* are in influencing people. That understanding has had widespread application by marketers in successfully shaping consumer behavior, although as you shall see in a later chapter these marketers now have sound science behind their application.

Nevertheless, psychoanalysis was not much help for why many patients sought therapy. It enjoyed a long run of popularity, but by the 1970s the treatment was in serious trouble. Woody Allen with his never–ending perseverations and neuroses was a poster child for its resonance in certain circles, but he also typified its failure since he was never able to swerve from the path of his ongoing anguish. Alarmingly for the profession, psychiatrists were failing to compete with other mental health professions for patients. Years of widespread use had provided a kind of public laboratory for testing the effectiveness of psychoanalysis. The results did not live up to the billing. Too often, the problems patients brought to their analysts were not remedied.

The ineffectiveness of the treatment became news. In 1975, Sir Peter Medawar, the Nobel Prize winning immunologist, wrote, "Psychoanalytic therapy is the most stupendous intellectual confidence trick of the twentieth century." Word spread among the public that psychoanalysis did not work. More and more people began choosing other types of talk therapy. On this playing field in which different psychological treatments were offered and health insurance honored each, psychiatrists, with their psychoanalytically oriented practices, were challenged. They struggled to attract and to keep patients.

A book about these times by two historians of health care, Drs. Stuart Kirk and Herb Kutchins, described psychiatry's growing disrepute:

> . . . problems with psychiatry were not only coming from the press, public, and policymakers, but also from social and behavioral scientists, who were raising new and equally ominous concerns about psychiatry's effectiveness as a helping profession.

Criticism of psychiatric diagnoses also became news. In the 1970s, DSM-II was the psychiatric manual that was in use for diagnosing mental disorders. Critics from all walks of life found the manual unreliable. I was in the full swing of my profession at this point, and as I mentioned earlier, neither many of my colleagues nor I took the manual seriously. Studies that demonstrated its weakness appeared widely in the press. One study, and it was representative, reported that psychiatrists who had the same information about a patient agreed on their diagnoses only 20% of the time.

Another prominently reported study used actors to secretly simulate patients. These "patients" told the psychiatrists who examined them that they were having hallucinations but no other abnormal symptoms. All were hospitalized with diagnoses of schizophrenia. These fictional patients had been instructed by Dr. David Rosenhan, the study's director and author, that once they were hospitalized to stop reporting any hallucinations, and to behave entirely normally. Yet the hospital's psychiatrists maintained the diagnoses they had given them upon admission, and they continued to be hospitalized as psychotic. This was a time when it was not unusual for patients to be kept hospitalized against their will. Dr. Rosenhan summarized the results as follows, "It is clear that we cannot distinguish the sane from the insane in psychiatric hospitals."

Even before these revelations, other doctors looked down on psychiatrists. Not surprisingly, doctors favor medical treatments over psychological treatments. Although psychiatrists had MD degrees, the treatment they offered had no relationship to their medical studies. Freud's theory regarded mental disorders as psychological in nature, not as physical diseases.

Today most people know that within medicine, there is a hierarchy of prestige and income associated with different medical specialties. These factors have an influence on how attractive different specialties are to medical students. Professions like surgery and cardiology are highly ranked, while geriatrics and psychiatry are less preferred and less lucrative.

As the public turned to other helping professions and psychiatric practices dwindled, ever fewer medical students chose a career in psychiatry. Its non-medical nature, relatively poor income, and its ineffectiveness contributed to its lower status. The New York Times described the profession's problems, reporting that the number of medical students going into psychiatry had dropped from 11% in 1970 to just 5% in 1980. Few doctors regarded psychiatry favorably.

****

Although the misguided biological theories and destructive practices related to eugenics and lobotomy had been discredited, that did not spell the end of biological psychiatry. Going back to the 19th century, doctors have prescribed drugs in an effort to alleviate distress; for example, morphine for pain, potassium bromide as an anticonvulsant, chloral hydrate as a sedative. Following World War II, lithium was prescribed for manic-depressive disorder (bipolar disorder) and chlorpromazine (Thorazine) for schizophrenia. A minority of psychiatrists continued to embrace a biological theory of mental illness and prescribed drugs. For the most part they treated patients with more serious disorders on referral from other psychiatrists. A fledgling pharmaceutical industry had begun marketing drugs to treat various mental disorders, mainly psychoses, such as schizophrenia. Drug treatments provided a less severe assault on the body than psychosurgery and sterilization. Medically oriented psychiatrists prescribed these drugs as their treatments for depression and other mental disorders.

Often, medically oriented psychiatrists worked in mental hospitals where their views prevailed. Many patients admitted to mental hospitals were diagnosed as psychotic (schizophrenic). Much of their behavior was distinctly odd. Some hallucinated and some had delusions; some were agitated and out of control; some were often in a non-communicative state. These patients were different from those who saw psychiatrists from the freedom of their own lives. They had been hospitalized because they were unable to function reasonably and independently. Aside from those diagnosed as schizophrenic, there were others who suffered from the physical effects of alcohol or drug abuse or from brain injuries.

And there were patients diagnosed as depressed, who fit with the DSM-II's definition I reviewed in the first chapter.

Although there was no scientific explanation for these reactions, psychiatrists assumed the brains of these patients must be ill for their behaviors to be so disturbed. Management of these patients could be difficult. Treatment was heavily weighted toward drugs rather than talk therapy. The main utility of these drugs was not therapeutic but operated to make patients more manageable. Mental hospitals came to be viewed as warehouses for the mentally ill. The conditions were callous, even cruel. Ken Kesey's, "One Flew Over the Cuckoo's Nest," informed the public about the awful conditions that existed in these hospitals and galvanized change. Beginning in the 1960s, in an effort to correct these abuses, many mental hospitalizations were replaced by community mental health centers, where patients were treated in out-patient facilities close to their homes.

Around this same time, these psychiatrists began treating patients diagnosed as schizophrenic with Thorazine (chlorpromazine), which suppressed their more florid symptoms. Thorazine was regarded as a wonder drug.

These medically oriented psychiatrists argued that mental disorder, not just schizophrenia, should not be conceptualized as a *psychological* disorder, but as a *biological* disease, requiring *medical* treatment. They advocated for a return of the medicalization of psychiatry, arguing for the prescription of psychiatric drugs as the treatment of choice for mental disorders.

However, even early on it was known that the positive results for these drugs came at a physical cost: heart attacks, pneumonia, uncontrollable tremors (tardive dyskinesia), and significant weight gain. Years later, the science journalist, Robert Whitaker, in his book, "Mad in America," reviewed the research reports on Thorazine, documenting how the drug companies skewed their research to hide how these drugs were no more effective than social/psychological treatments, which were safer.

By the 1960s, there existed a *scientifically based psychological approach* to understanding human behavior that was quite different from psychoanalysis. This was the viewpoint espoused by behavioral psychologists that *mental disorders were composed of behaviors learned according to objectively definable principles.* Behavioral psychologists are strict empiricists who are skeptical of theories that are unsupported by data. On the basis of their research, they concluded that the commonly occurring mental disorders are products of negative experiences that lead to the learning of dysfunctional behaviors (for example, a poor response to loss). By applying principles that grew out of carefully designed experimental and clinical studies they developed procedures for treating a number of mental disorders. Their treatment, called *behavior therapy*, was found to be more effective than psychiatric drugs, as well as psychoanalysis.

Several psychiatrists chose this psychological path and were collaborating with behavioral psychologists in developing *behavior therapy*. In the early 1970s, making use of the research that had taken place in psychology laboratories, Dr. Joseph Wolpe showed that he had devised a highly successful behavior therapy for phobias. Dr. Aaron Beck, also a psychiatrist, demonstrated that he had devised a very successful behavior therapy for depression. In 1977, a well-designed study showed that behavior therapy significantly outperformed drug treatment with depressed patients (80% improved vs. 23% improved, with significantly fewer seeking therapy six months later). Thus, in the decade before publication of DSM-III and psychiatry's medicalization, behavioral treatments had been shown to be the best treatment for two diagnoses of mental disorder.

So, at this point in time, psychiatrists had a choice as to how to arrest the decline in their profession. Behavioral treatments were being tested according to scientific standards and yielding consistently positive results. Research data were being published that showed behavior therapy was succeeding in a way that psychiatric drugs and psychoanalysis was not.

Psychiatric leaders could have chosen to psychologically re-tool the profession. They could have followed where the behavioral data led. They could have adopted an orientation that fit with this promising beginning. Or they could reject any psychological stance in favor of a biological theory for mental disorder, for which, as you shall see in Chapter 4, there was no good data. They could instead define mental disorder as a brain illness and advocate medical treatment. And that is what they did.

If all mental disorders, not simply the psychoses, were defined as brain illnesses, psychiatrists with their MDs and prescription rights would be indispensable, ensuring the security of their profession. Moreover, this change would have the advantage of increasing their acceptance by other doctors. If they chose a psychological theory and treatment for mental disorder, they would have to accept parity with other mental health professions. It would mean losing their pride of place as physicians.

Ultimately, most of the profession followed the choice by its leaders to medicalize psychiatry. It was done strategically, over time and, ironically, those who spearheaded this transformation claimed they were making the profession "more scientific." Looking at it from this remove in time, and knowing exactly how little evidence they had, it is clear that the changes were based on ideology, financial considerations, and anecdotal evidence and not on an appropriate adherence to science. In succeeding chapters, you will see for yourself the absence of scientific evidence for the medicalization of psychiatry.

****

The changes that were made in DSM-III were designed to facilitate a new version of a medical orientation. All of the psychologically tinged language was eliminated from the manual and replaced by language more amenable to a biological/medical orientation.

In the early 1980s, after many decades of intense and often passionate espousal of Freudian psychoanalytic theory, the official organs of the psychiatric profession declared "a biological revolution." Their *chemical imbalance theory* declared that mental disorder was caused by a diseased brain, a brain made ill by an imbalance of neurotransmitters. As physicians, they advocated medical treatment. Prescription of psychiatric drugs being marketed by the pharmaceutical industry became the treatment of choice.

With regard to the main belief systems that existed in psychiatry at that time, on substantive grounds the evidence for a disease viewpoint and for the value of drug treatments was no better or worse than the case histories the psychoanalysts cited for their psychological theory and practice. In other words, the science wasn't there for either position. But given the profession's dire circumstances, these fervent, biologically oriented psychiatrists were able to seize control of the American Psychiatric Association. Eventually they persuaded the Freudians that survival of the profession required them to act like "real doctors" and to prescribe medicines.

Since the Freudians were in the majority, it was not an easy transition. Most psychiatrists had chosen to go to medical school for an MD degree rather than go to graduate school in psychology for a PhD degree because they saw that choice as the way to make a better living, not because they were interested in practicing medicine. Practicing psychoanalysis or some variant of the treatment of it was what mattered to them. After finishing medical school, most psychiatrists were not interested in practicing medicine. They largely abandoned their medical training in favor of investing themselves in learning psychoanalytic theory and one of its treatment variants.

They had spent their professional lives, adding up to years of training and experience, engaged in this version of a psychological treatment. Years past medical school, with little accompanying experience practicing medicine, they were told their continuation in practice depended upon learning how to treat patients medically. Moreover, because the medically oriented psychiatrists had taken control of psychiatric education, the psychoanalysts now were facing increased competition from newly minted psychiatrists with a medical orientation.

Imagine yourself in such a situation. Changing your practice required re-educating yourself in an alternative viewpoint you had rejected. The choice would be an unwelcome one, but under the circumstances, you can see that your need to preserve your reputation together with having a family to support might influence a decision to go along.

Psychiatrist Peter Kramer's 1993 best-selling book, "Listening to Prozac," became the capstone that ensured the ultimate success of the medicalization of psychiatry. Dr. Kramer recounted case after case of patients who, with the help of Prozac, not only overcame their depression, they became the ideal selves they always wanted to be. It was the same claim the psychoanalysts made for their treatment; that is, they offered a narrative that has great appeal. To my knowledge no one else has ever made such an astonishing claim for Prozac or any other antidepressant. And, as you shall see, there is an abundance of highly contradictory scientific evidence. Ironically, by then the advertising world was showing industries how to apply *psychological science* to the *marketing* of their products. Drug companies use the principles they borrowed from behavioral research to sell their drugs widely for great profit in the same way that liquor companies sell whisky. Aside from Dr. Kramer's influence, psychiatry's successful medicalization is bankrolled by the pharmaceutical industry, which plants stories in the media and slants medical journal articles to promote a biological explanation and medical treatment for mental disorders. This part of the story will be told in later chapters of this book. We must first look into what medical science has to tell us.

To sum up, for the last 60–70 years, two systems of psychiatric care, each lasting 30 to 40 years or more, have dominated psychiatry: psychoanalysis until the latter years of the 20th C and medicalized biological psychiatry since then. Both have claimed a scientific basis for their practices. Each has offered an explanation for depression and a remedy related to that explanation. Freud was just as certain of his scientifically unverified theories as today's psychiatrists are of theirs. However, we now know that neither of these systems has provided scientific validation for how they diagnose, explain, and treat depression.

Fast forward 50 years to today and we see that psychiatry is no longer under attack. The percentage of medical students choosing psychiatry has held steady at about 5%. Psychiatric diagnoses and treatments based on a medical model are well accepted by doctors and the public. So how was this accomplished? Psychiatrists have answered that their improved status did not result from hype but on the substantive grounds of psychiatry coming to rely on medical science in diagnosing, treating, and explaining mental disorders.

****

So, to evaluate this claim, let's look first at the *quality* of the *medical science* that is applied to the *diagnosis* of mental disorders. Since the new diagnostic manual, DSM-III, was the instrument through which the psychiatric community declared it had established itself as a scientific discipline, then it is necessary to ask: Was there scientific verification for the changes made to DSM-III?

DSM-III was publicized as having been constructed according to a strict application of the scientific method. The President of the American Psychiatric Association declared that publication of DSM-III provided proof that psychiatric diagnoses were now as scientific as diagnoses made by other medical doctors. Considerable publicity accompanied DSM-III's publication, and the manual significantly elevated the status of psychiatry with the public and other doctors. Psychiatry was no longer regarded as medicine's hapless stepchild.

What are the facts? Psychiatry's legitimacy as a medical profession needs to be judged by applying the same principles used to judge the scientific soundness of diagnoses and treatments of physical illnesses. To do so we must first examine what is meant by *the scientific method* and what constitutes *scientific evidence.* I briefly discussed the phrase "the scientific method" at the beginning of this chapter. It is the *sine qua* non for any branch of scientific endeavor and it is the cornerstone of every advance in technology, essential to the understanding of many complex processes. Let's look at it in a little more depth. Its principles are not difficult to understand.

The scientific method is a system for arriving at conclusions *objectively.* It accomplishes this aim by means of the systematic collection and analysis of *data.* These data constitute the evidence to be studied. *Strict rules* govern how data are collected and what conclusions are justified. Often the scientific method entails the analysis of results of experiments that test *hypotheses.* Hypotheses are educated guesses. They seek to test the likelihood that a presumed cause and effect relationship can be trusted. This *objectivity* is what makes scientific evidence superior to anecdotal evidence. Anecdotal evidence is *subjective.* When things are decided subjectively there is no way of knowing if the conclusion is right or wrong.

The scientific method is designed to minimize the influence of an investigator's *bias.* Bias is the enemy of science because it can influence how the results of an experiment are interpreted. The following is a wonderful phrase, and if you think about it should probably apply to much else in our lives: The results of scientific experiments must be *falsifiable.* In other words, preconceived ideas can be proven wrong. The requirement of falsifiability was formulated by Karl Popper, one of the great philosophers of science of the 20th century. Falsifiability is the foundation of scientific experiments. It distinguishes the scientific from the unscientific.

Data, not assumptions, must dictate conclusions, including conclusions that conflict with the experimenter's predictions. When conclusions from scientific studies follow directly from the data and not to support a scientist's beliefs or, worse yet, deliberately falsified to do so, then and only then do they meet scientific standards for acceptability. This was the problem with psychoanalysis, where conclusions were based on case studies, not on testing hypotheses. And as you shall see, the data from studies bearing on the chemical imbalance theory (Chapter 4) and of the effectiveness of antidepressant drugs (Chapters 5 and 6) do not support the *theory* or the *treatment.* Before we discuss these important issues we need to look at some scientific principles applicable to the construction of DSM-III, that relate to *psychiatric diagnosis.*

Reliability and *validity.* These two variables are central when evaluating the quality of the conclusions drawn from the DSM-III data. A diagnosis is a kind of measurement. Just as a clock is a measurement of time and a scale is a measurement of weight, a diagnosis is a measurement of pathology, a measure of deviation from a norm.

If your clock is always five minutes fast, it is reliable. This is because reliability is a measurement of *consistency.* The fish you buy at a market is sold by the pound. You want the scale to be consistent. If the same piece of fish on repeated weighings registers as half a pound, then one and a half pounds, then one pound, the scale is not reliable. *Reliability is a statement about agreement between measurements.* The study I cited earlier in this chapter of 20% agreement among psychiatrists in their diagnoses, showed the unreliability of psychiatric diagnoses.

Validity, on the other hand, is a measure of accuracy. One cares about consistency, but accuracy is even more important. Validity refers to the *truth* of a measurement. If the fish you bought weighs one pound, you want the scale to show it as one pound. For commerce to function smoothly, the scale at the fish market should be both consistent *and* accurate. The same rule applies to diagnoses and treatments in health care.

A clock's validity is measured by how accurate a measure it is of Greenwich Mean Time, which is the established standard for time. The official standard for weight is the international avoirdupois pound. In science, the validity of a measure is judged by how well it *predicts* something of interest, such as how a blood pressure monitor has been verified as accurately predicting heart disease when it is present. The Rosenhan study I cited earlier in this chapter was a study that showed the absence of validity of psychiatric diagnoses.

Reliability and validity are *variables*. Researchers use mathematical formulas to assess the degree of reliability and validity of the measurements they take. By making use of these statistical tests, scientists can determine the merit of the instruments they are studying.

Now let's look at a different example that illustrates the difference between *beliefs* and *objective measures* taken from instruments. For centuries people believed that since the sun rose in the east and set in the west, the sun rotated around the earth. After all, it was obvious, wasn't it? There was consensus on this conclusion. People agreed about it. Therefore, the belief that the sun rotated around the earth was reliable because reliability has to do with agreement.

By applying the scientific method to his observations, Galileo found that the earth rotated around the sun and not the other way around. Astrophysicists, making use of improved technology tracking the movement of celestial bodies in the universe, have corroborated Galileo's conclusions, so they meet the requirement for validity.

You can see that there are several lessons to be taken from this discussion. Reliability does not guarantee validity. Just because a conclusion appears obvious, this does not mean it is true. Also, many and even everyone can agree about something, and it can still be dead wrong. Thus, it should be obvious that validity is more important than reliability. *The determination of validity is essential and requires its own separate, objective measurement.* In Chapter 4 you will see that the chemical imbalance theory of depression qualifies by one measure of reliability (people agree with it), but it is not valid (the data contradict it).

So, now that we have reviewed the basics of the scientific method as it applies to diagnosis, we can ask what the application of these principles determined about the scientific respectability of DSM-III diagnoses. Does the data back up what psychiatrists claimed about DSM-III when it was published and that they have continued to believe about the DSM right up to today? That will be the subject of the next chapter.

****

However, before leaving this discussion of the scientific method, I want to comment on the appeal of anecdotal evidence. Anecdotal evidence is a rich source of ideas. In becoming adults, we take lessons from our experience that usually are correct, but sometimes are not, especially regarding cause-and-effect relationships which can be difficult to discern. Many of our assessments are governed by anecdotal evidence. As I have indicated, anecdotal evidence refers to beliefs that are subjective. They are attempts to make sense of our experience, but they are not falsifiable. I have referred to psychoanalytic theory and to Dr. Kramer's book as examples of anecdotal evidence. Opinions of therapists about the success of their efforts are anecdotal; they are subjective, not objective. My cousin drank carrot juice for a month, and it cured her sciatica, is an anecdote. It does nothing to prove the efficacy of carrot juice in curing sciatica. Many other factors might have come into play that my cousin did not consider.

Someone else, also with a back problem, began practicing Pilates and concluded this exercise eliminated her back pain. Another felt better after buying a new mattress. Are any of them right, all of them right, or none of them, right? Had they identified what reduced their pain or was it coincidence? We don't know the answer for certain because this is a malady where medical science is weak. Doctors have insufficient knowledge to provide a valid accounting for many people's back pain. When science is lacking, anecdotal evidence flourishes. Welcome to the world of mental health and mental disorder, where even less scientific evidence exists to justify current psychiatric diagnoses, explanations, and drug prescriptions. In a chapter that follows I will examine how conflicts of interest have fostered egregious departures from the dictates of the scientific method and have adversely affected mental health care.

Neil DeGrasse Tyson is an astrophysicist at the American Museum of Natural History and director of the Hayden Planetarium. He is the author of a number of books explaining science to the public. He has written,

> Science is not just about seeing, it's about measuring, preferably with something that's not your own eyes, which are inextricably conjoined with the baggage of your brain. That baggage is more often than not a satchel of preconceived notions, and outright bias.

Quite often in life, there is a dangerous inclination to balk at the reins of scientific testing and to embrace anecdotal evidence instead. We have great reason to know this is untrustworthy. When matters are decided scientifically, the observations that are the stuff of anecdotal evidence are the source of *hypotheses* tested by the systematic collection of *data.* With respect to the subject of this book, the value attributed to a drug may be related to the passage of time, which brings about its own healing. Or it may be related to the power of the mind as evidenced by the placebo effect. Or other unrecognized factors, including those that are accidental. There is an abundance of scientific evidence for these alternative explanations, rather than any benefit coming from the chemicals in these drugs. As you will see, the best results occur when there is purposeful action *dictated by data*. This is the basis for behavior therapy, which I will discuss in the last three chapters of this book.

In my work with patients, I found that when patients are given the opportunity to operate on the basis of data, presented logically as it relates to their behavior, they readily take to this approach. Behavioral data concerning the causation of distress, accumulated systematically in the course of therapy, are more persuasive than suppositions. If given the choice, people prefer verifiability. In therapy, after a number of sessions, I would sit side by side with my patients and diagram on paper the behavioral connections so that we could examine together the processes I had observed. That formulation was my "prescription" for what changes needed to be made for a resolution of the problem.

My patients pursued testing what I had suggested even when, in the short run, this was discomforting. They found in the end that their trust and their efforts paid off. The process was self-enhancing. If given the opportunity, we prefer data-driven explanations to anecdotal ones, in large part, because they are so prescriptive.

As convincing as it may sometimes seem, anecdotal evidence is untrustworthy. It is not prescriptive. As Thomas Boswell, the noted sports columnist for the Washington Post, has asked, "Are we going to believe the facts or our lyin' eyes?"

3

The DSM-III Data: Truth vs. Truthiness

What was at stake (in developing DSM-III) was the fate of the psychiatric profession and the enormous, multibillion dollar mental health industry.

—Stuart Kirk, PhD and Herb Kutchins, PhD

Health practitioners have catalogued diseases and their treatments for centuries. These catalogues were little more than specialized even arcane lists that were relevant only to medical practitioners. Little by little, the use of these catalogues has changed. In post-World War II Europe and the United States, they have become the instruments for Western governments to define public health issues and for insurance companies to determine payouts. In our day, diagnostic manuals have achieved vast economic and political importance. This is strikingly evident with respect to the DSM, the diagnostic manual for mental disorders. DSM-III played a special role in elevating the DSM's prominence.

Before we examine together the scientific evidence regarding the reliability and validity of DSM-III, let's review the impact it had on the medicalization of mental disorders. This will give us a better perspective on its effect and on its worth.

The narrative that accompanied publication of DSM-III emphasized two points: the manual was constructed by a strict application of the scientific method and the manual's diagnoses were as medical as those rendered by other doctors. Jack Weinberg, the President of the American Psychiatric Association at that time said that the revision provided proof that psychiatric diagnoses were now as scientifically trustworthy as diagnoses made by primary care doctors. Dr. Weinberg stated that DSM-III enabled the profession of psychiatry to operate as a full-fledged medical specialty. Dr. Gerald Klerman, who was Director of the Alcohol, Drug, and Mental Health Administration, was one of psychiatry's chief spokespersons at the time. He stated,

> The decision of the APA (American Psychiatric Association) to develop DSM-III and then to promulgate its use represents a significant reaffirmation on the part of American psychiatry to its medical identity and its commitment to scientific medicine.

Take note of what they both emphasize: *DSM-III's commitment to science and its medical identity* because, as you shall soon see in this chapter and the next, DSM-III manifests neither of these.

Within a short time, the bulk of the psychiatric community adopted the new brain disease theory, which soon accompanied the publication of the new manual. Other doctors did, too, as did the public. Prescription of psychiatric drugs became the treatment of choice. People became invested in a medical viewpoint as increasing numbers of them took these drugs.

The chemical imbalance theory of depression soon became common currency. Magazines popularized it and touted it in commercials. Pharmaceutical companies and the psychiatric community presented the theory as a *fait accompli* to other doctors. The public, along with many medical experts, began to take it for granted that we suffered from what was now called "depression" because something was wrong with the way that our brain worked; that is to say, we were no longer sad because of the effects of negative events in our lives. We were depressed because our brains did not function correctly. *Our brains were ill.*

The National Institute of Mental Health (NIMH), which is led by psychiatrists, actively endorsed DSM-III's merit and selectively favored proposals of studies of drug treatments for DSM-III diagnoses. In addition, to cement the change from a psychological to a medical viewpoint, they re-organized the institute. At that time, the NIMH had two co-equal offices, one for processing grant applications for biologically oriented research, the other for processing psychologically oriented research proposals. Shortly after publication of DSM-III, the office that handled grant applications for psychological research was eliminated.

Medical science advancement was in the news. A book aimed at the general public described the great progress that had been made in the diagnosis and treatment of physical illnesses as a result of scientific advances. A psychiatrist, Dr. Jerrold Maxmen, following in those footsteps, wrote a book for the general public extolling the revolutionary value of DSM-III. He described the new diagnostic manual as being a major scientific advancement in psychiatry's medical care for mental disorders. He wrote,

> On July 1, 1980, the ascendance of scientific psychiatry became official. For on this day, the APA published a radically different system for psychiatric diagnosis called . . . DSM-III. By adopting the scientifically based DSM-III as its official system for diagnosis, American psychiatrists broke with a fifty year tradition of using psychoanalytically based diagnoses. Perhaps more than any other single event, the publication of DSM-III demonstrated that American Psychiatry had indeed undergone a revolution.

In short, the rhetoric about DSM-III hit the psychiatric and medical community in 1980 like a tidal wave, upending established beliefs and practices. Over a few short years, the effect rippled out, the number of people being treated medically with psychiatric drugs increased significantly. This was particularly true for diagnoses of depression and prescription of antidepressant drugs. These developments enhanced the prominence of the psychiatric profession and created widespread changes in insurance and government health policies. The medicalization of psychiatry had succeeded, probably beyond the wildest dreams of the psychiatrists who were responsible for it. In the next chapter you will see that there was no scientific merit to the studies that supposedly justified the medical theory for depression, but first let's look at diagnoses.

****

We come now to the critical issue: Did the contents of DSM-III justify the enormous impact it had on the diagnosing of mental disorders? In other words, did the construction of DSM-III provide a sound basis for the claims that the manual had established a new science and medical basis for psychiatric diagnoses? Were the diagnoses in DSM-III valid? Were they reliable?

In addressing these questions, it is important to understand the chain of events and to point out that despite the rush to laud DSM-III as a scientific breakthrough, the actual research data for DSM-III were not released at the time of its publication. The health community, as a whole, just relied on the reputation of the men who were responsible for DSM-III and the subsequent propagation of a biological theory for the diagnosis and treatment of mental disorders. The implication seems to be that if such prominent psychiatrists did not have ample scientific proof, they would not have initiated such changes. Surely, they would not, could not have done so with such absolute conviction. Still, why did no one request the data to verify the sweeping assertions made by the architect and proponents of DSM-III?

It is not a question we can answer. Perhaps they believed that no one could step forward with such assurance unless they had incontrovertible proof. Evidently, no one wanted to challenge the psychiatrists who lauded DSM-III since their reputations made them redoubtable. Certainly, the great fanfare surrounding the new manual contributed to its acceptance.

Fortunately, ten years later there arose two of those curious and industrious souls who are not content with accepting the popular "wisdom" and who want to see and know for themselves the basis for things that happen. Such were two reputable and respected researchers and scholars, Dr. Stuart Kirk and Dr. Herb Kutchins. By means of a Freedom of Information Act request, they gained access to the data that went into the construction of DSM-III. They could do so because, under the Freedom of Information Act, government funded projects must release their data when a request is filed. Since DSM-III was a government funded project through the National Institute of Mental Health (NIMH), the data in the research fell under this ruling.

Dr. Kirk is professor emeritus at the Luskin School of Public Affairs, University of California, Los Angeles. He previously was Dean of the School of Social Welfare at the State University of New York at Albany and a professor at the Columbia University School of Social Work. Dr. Kutchins is a professor in the School of Health and Human Services at California State University, Sacramento, California, and holds the Marjorie Crump chair in the School of Social Policy at the University of California, Los Angeles.

Drs. Kirk and Kutchins discovered something as surprising as it was unexpected, and they published their findings in 1992. Not only had no new scientific discoveries justified the change in how depression was diagnosed, *no new scientific data were behind any of the diagnoses listed in DSM-III.* There was no empirical basis for the changes that were made in how the disorders were diagnosed. *Nor were decisions about the disorders in the manual medically based. No new medical data were cited for the diagnoses.* They were based simply on a psychiatric preference for a biological (medical) explanation for mental disorder as opposed to a psychological explanation.

The British psychologist, Dr. Lucy Johnston, has written about the absence of science behind the construction of DSM-III and all of the subsequent DSM manuals. She points out that beginning with DSM-III, DSM diagnoses *have been voted into existence by committees.* Medical manuals for physical illnesses are objective. They are based on empirical physical data; they are not based on doctors' unverified personal opinions. The claim that DSM-III matched the science of medical manuals for physical illnesses, which was the cornerstone for the acceptance of DSM-III by doctors, the public, and the media, was false. Dr. Lapouse's observation is as true today as it was in 1969.

As I have reviewed, explanations not backed up by empirical physical data would be considered anathema for any other medical diagnostic manual. Nevertheless, by these means DSM-III became the flagship for the medicalizing of psychiatry.

Let me repeat: Following the advent of the scientific method in the latter years of the 19th century, diseases of the body have been diagnosed on the basis of scientific evidence. Diagnoses and treatments are based on knowledge of the cause and course of a disease. *They evolve from an empirical base.* Diagnoses are not based on unsupported opinions held by those constructing the manuals. DSM-III turned out to be the cuckoo in the bird's nest.

Although their book was published more than 25 years ago, you probably never heard about what Drs. Kirk and Kutchins found, which completely refute the claims made by psychiatrists then and ever since for the scientific worth of the DSM. *The success with which these findings have been buried is significant in its own right*; it is the first indication I will be citing of the control psychiatry and Big Pharma have been able to wield in managing information contradictory to their interests.

The construction of DSM-III was put under the direction of Robert Spitzer, professor of psychiatry at Columbia University. Dr. Spitzer had achieved some notice in the 1970s because of his efforts to improve the reliability of psychiatric diagnoses by developing a structured interview for diagnosing depression.

After reviewing the construction of DSM-III, here is what Drs. Kirk and Kutchins had to say about what they found out:

> By developing a massive superstructure consisting of dozens of committees, and involving hundreds of participants, the Task Force created the illusion that the development of the manual was the result of an enormous research effort. Despite the widespread participation of psychiatrists and other mental health professionals, actual decisions were made by a small group of participants in the Task Force. Research, including the data generated by a large federally supported study, was

> used selectively to support the goals of the Task Force and to undermine the objections of their opponents, particularly psychotherapists with a Freudian orientation, who constituted the majority of the APA (American Psychiatric Association). The eventual coup(. . .)successfully used the language, paradigms, and technology of research to(. . .)(present DSM-III) not only as a solution to the problem of psychiatric reliability, but as the embodiment of a new science of psychiatry.

In his own words, describing the construction of DSM-III, Dr. Spitzer stated (in an interview in 1989) that he selected people to serve on the Task Force that "he was comfortable with" and although there were complaints that he ran things in a "high handed manner," he declared, "I could just get my way by sweet talking and whatnot." In another interview, quoted in one of his obituaries, "he recalled that the publication of DSM-III had been 'wonderful for the mood of psychiatry' helping professionals to feel: 'Gee, we're more scientific. We're part of medicine.' "

In 2012, in an interview with Dr. James Davies, the British psychologist and author, Dr. Spitzer *acknowledged the absence of any known physiological basis for the great bulk of the mental disorders listed in DSM-III*: "There are only a handful of disorders known to have a clear biological cause . . . known as the organic disorders . . .." Otherwise, Dr. Spitzer admitted, there were no physiological markers for the great majority of the disorders in DSM-III.

Initially, it was entirely possible that Dr. Spitzer and his colleagues hoped that it was only a matter of time before corroborating evidence was uncovered. This may be important for each of their individual conscience and culpability, but when diagnoses and treatments are founded on a commitment to an unverified theory, when that theory is dished up as fact, and when the system created serves the self-interest of its proponents, sincerity becomes immaterial in evaluating the welfare of the people affected. The good faith of Dr. Spitzer and his colleagues is irrelevant for the purposes of evaluating the scientific value of their systems.

When Drs. Kirk and Kutchins reviewed the data from the field trials of DSM-III that supposedly affirmed its scientific merit, the evidence was damning. The first thing that stood out is what is missing: *There is no evidence for the validity of DSM-III diagnoses.* This is true of all the diagnoses, not just the ones for depression. No effort was made to test the validity of any of the diagnoses. Given the importance in medical science of establishing validity, this is shocking. As we saw in Chapter 2, *a diagnostic system that does not demonstrate validity fails the prime requirement of science.*

Of the 265 diagnoses that appear in the manual, a small number had been validated prior to DSM-III as having a physiological basis. These are the organic diagnoses of Huntington's Disease, Down Syndrome, Senile Dementia, Paresis (syphilis), and alcohol and drug related organic mental disorders. Aside from including these diagnoses in DSM-III, no effort was made to establish the validity of any of the other diagnoses in the new manual.

In the interview with Dr. Davies, I referenced above, Dr. Spitzer explained to Dr. Davies how he established the validity of the diagnoses in DSM-III: "It became a question of how much consensus there was to recognize and include a particular disorder," to which Dr. Davies responded, "So it was agreement that determined what went in the DSM?" Dr. Spitzer replied, "That was essentially how it went—right."

As you will recall from Chapter 2, *agreement is the definition of reliability, not validity*. And validity is the more important of the two because it has to do with verification, not just agreement. Not only did Dr. Spitzer conflate sadness with depression, he conflated validity with reliability. On this basis alone, the statements hailing DSM-III as having established the scientific/medical respectability of psychiatric diagnoses were unfounded.

Dr. Spitzer died in 2015. It is easy to speculate that he was aware that attempts at validation would lead to insurmountable problems. He had to know the difference between validity and reliability and that he could not find any scientific evidence to validate the diagnostic system he had created. As he acknowledged to Dr. Davies, he knew that the check lists for the diagnoses could not be grounded in any physiological causation and could not be substantiated as predictors of effective medical treatments. As any genuine medical scientist knows, this knowledge is fundamental to a medical system's *validity*.

So, Dr. Spitzer chose to focus solely on testing reliability, which was his area of interest, ignoring the issue of validity. Recall that DSM-II diagnoses had been highly publicized as both invalid and unreliable, discrediting the manual's diagnoses. Doctors could not agree when diagnosing patients with a mental disorder. Dr. Spitzer declared that DSM-III had rectified the reliability problem. He declared reliability to be

> (. . .)much higher for DSM-III(. . .)For most of the diagnostic classes the reliability is quite good and in general is higher than that previously achieved using DSM-I and DSM-II. It is particularly encouraging that the reliability for such categories as schizophrenia and the major affective disorders is so high.

Other prominent psychiatrists agreed. Dr. Gerald Klerman, the senior psychiatric spokesperson I referred to earlier, stated, "In principle, the problem of reliability has been solved."

These claims were false. When Drs. Kirk and Kutchins reviewed the DSM-III data with respect to reliability; it became obvious that *there was no evidence that psychiatric diagnoses were any more reliable than those that had been based on the previous manual.* They found that, "(Dr. Spitzer) actually did not have any new data that systematically compared the overall reliability of DSM-III with previous editions." In fact, there is good reason to conclude that DSM-III's reliability probably is worse since the manual increased the number of diagnoses by more than 40% (subsequent editions of the DSM have added even more diagnoses). Whereas DSM-II had 182 diagnoses and ran for 134 pages, DSM-III's 265 diagnoses required 494 pages.

These results bear repeating: *Objective analyses of the data reveal there was no scientific evidence that DSM-III diagnoses were valid or reliable.* In fact, the evidence points to the exact opposite conclusions. The diagnostic system that psychiatry devised to pave the way for the medicalization of psychiatry, that was trumpeted as based on science, and that established the psychiatric profession's reputation with the public and with other doctors, *was without medical or scientific merit.*

The importance of this finding is amplified because, as I have indicated, DSM-III set the mold for construction of all the revisions that followed. All of these manuals have adhered closely to DSM-III's structure and none of them has been demonstrated to be valid or reliable.

****

Let's get specific. Let's look at Drs. Kirk and Kutchins did, at the actual data that were collected in the construction of the manual. These were the data that led to the lofty claims that were made for DSM-III. The language I use in what follows may be technical, but I urge you to bear with me even if you do not have a scientific background and may not follow the argument in detail. As Bob Dylan says, you don't need to be a weatherman to know which way the wind is blowing. The overall picture will become clear, and this is essential.

It is important for the public not to allow infractions of this magnitude to go undetected and ignored because doing so will allow mistakes that are harmful to be perpetrated. This is often done by embedding them in elaborately detailed explanations or by complex and confusing statistical analyses. As the comedian John Oliver has said, "If you want to do something evil, put it inside something boring."

Arriving at a measure of reliability is accomplished by means of statistical analyses. They are correlation coefficients. Correlations measure the amount of agreement among raters; in this case, the amount of agreement there was among doctors making a diagnosis of a patient as having a mental disorder. A number of different correlation coefficients are in use. They all range from -1.00 to +1.00. A correlation of .00 means there is no agreement, that the ratings are governed by chance; you could do as well by flipping a coin. A correlation of +1.00 indicates perfect agreement, that the two variables are exactly associated—they move in synchrony. A correlation of -1.00 indicates perfect disagreement, which means that as one variable goes up, the other variable goes down to the same extent, which also indicates a relationship.

Dr. Spitzer chose a correlation of + .70 as the requirement for demonstrating satisfactory reliability. A correlation of .70 is a common standard, but it is not a strenuous standard. There are researchers who favor a higher standard (.90), but Dr. Spitzer's choice was not out of line with the criterion chosen in other studies.

Dr. Spitzer first made assessments of the reliability of DSM-III's major diagnostic categories, called Axis I and Axis II. Axis I is made up of diagnoses that fall under the major headings of Schizophrenia, Mood Disorders (which includes Depression), and Anxiety Disorders. In assessments of medical diagnoses, it is expected that there will be satisfactory reliability for the major categories, such as Axis I, even though reliability may not be demonstrated for all of the individual diagnoses that fall under these major headings.

Recall that Dr. Spitzer had praised the reliability of the findings for Axis I, with respect to schizophrenia and the affective disorders (depression) being high. But the correlation found for Schizophrenia was .57 and for the Affective Disorders (depression) was .41. Neither met his .70 requirement for reliability. Only 31 of the correlations testing the reliability of Axis I diagnoses met the .70 criterion. 49 did not. These are very poor results indeed. You don't have to be a statistician to see that *31 represents less than half of the total and that therefore the claim for the reliability of these diagnoses was spurious.* Drs. Kirk and Kutchins report: "Not a single major diagnostic category achieved the .70 standard." Perhaps these results were exceptional and others within Axis I were more reliable?

Not at all. DSM-III results *for children and adolescents are even worse.* If one looks at the results for children and adolescents on Axis I, certainly an important area of interest, only 8 of the 24 correlations met the .70 standard. If this were not enough, it turns out that half of the correlations were based on only one patient. Basing results on just one case is a violation of one of the requirements for using this statistic. It is a striking indication of how fast and loose the judgements were in constructing this manual.

Let us turn now to the results for Axis II. Axis II has to do with diagnoses of Personality Disorders (for example, Paranoid Personality, Narcissistic Personality, and Passive-Aggressive Personality). Only one of the seven correlations for Axis II diagnoses met the .70 standard. So, *Axis II diagnoses also failed to show reliability.*

Then there is the issue of how much agreement there was on the *specific diagnoses* that fall under the broad headings of Axis I and Axis II. Demonstrating reliability for these diagnoses is important because these are the diagnoses that are rendered by psychiatrists, psychologists, and other mental health professionals in clinical practice. What are the results for these diagnoses? *Mostly there are none.* DSM-III listed 200 specific diagnoses under Axis I. Results were reported on a grand total of 16 of them (8%). There were 26 reliability studies completed for these 16 diagnoses, of which only 9 met the .70 criterion of reliability (35%). Small numbers (cells with only one or two cases) occur throughout the tables for these diagnoses, further discrediting the value of the conclusions reached for many of the individual diagnoses.

Clearly, *there was no satisfactory demonstration of reliability for the specific diagnoses listed in DSM-III.* This is exactly what had been true of DSM-II. Ordinarily, researchers who get results such as these do not put out press releases, they go back to the drawing board.

As I wrote earlier, it is not necessary to understand the statistical analyses in any detail to realize that the authoritative-sounding claims made for the medical and scientific value of DSM-III were completely unwarranted. That said, it is easy to skip over the import of these statistics. In the case of science where numbers are measurements of life's quality or the possibility of survival, we cannot afford to dismiss their significance. Let's recognize what this wrought. Unchallenged, these statistics have been unknown or ignored, always undermining and never recognized. DSM-III set the mold for subsequent editions of the DSM. Changes to the basic model initiated with DSM-III have been minimal in subsequent editions of the DSM. Mostly the changes to the DSM have had to do with adding diagnoses.

The highly touted diagnostic system psychiatrists employ to diagnose mental disorder, that began with DSM-III and continues to this day, and that paved the way for the medicalization of treatments for mental disorder, is *devoid of empirical justification.* Dr. Spitzer's endorsement of DSM-III's value as a diagnostic instrument is a quite glaring example of a violation of the scientific principle of falsifiability. His bias, not the data, determined his interpretation of the results.

There is a postscript to this story. Two reliability studies of the DSM subsequently were undertaken. The American Psychiatric Association received a grant from the MacArthur Foundation to conduct a reliability study of DSM-IV. A second DSM-IV reliability study was conducted at six sites in the United States and a site in Germany of some 600 patients. The results of these studies were never published, telling its own story. The investigators stated they had expected higher reliability values. Drs. Kirk and Kutchins reviewed the data and stated that the results were "not different from those statistics achieved in the 1950s and 1960s (with DSM-I and DSM-II) and in some cases worse." They conclude, "*The DSM revolution in reliability was a revolution in rhetoric, not in reality.*"

As for the current manual, DSM-V, there has been no demonstration of validity or reliability. With respect to diagnoses of depression, those in charge stated, "The questionable reliability of major depressive disorder, unchanged from DSM-IV, is obviously a problem."

Dr. Spitzer, himself, in an interview with Alex Spiegel, the science journalist who wrote a review of the DSM in 2005, stated, "To say that we've solved the reliability problem is not true." Let's be clear about what Dr. Spitzer was acknowledging about DSM-III and the subsequent DSM manuals. Although once again he was omitting mention of validity, the math that applies to these calculations tells us that *a system that fails to show reliability cannot have validity.* Dr. Spitzer had expertise in statistics, so he certainly knew this to be true. And when he acknowledged to Drs. Horwitz and Wakefield that DSM-III diagnoses of depression conflated normality with abnormality, he was admitting that the manual's diagnoses of depression were not valid diagnoses. As I have indicated, validity and reliability are the fundamental requirements of any system of measurement, whether the system pertains to weights or to diagnoses.

If we recall the earlier discussion of validity and reliability, we can put Dr. Spitzer's admission into the context of everyday life: if you knew that the scale in your supermarket was untrustworthy, would you continue to shop there?

****

Mental disorder is different from physical illness and the implications of this difference go beyond the false claims made for DSM diagnoses. Research results show that unlike physical illnesses, the common mental disorders cannot be identified physiologically. They cannot be distinguished from normality physiologically nor from one another on physical grounds.

Behavior is disordered, not physiology. As I discussed in relation to the conflation of sadness and depression, for the great majority of these patients there is nothing wrong with their brain's wiring; their brain is operating the way it is supposed to. *The problem is attributable to negative experiences and the patient's response to these experiences, not to a disease process.* It is why the term mental "disorder" is preferable to mental "illness." Although Dr. Spitzer and other psychiatric leaders were intent on medicalizing psychiatry they could not escape from this reality. *They were unable to cite any verified physiological processes as being responsible for these diagnoses.*

So, instead, Dr. Spitzer's check lists for making the diagnoses in DSM-III are descriptions of behaviors, not of physical defects. Despite this being an apparently "behavioral" approach, what matters scientifically is *which* behaviors are selected and *how* they are selected. The behaviors cited to diagnose depression were familiar because they were recognized as being associated with sadness as well as depression. *The DSM check lists are unreliable and invalid because they were selected anecdotally, not by scientific research that established a functional relationship between those behaviors and depression.* Just as there are specific bacteria and viruses that cause particular illnesses, there are specifiable experiences and behaviors that are responsible for particular mental disorders.

In later chapters I will be discussing how research carried out by behavioral psychologists has revealed that the obvious behaviors on the DSM check lists are not the pathological behaviors that are responsible for depression. The behaviors on the check lists are *effects* associated with sadness or depression, *not the cause* of either condition. They tell us nothing about the cause of depression.

We now know that the check lists for making diagnoses of mental disorders that began with DSM-III are every bit as untrustworthy as a cough is for diagnosing tuberculosis. The problems with psychiatric diagnoses when Dr. Lapouse made his statement in 1969 are still present today.

Diagnoses of depression are the prime example of how things *got worse* after DSM-III was published in 1980 rather than better. In Dr. Lapouse's day, depression was a rare diagnosis. As I have indicated, today, depression is the #1 psychiatric diagnosis. It is the third most frequently made diagnosis of all diagnoses rendered by doctors. It is the most frequent of all diagnoses for people aged 18–44. As we will see ever more clearly, we now have millions of people with a cough being told they have tuberculosis, or to put it directly, we have millions of people being told they are mentally ill when, in fact, they are experiencing normal responses to painful life experiences.

By contrast, behavioral psychologists have conducted experiments that reveal the behavioral mechanisms responsible for various mental disorders. Although the mechanisms are psychological, not physiological, they were discovered by the same empirical process pioneered by Pasteur when he established the germ theory, the mechanism governing many physical illnesses.

Behavioral psychologists have been able to devise effective treatments based on this kind of empirical research. The behaviors they cite have been used to predict treatments that work. Later on, you will see that the behaviors identified differ from those that comprise the check lists in DSM manuals. And you will see how directing behavioral treatment at correcting these faulty behaviors has led to greater success.

The British psychiatrist, Dr. Peter Tyrer, who is emeritus professor of community psychiatry at the Imperial College of London, recently suggested that the DSM, right up to DSM-V, could stand for "Diagnosis as a Source of Money" or "Diagnosis for Simple Minds."

Finally, I would be remiss if I did not repeat and emphasize that the data revealing the absence of any empirical justification for the drastic changes made for this edition of the DSM only became known through the Freedom of Information Act. Had there been no Freedom of Information Act would this information ever have been made public? And now that this has been known for nearly three decades, why is the DSM still an acceptable diagnostic system? Although DSM-V has come under some criticism, it has been accepted, on the whole, as today's psychiatric manual for diagnosing mental disorders. There is no excuse for continuing to use a diagnostic system that is invalid and unreliable, particularly one that fosters misdiagnoses that often lead, as you shall see, to medical treatments that can endanger the life and welfare of patients.

4

Psychiatry's Brain Disease Theory

The main problem with the (chemical imbalance) theory is that after decades of trying to prove it, researchers have still come up empty-handed.

—Marcia Angell, MD

Part One

If you have been diagnosed as depressed your doctor probably told you that your depression is caused by a chemical imbalance in your brain of serotonin, one of the brain's neurotransmitters. To put it bluntly, you have been diagnosed as having a brain disease.

The idea that antidepressant drugs correct a chemical imbalance of the brain has become common currency. Most people accept this explanation, believing that all that remains is some tweaking by their doctor to find the right drug and the right dosage for their brain to be healed. Most doctors have accepted this explanation to be true as well. However, scientists who have examined the evidence, who are not in the employ of the pharmaceutical companies, disagree. After studying the research related to these claims, they have concluded *there is no good science behind the brain disease theory of depression*. One of these scientists referred to the theory as "neurobollocks," another as "biobabble" having replaced psychoanalytic "psychobabble."

Let's take a quick look at the history of the theory that mental disorder is a chemical imbalance brain disease. The theory stems from accidental findings dating from the 1950s, when researchers became interested in the side effects of several drugs being tested for other purposes. Marsilid (iproniazid), the first drug offered as an antidepressant, was discovered during research on tuberculosis. Miltown (meprobamate), the first drug marketed to treat anxiety, was discovered during research aimed at finding an effective agent against gram-negative microorganisms (also related to tuberculosis). Lithium, the first drug used to treat bipolar disorder, was discovered because of its industrial usefulness in metallurgy and ceramics.

Researchers noticed that when people were exposed to these compounds, some of these chemicals induced a sedative effect and others an energizing effect. Psychiatric researchers whose research was supported by drug companies began to study these findings.

They speculated that different neurotransmitters in the brain might be regulating different emotional states. With respect to depression, two particular drugs took center stage, iproniazid and reserpine. Reserpine was a familiar drug because it had been in use in mental hospitals to calm down schizophrenic patients when they became agitated. Its use for this purpose came about as a result of studies that showed when reserpine was given to animals, they became inactive and unresponsive. Iproniazid, on the other hand, the drug doctors prescribed to treat tuberculosis, had the unfortunate tendency for some patients to become problematically euphoric.

When they looked into the effects of both these drugs on the brain, they found that reserpine reduced the action of the neurotransmitters, epinephrine and serotonin, whereas iproniazid enhanced the activity of these neurotransmitters. They concluded that reserpine instigated depression (because it led to inactive, unresponsive behavior) and iproniazid eliminated depression (because it induced euphoria).

They claimed they had identified the brain mechanism that explained depression. Their explanation was accompanied by an impressive looking, colorfully illustrated diagram that depicted chemical actions at receptor sites in the brain.

They declared that a deficiency of norepinephrine or serotonin accounted for depression. And they claimed that iproniazid, by keeping the levels of these neurotransmitters higher, cured depression. Thus, the chemical imbalance theory was born to account for depression and antidepressant drugs, alleged to correct this imbalance, became the treatment for depression.

So, what is wrong with the science behind the chemical imbalance theory? To begin with, the theory violates a fundamental principle of science. It is based on *backward reasoning*. The effects of these drugs were just that: *effects*, but the researchers assigned those effects to create a *cause*, declaring that they had found the neurochemical basis for depression and now knew how to treat depression successfully. This is the same reasoning process as deciding that you have a fever because you feel hot—and it is just about as valid. There are, after all, so many possible causes for the feeling of heat. You may just have run several miles, you may be in an overheated room, you may be in the tropics, or on a crowded bus.

Let's be clear. Reasoning backward from effect to cause may not always be a problem in our everyday life, but it is anathema to good science. Backward reasoning violates the scientific requirement of falsifiability. In addition, a fundamental tenet of science is that a correlation does not imply causation. Carrying an umbrella when rain has been forecast does not cause the rain to fall, which doesn't really matter when we are just trying to increase the odds of staying dry on our way to and from work. It is disastrous if we are trying to specify the basis for why things happen.

Before the discovery of the germ theory of disease, and going back to ancient times, doctors believed in the *miasma theory* of disease. The miasma theory held that diseases were not due to person to person contact but to polluted air, which came from rotting organic matter. People got sick/there was rotting organic matter/therefore the rotting organic matter caused the sickness. The serotonin chemical imbalance theory, like the miasma theory, is an example of backward reasoning, and it, too, clearly shows the danger of reasoning from an effect to a cause.

****

From the very start there were fundamental problems with the formulation of the chemical imbalance theory. For one thing, the animal studies were questionable experimental models for depression. How would we know what depression is in an animal? Is sadness in response to loss common in animals, too? How would we know and how would we tell the difference?

As for the human studies, the researchers ignored the results of studies that failed to show reserpine was related to depression. And how much sense does it make to attribute depression solely to actions related to the few neurotransmitters we happen to know something about when there are hundreds of other neurotransmitters we know next to nothing about?

In addition, what was being measured in these studies was open to question. The great bulk of serotonin activity in our bodies is not in our brains but is engaged in the functioning of many other organs and the circulatory system. Serotonin is produced in these other organs, and it binds to multiple receptor types that are different from those in the brain, facilitating a great variety of physiological processes in the body that have nothing to do with brain functioning. Complicating matters still further, serotonin levels in the brain cannot be measured directly. Serotonin levels reported for the brain actually are estimates based on analyses of urine samples or from cerebrospinal fluid. How valid are these samples as measures of serotonin in the brain, not the rest of the body?

Questions also arise because of the timing of the effects of antidepressant drugs. Within a day or two of taking the drug the levels of serotonin in the brain spike to their highest level. By the time some patients report improvement, usually two or three weeks later, the higher levels of serotonin have been reversed because the brain has reacted to combat the effects of the drug. Thus, this finding fits far better with a *psychological explanation* of a placebo effect rather than a neurotransmitter explanation. Understanding the placebo effect is critical to understanding why patients and doctors believe in these drugs. It is an explanation that I will discuss in detail in a later chapter.

Other studies suggest serotonin levels reflect stress (an effect rather than a cause). This would mean that serotonin levels are not a cause of depression but rather an effect of stress (another psychological explanation). Stress implicates environmental factors as being responsible, not genetic/biological factors.

Several years after this took hold, the data that were alleged to support the relationship between reserpine and depression and that gave rise to the chemical imbalance theory were examined by other scientists. They discovered that the conclusions did not come from controlled clinical trials but were clinical impressions. In one study that was cited prominently, the results actually were contradictory to the theory. In this study, very few of the patients given reserpine became depressed, even after taking the drug for an extended period. And most of them had been diagnosed as depressed previously, suggesting that their depression was not a response to reserpine, but an unrelated relapse.

Over the course of the past thirty years, the drug companies and the NIMH have spent an enormous amount of money with the goal of establishing the chemical imbalance theory. By the year 2000, a large number of privately and publicly funded studies had been conducted aimed at verifying the theory.

In 2005, a comprehensive review of published research testing the chemical imbalance theory concluded, "(. . .)there is no direct evidence of serotonin deficiency despite thousands of studies that have attempted to validate this notion." Another review published in 2008 in the New England Journal of Medicine, concluded, "(. . .)numerous studies of norepinephrine and serotonin metabolites in plasma, urine, and cerebrospinal fluid as well as postmortem studies of the brains of patients with depression, have yet to identify the purported deficiency reliably." Still other reviewers of the scientific literature reported being unable to find a single peer-reviewed study that supports the serotonin chemical imbalance theory for any mental disorder.

Elliot Valenstein, emeritus professor of psychology and neuroscience at the University of Michigan, spent a distinguished career studying this area of research. He concluded there is no scientific justification for psychiatry's brain-based explanation for depression and other mental disorders. Dr. Valenstein has summarized the research results regarding depression:

> No single neurotransmitter or combination of neurotransmitters (serotonin, norepinephrine, dopamine, acetylcholine) has been shown to be the cause of depression. Although depression is attributed to a deficiency of serotonin in the brain and antidepressant drugs are prescribed to boost serotonin, most depressed patients do not have low levels of serotonin or norepinephrine and some have very high levels; patients with no history of depression have been found to have low levels of serotonin and norepinephrine. Studies have shown that reducing the levels of these neurotransmitters (with cocaine, for example) doesn't cause depression, nor does increasing the levels of these neurotransmitters reduce depression.

His best guess is that any relationship between serotonin or any of the other neurotransmitters and depression is indirect and far from causal.

In reviewing the absence of a scientific basis for this theory, Dr. Irving Kirsch, at Harvard Medical School, wrote:

> The chemical imbalance theory rode to fame on the basis of uncontrolled case reports of improvement on some drugs and deterioration on others, while contrary data-some of it from carefully controlled studies-were simply ignored. Later attempts to test the theory by experimentally reducing serotonin or norepinephrine in healthy volunteers disproved the theory completely.

He summarized the negative results with a warning:

> The serotonin theory is as close as any theory in the history of science to having been proved wrong. Instead of curing depression, popular antidepressants may

induce a biological vulnerability making people more likely to become depressed in the future.

Dr. Marcia Angell, the former Editor-in-Chief of the New England Journal of Medicine, one of our most prestigious medical journals, has summed this up as follows, "(. . .) the main problem with the (chemical imbalance) theory is that after decades of trying to prove it, researchers have still come up empty-handed."

In short, *research results have failed to verify any neurotransmitter, biochemical, or neurophysiological theory for depression.* No consistent serotonin abnormalities have been identified in patients diagnosed as depressed. Nor has any other individual neurotransmitter or any combination of neurotransmitters been found to be the cause of depression.

And yet, psychiatry has continued to endorse brain theories to account for depression and has promoted the treatment of depression by means of several classes of drugs supplied by the pharmaceutical industry that have an activating effect on one or more of the brain's neurotransmitters. The drug companies have marketed these drugs as antidepressants and the treatment is as popular as the toxic chemical mercury was in the 19th century.

Thomas Bayes' foundational scientific theorem calls for updating beliefs when there is new contradictory evidence. Instead, in a parody of the old saying, "Begin as you mean to go on," psychiatry's initial errant reporting set the tone for what was to come, for the way that psychiatry would depart from good science to yield an economically favorable outcome. Perhaps another old saying also applies, that it is difficult for a man to understand something when his paycheck depends on his not understanding it.

****

As we saw in the previous chapters, psychiatric leaders were intent on medicalizing psychiatry. Doing so required establishing a compelling physiological rationale for mental disorder. The chemical imbalance theory was chosen as the explanation despite the lack of scientific verification. Over the years, psychiatrists and their allies in the pharmaceutical industry have worked intensively to fashion a plausible brain-based narrative for depression and other mental disorders.

We have been conquered by the terrible power of words, in close alignment with business interests, not by empirical evidence that qualifies as good science. It took time and careful crafting to develop this narrative, one which most people, including most doctors, have come to accept. As the years have gone by, this joint marketing effort has imposed itself. Doctors and the general public now believe that depression and other mental disorders are brain-based illnesses.

I have used terms like "fashioned," and "crafted" because that is what has been done. Look at other enormous markets like clothing, cosmetics, cigarettes, and automobiles where the industry in question has designed, named, and cultivated a target market. This is exactly what has happened with mental disorders. The idea that people diagnosed with a mental disorder have a brain disease best treated medically with drugs relies not on science, but on the same kind of intensive, sophisticated marketing. The pharmaceutical industry went full bore in selling this notion to the public-and to doctors.

The marketing of psychiatry's biological revolution succeeded in large part because at its core, it sounds good, and this gives it a spurious credibility. After all, we know we are made of flesh and blood and the capability for our behavior resides in our nervous system. It has proven easy to characterize depression as an illness in the brain just like diseases of other organs in our bodies.

The brain's operations are still mostly a mystery. People love magic and the brain is magical. The secrecy of the brain adds to this effect. When new findings from brain research were announced that were alleged to disclose chemical imbalances in the brain, and when these imbalances were alleged to be the basis for depression and other mental disorders, how many were qualified to dispute these conclusions? When new drugs were said to remedy these brain conditions, many people were relieved a pill was available to rescue them from their distress. Over the last thirty some years, when doctors have recommended antidepressants, most people, at least initially, have filled the prescriptions.

The Monoamine oxidase inhibitors came first. Iproniazid, later marketed as Marsilid, was an early MAOI. Others marketed since then are Marplan, Nardil, and Parnate. Then came the Tricyclics (TCAs). Elavil, Anafranil, Sinequan, and Tofranil are TCAs. And now we have today's preferred antidepressants, the Selective Serotonin Reuptake Inhibitors (SSRIs). Prozac, Paxil, Celexa, Zoloft, and Lexapro are SSRIs, which actually are a subclass of Tricyclics that act more selectively on serotonin. There also are variants of the SSRIs that act selectively on norepinephrine and dopamine.

None of these classes of drugs has been shown to be any more effective than the previous class and numerous studies have found them to be no more effective than placebo. The prime difference, as each new class appeared, was some reduction in the side effects associated with their use, thus enabling a larger number of people to tolerate the drug. The irony associated with this "advantage" is that this factor contributes directly to the potential harmfulness of these drugs by facilitating their long-term use.

There is another difference that is of interest to those who are selling the drugs and to you, the buyer. New drugs cost more than the previous drug when they enter the market. Costs and profits increase with each new drug.

When I was in practice it was not unusual to meet with patients who were dissatisfied with the antidepressant drugs prescribed by their psychiatrist or primary care physician. They had embraced the idea that a pill would be the answer, but it hadn't happened, and they were confused. In psychotherapy, they discovered how to help themselves. In the next two chapters I will review studies of the effectiveness of these drugs and in Chapters 11 and 12 I will review the successful behavioral therapies that have been developed

****

Psychiatry's chemical imbalance explanation for depression can be constructively contrasted with the history leading to the *germ theory* for physical illness. As I have indicated, until the 19th century, scientists and the public believed in the miasma theory of disease. Diseases were thought to be caused by a poisonous vapor, a miasma, made up of suspended particles of decaying matter, identifiable by the foul smell. No one thought that disease might be passed from person to person.

In the 1840s, a Hungarian obstetrician, Dr. Ignaz Semmelweiss, noticed that there were far more postpartum infections in women delivering in his hospital than women attended elsewhere by midwives. He found that doctors often were making deliveries immediately after coming from autopsies and speculated that they were spreading some contagious matter–person to person, a cause and effect relationship. He required doctors to wash their hands with chlorinated water, reducing mortality from childbirth in his hospital from 18% to 2%. Despite these favorable results, the medical establishment rejected his speculation and solution, ostracizing him for his views. He was considered an untrustworthy eccentric. As so often happens, the path to progress was blocked by the determination to maintain entrenched beliefs and practices.

Gradually, as the 19th century progressed, the value of empirical evidence became recognized. It was a time when travelers encountered the most contagious of diseases, cholera. Cholera was epidemic in Egypt and India. The British government resisted the idea of person-to-person transmission of the disease since it entailed extensive quarantines that had negative effects on trade—an early example of the response to Covid-19. Science does not exist in a vacuum, and for good or for ill, states and commerce have affected its acceptance. Dr. Robert Koch, a German microbiologist, examined the intestines of those who had died of the disease and discovered a particular bacterium in them. But he didn't stop there in identifying the cause of the disease. He looked for the source of the bacteria. He found that the germs were present in water from a nearby tank that was the source of their drinking water and used for washing.

Then, after the invention of the microscope, Louis Pasteur was able to conduct experiments on the relationship between germs and disease that verified the germ theory. In laboratory studies he discovered the pathology of puerperal fever (postpartum infections), identifying the bacteria that were the cause of that disease, providing the basis for the observations of Dr. Semmelweiss. Dr. Pasteur's suggestion that brewers heat their beer to kill bacteria (pasteurization) greatly reduced spoilage. Interestingly, it was the profitable effects of this recommendation on the beer industry that eventually proved persuasive in making the case.

Drs. Koch and Pasteur are regarded as among the founders of scientific medicine. Dr. Koch is esteemed as the father of *public health* because, based on his advice, cholera disappeared when structures were built to deliver clean water-an environmental solution. Noteworthy among Dr. Koch's contributions was his detailing of the requirements of the scientific method that must be met to establish cause and effect relationships. He prohibited *backward reasoning* and this stricture still stands as an integral part of any valid scientific exploration.

The germ theory has been validated. Evolving as it did from empirical results, the theory has demonstrated its validity in sanitation, pasteurization, and vaccination. The biology that the theory invokes has provided the basis for development of antibiotic drugs and has been highly useful in preventing and treating disease. Predictions based on the germ theory pan out. Witness the success of vaccines against the coronavirus.

Psychiatrists like to draw an analogy between depression and diabetes, as if both conditions are *chemical imbalance illnesses*, both requiring the regular administration of drugs to correct an illness caused by a physiological imbalance.

In the case of diabetes, research results have informed us about the mechanisms responsible for the disease, how they are manifested, and what we can do to remedy the illness. *Scientific knowledge underlies and justifies calling diabetes a chemical imbalance disease.* Medical science has taught us there are several forms of diabetes, that type 1 is an autoimmune condition and type 2 is not, and how to differentiate them. We know how the symptoms reflect the illness, and we can predict what needs to be done to remedy it. We know in detail how all this happens physiologically in the different forms of diabetes. That's the basis for citing a chemical imbalance and for what is printed in the medical manual that dictates the diagnosis and treatment of diabetes. It is an illustration of the beneficial outcome of applying the scientific method when determining diagnoses and treatments.

The mechanisms postulated for the chemical imbalance theory of depression fall apart when tested. Symptoms of depression cannot be traced back to root physiological causes as is the case for the symptoms found in diabetes. Psychiatrists have advanced the chemical imbalance theory of depression but saying something does not make it so. No scientific evidence exists for the chemical imbalance theory for depression as it does for diabetes. Nor is there any science that directs drug treatment for depression to correct a chemical imbalance. We have seen how the DSM, furnishing diagnoses of depression, has failed scientific testing. Just as was the case with DSM-III diagnoses, the biological theory of depression, the chemical imbalance theory, was not derived from medical science, but has been marketed as if it was, promoting the sale of medicalized treatments for patients unreliably and invalidly diagnosed as depressed.

In fact, the chemical imbalance theory of depression does not even qualify as a scientific theory. Scientific theories are constructed on the basis of hypotheses that have been confirmed, not on hypotheses that have failed. Over time, scientists have developed a common "language" of science and the method they have developed has rules and definitions that accompany it just as grammar and vocabulary accompany the elaboration of a language. In the context of that "language" then, brain disease conversation is a *hypothesis* that has failed experimental testing.

Despite the use of apparently scientific jargon in the presentation of this "theory" and despite the colorful diagrams, those advancing the chemical imbalance theory have violated the deepest grammar of the language of science. As I have indicated, after more than a hundred and fifty years of effort, no brain pathology (disease) has been found to be the cause of any of the common psychiatric diagnoses, including depression. The miasma theory—not diabetes—is the appropriate analogy.

The psychiatrist Dr. Allen Frances, formerly chairman of the Department of Psychiatry at Duke University's School of Medicine, and a founder of the Journal of Psychiatric Practice, has written:

> Billions of research dollars have failed to produce convincing evidence that any mental disorder is a discrete disease entity with a unitary cause. Dozens of

different candidate genes have been "found" but in follow-up studies each turned out to be fool's gold.

****

Part Two

The medicalization of psychiatry implies that there is a genetic basis for mental disorder. In the ongoing debate regarding the pre-eminence of nature versus nurture, psychiatry has taken a sharp turn in favor of the former. Genetic explanations are so appealing that people pay quite substantial sums of money for genetic analyses that go back hundreds of years.

You may have heard that depression is genetic and runs in families. Maybe you are concerned because you have family members who were diagnosed as depressed. Belief in a genetic explanation for depression goes back all the way to the German psychiatrist, Dr. Emil Kraepelin, in the early 1900s.

Despite what you have read or heard, *the evidence for a genetic cause for depression is far from established.* Families share environments as well as genes. Moreover, the field of epigenetics is about how environments affect gene expressions. How much to attribute to genetics and how much to environmental influences is unknown. While it is plausible to hypothesize that both genetics and the environment make contributions to different mental disorders, determining their relative weights is not nearly as simple as many researchers in this field have claimed. "Definitive" studies are not definitive at all. Sorting this out is complicated and the jury is still out, but the weight of the evidence is not on the side of genetics.

Research reports that mistakenly attribute a genetic case for depression have confused doctors and the public. For example, in 2003, a study was published in Science, a very prestigious journal, that purported to give definitive evidence that some patients had a genetic vulnerability to depression. Six years later, after a re-examination of the data, an article was published in the Journal of the American Medical Association that overturned this reported finding. The researchers concluded there was no evidence to support the genetic explanation for depression that had appeared in Science. In 2019, an even more extensive study of 620,000 patients verified these negative findings. *The study found that the 18 most frequently cited candidate genes for depression, including the mechanism for serotonin, were no more associated with depression than randomly chosen genes.*

Twin studies have been central to making the argument that mental disorder is genetically determined. For many years this research focused on comparing traits of identical or monozygotic (MZ) twins with those of fraternal or dizygotic (DZ) twins. MZ twins share the same genes, whereas DZ twins share about 50% of their genes, as is the case with other siblings. The assumption is that if identical twins are more similar than fraternal twins with regard to a particular trait, such as introversion/extroversion, it must be because of genetics, not environmental factors. However, it has been well documented that parents, teachers, and peers treat identical twins more similarly than fraternal twins. The environments of identical twins, as well as their genetics, are more similar than for fraternal twins. In scientific terminology, their environments are confounded with their genetics, meaning that the relative contributions cannot be sorted out in these studies. It is easy to believe in genetic explanations for traits, but just as easy to doubt their predominance.

A case in point is the "Genain" sisters, which often is cited as evidence for a genetics viewpoint ("genain" is a pseudonym derived from the Greek for "dreadful gene"). These sisters were quadruplets, and all were alleged to be schizophrenic. They were written about in the 1970s, when they were in their 40s, when psychiatry was gearing up for the medicalization of mental disorders. However, the diagnoses of schizophrenia assigned to these sisters are open to considerable question, as is the attribution of a genetic basis for whatever mental disorder some or all of them may have had. One of the sisters was never in treatment for a mental disorder and refused to have anything to do with the researchers. As for their being a prime example of a genetic origin for mental disorder, consider the following: (a) their father was an alcoholic who repeatedly molested his daughters, (b) the parents had two of the sisters circumcised after discovering that they engaged in mutual masturbation, and (c) one of the daughters was forced by her parents to stay at home during her senior year in high school. These environmental factors were not considered by the researchers to be relevant.

The twin studies that are cited as the gold standard for a genetic basis for mental disorder are of identical twins who have been adopted and reared apart. The authors of these studies claim this has solved the confounding of nature and nurture. Dr. Jay Joseph, a psychologist who has studied this subject closely, has reviewed the research that has been done. He found the studies to be highly biased in favor of a genetic viewpoint, beginning with the assumption that any difference found had to be due to nature, not nurture. In many cases the identical twins had lived together for as long as five years and their separation occurred late in childhood; many were in contact with one another following their separation;

they were the same age; of the same sex; and had very similar physical appearance, which tend to lead to similar reactions from others.

Moreover, the pairs were usually in homes that were similar culturally and economically. All the assessments that went into the comparisons were made by researchers who had a bias in favor of a genetic viewpoint. As if this were not enough, some of the twins' accounts were of questionable credibility because they had incentives to exaggerate aspects of their stories to researchers who favored a genetic interpretation.

The most often cited twin study in support of a genetic explanation for behavior is Thomas Bouchard's Minnesota study (MISTRA), published in 1990. Dr. Bouchard concluded from his results that IQ, personality, and behavior were strongly influenced by genetics. However, in reviewing this study, Dr. Joseph points to several glaring defects. To begin with, the researchers did not apply a test ordinarily used to distinguish between MZ and DZ twins, raising questions about the accuracy of the assignments. In addition, the researchers themselves acknowledged that they had made assumptions in analyzing their data that "are not likely to hold up" and are "generally oversimplifications of the actual situation and their violation can introduce systematic distortions in the estimates." Dr. Bouchard and his colleagues refused to grant other researchers any access to their raw data or to their case history information, underlining this point.

A study by Shields illustrates how there is only one right answer for some of these researchers. Twins not separated until age nine or for only five years during childhood were counted as "separated pairs." A pair brought up by two aunts who lived next door to one another qualified as a "separated" pair. Some of the reports of this area of research have been embellished with details such as the identical twins who named their children with the same name as if this name was imprinted in their DNA rather than having a more obvious explanation.

Another interested scientist, Richard Bentall, has discussed the statistical methods that are employed to measure whether variations in the genetic relationships between relatives are predictive of mental disorder. This is known as "concordance." As the distance between genetic relationships increases, concordance should be lower. Many studies have been done comparing the rates of mental disorder in MZ twins to DZ twins. One of the largest such studies ever undertaken was by Franz Kallman in 1946. Dr. Kallman reported that 80% of the identical twins of schizophrenic parents were schizophrenic, whereas only 15% of non-identical twins were diagnosed. But Dr. Kallman made his own ratings and he decided which twins were identical by their appearance, not by means of objective testing. Despite our ability since then to objectively distinguish between MZ and DZ twins, no other researcher has ever found such resounding results.

The statistic that is used in these studies is known as "heritability" or "h^2," which is interpreted as the amount of variation in a disorder that can be attributed to genes. However, this attribution is false: h^2 depends on the variation in environmental factors as well as on the variation in genetic factors. Dr. Bentall gives the example of intelligence, citing how IQ is found to be highly related to genetics in high-income families because of the consistency of intellectually stimulating environments these children enjoy, but much less related to genetics in low-income families, where environmental factors are far more varied and influential.

In addition, environmental factors in h^2 studies are calculated indirectly, as that portion left over after calculating for genetic factors. Dr. Bentall, in commenting on the calculation of the relative weights of genetic vs. environmental influences on behavior, writes, "In reality, however, the only way of discovering whether environmental influences are important is by looking for them."

He goes on to state, "Unfortunately, h^2 is one of the most misleading (and most misunderstood) statistics in the whole of psychiatric research." Judging from this present review of psychiatric research, the faulty interpretation of h^2 appears to be quite consistent with other psychiatric self-serving interpretations of data that we have already considered, with many more to come. It is no simple matter to decide which psychiatric manipulation of the data wins the prize as the most misleading. In summing up how the h^2 statistic has been used as a measure of concordance rates in family, twin, and adoption studies, Dr. Bentall writes:

> In fact, numerous biases in the measurement of concordance can be demonstrated and, given the way in which the genetic cause of mental illness has been treated as an axiom rather than a hypothesis, it is perhaps not surprising that these inevitably resulted in the inflation of h^2.

He concludes that results for the h^2 statistic indicate that:

> . . . genes play some role at some point in increasing risk of mental illness, but nothing else. Hence, even when it is calculated from reliable and meaningful data, the statistic is almost completely mis-informative about the influence of environmental factors.

Clearly the twin studies do not qualify as meeting a gold standard.

There is nothing foreign about the idea that mental disorder, including depression, is due mainly to behavioral/environmental factors, not genetics. Most physical illnesses are caused in this way. Public health officials regularly make this point. Alcohol, drugs, tobacco, pollutants in air and water, radiation, guns, and automobile accidents are cited as being among the largest environmental causes of illness, injury, and death. The most common causes of death are heart disease, cancer, respiratory disease, and accidents, all of which largely are the outcome of behavioral/environmental factors. A good example relevant to mental disorder is Parkinson's Disease. A study of Parkinson's Disease (which is known to be associated with antidepressant drug prescriptions), found the disease is caused by exposure to the chemicals in pesticides, and that it rarely has a genetic origin.

There also are many examples on the positive side, of how environmental factors enhance our brain functions, our behavior, and our health. To give just one example, there is evidence that exercise strengthens neural connections in the brain involved in memory and learning. There is ample reason to conclude that our environment and how we respond to it, influence our health and well-being more than our inheritance.

This realization is basic to the field of epigenetics. Epigenetics refers to the finding that genes respond to environmental influences. Genes can be expressed or silenced by lifestyle, with no underlying changes in DNA. Causation is complex. Not many physical illnesses are known to have a purely genetic origin: A causal gene has been isolated for Huntington's Disease, Down Syndrome, BRCA1, Hemophilia, Sickle-cell Anemia, and Cystic fibrosis. Not a long list. With respect to mental disorders, the better-designed studies and the Human Genome Project have reported very weak genetic connections to DSM diagnoses.

Other studies sometimes cited for a biological explanation for mental disorder are based on brain pathology. Postmortem studies comparing the brains of mentally disordered patients with other people's brains have found differences. Many people diagnosed with a mental disorder have been on drugs long-term, exposing them to the risk of brain damage. I will review the evidence bearing on this in Chapter 7. We know behavior leads to changes in the brain. Learning to ride a bike changes the brain, just as altering one's diet changes the digestive tract.

The behaviors characterizing sadness and depression include reduced physical activity, which affects the body and induces changes in brain chemistry and even brain structure. Stress, an environmental factor, changes many organs in our body. High blood pressure is an example. Since learning and emotion are affected by interactions with our environment, why wouldn't responses to our environment and to stress cause changes in the brain? A perfectly reasonable argument can be made that any differences in the brain found on autopsy are more likely effects rather than causes.

We now know there are hundreds of neurotransmitters interacting with billions of neurons and trillions of synapses in complex and largely unknown ways. Arriving at a biological understanding of how the brain orchestrates different emotions and behaviors at a specific time, under different internal and external conditions, and discovering a drug that affects the nervous system so precisely in the moment to control these reactions to our wishes is much more than a tall order. It is preposterous.

As H. Allen Orr, a distinguished professor of biology at the University of Rochester, has written:

> Geneticists have had an extraordinarily hard time finding genes that make substantive contributions to complex diseases like Type 2 diabetes. This doesn't bode well, to put it mildly, for finding genes that allegedly underlie subtle differences in predisposition to middle-class behavioral traits.

Research results point to life experiences as far more significant than genes as determinants of mental disorder. Even in the case of intellectual impairment, where Down Syndrome is one of the rare examples of a biologically based mental disorder (brain tumors and brain injuries are others), the environmental effects of insufficient stimulation of infants and young children are known to be far more pervasive causes of intellectual deficits.

Neurologically, we are exquisitely connected to be responsive to our environment. Our experiences, what we make of these experiences, and how we behave in our interactions with our environment, that is, psychological factors, appear to be far more important than our biology as explanations for mental disorders. This basic truth has been lost in the medicalizing of psychiatry.

Brain research is valuable. We know much more about the brain's structure and functioning than was the case even ten years ago, but it is important to recognize that our knowledge of the brain is still at the level of basic research. We do not have knowledge of the brain to explain depression or any of the other common psychiatric diagnoses. The current explanation of depression, the chemical imbalance theory, has been shown to be superficial and erroneous.

****

Recently, psychiatry has been promoting fMRI studies that monitor metabolic activity in the brain, which is related to the uptake of oxygen. The brain is an electric organ fueled by oxygen. Monitoring oxygen levels in the brain identifies regions engaged in a mental task. Some psychiatrists are now attaching great significance to biomarkers of brain circuit activity shown in fMRI studies, attributing causative significance to these colorful brain images. But since these biomarkers are common to a wide range of brain functions, neuroscientists who have no conflict of interest have dismissed these causative attributions as unwarranted.

Sally Satel is a psychiatrist who teaches at Yale Medical School and is a resident scholar at the American Enterprise Institute for Public Policy Research. Scott Lillienfeld is a clinical psychologist and a professor in the Psychology Department at Emory University. In a book they have written on fMRI research, they conclude,

> Naive media, slick neuroentrepeneurs, and even an occasional overzealous neuroscientist exaggerate the capacity of scans to reveal the contents of our minds, exalt brain physiology as inherently the most valuable level of explanation for understanding behavior, and rush to apply underdeveloped, if dazzling, science for commercial and forensic use.

A number of problems have been identified with analyses of fMRI images. A researcher discovered ". . . that the most common software package for fMRI analyses can result in false positive rates up to 70%. These results question the validity of a number of fMRI studies . . . ." As an example, when a researcher put a dead salmon in an fMRI scanner, the machine detected neural activity. When the dead salmon was asked, just like a human test subject, "what emotion the individual in the photo must be experiencing," the fMRI scan repeatedly reported that the demised creature was thinking about the pictures being shown.

Transformational data frequently is used in fMRI studies. This data is problematic. Conclusions are drawn from averaging groupings of scans. Averaging *questionnaire responses of dubious validity*, which is frequently the case, does not produce trustworthy results. When these groupings are based on *DSM diagnoses*, they are filled with error because of the failure of DSM diagnoses to be valid or reliable. One psychiatrist's diagnosis of social anxiety is another's diagnosis of depression, that diagnosis of depression is someone else's diagnosis of bipolar disorder, and so on. Diagnoses of depression conflate sadness with depression, two quite different conditions. The attempt to analyze fMRI images grouped according to flawed questionnaires or diagnoses is akin to attempting to understand what goes into the structure of an orange by studying a sample composed of oranges, bananas, and beets.

fMRI images are rather gross representations of the brain. Although these images record activity occurring in about a cubic millimeter of the brain, there are hundreds of thousands of neurons exchanging signals in this tiny area that are undetectable by fMRI scans. Not only that, any one neuron may have as many as ten thousand synaptic inflections. Because fMRIs measure the amount of oxygen in the blood being delivered to the brain, it takes about a second for the device to follow the stream. This may not seem like much time, but it is significant in terms of brain activity. It means fMRIs are not displaying the origin of the electrical signals, since they travel almost instantaneously throughout the brain.

Neuroscientists know that prior to these images, undetectable, hundreds of thousands of neurons were firing in unknown patterns. Since these activities have occurred already, the mechanisms controlling how these reactions to reactions to actions of neurons led to the fMRI images are unknown. While fMRI's can give valuable information, there is no scientific support for attributing causative significance to these findings.

When fMRI differences are found between someone who has been diagnosed with a mental disorder and someone who has not, it proves nothing about causality. *Backward reasoning* is rampant. The difference could just as easily be that the person's behavior was the cause of the findings rather than the effect. No causative relationship is demonstrated by these findings.

An article was published recently on the advances being made in fMRI research. When neuroscientists engaged in this research, ones who believe in the value of this instrument, were asked about clinical application of their findings, they responded by emphasizing the limits to what they had learned regarding mental disorder:

> "There are ridiculously simple questions about the cortex that we can't answer at all;" "We can't tell a schizophrenic brain from an autistic brain from a normal brain;" "We have so far to go before we can affect treatments that I tell people, 'Don't even think about that yet.' "

Drs. Satel and Lillienfeld make the basic point,

> Brain based explanations appear to be granted a kind of superiority over all other means of accounting for human behavior. We call this assumption 'neurocentrism'—the view that human experience and behavior can be best explained from the predominant or even exclusive perspective of the brain.

In a similar vein, Giovanni Fava, a psychiatrist, and psychiatric journal editor, has written, "It is ironic that, while psychiatrists tend to view treatment and prevention of relapse purely in pharmacological terms (as if it were a disease such as diabetes) diabetologists, as other medical specialists, emphasize the importance of nonpharmacologic strategies." Dr. Fava goes on to describe the disease model in psychiatry as "pharmaceutical reductionism," which has led to "under-treatment, over-treatment, and mistreatment."

5

Measuring Antidepressant Effectiveness: STAR*D

The unfortunate truth is that current medications help too few people to get better and very few people to get well.

—*Thomas Insel, MD*

Part One

We have come now to the third of the three critical issues: How good are antidepressant drugs? Are people getting better because of them? For some, these questions may seem academic. It is the practical implications that concern them, and if you have taken or are taking antidepressants, or if you know those who have done or are doing so, then it is understandable that the following question is what matters to you. Do antidepressant drugs make us well?

The National Institute of Mental Health (NIMH) has attempted to answer this question. The NIMH has conducted several important studies, and in 2006, they funded a huge study of the effectiveness of the antidepressant drugs currently prescribed to treat depression, called the STAR*D study. This was a significant event. The most prestigious health research institution in the United States undertook a major study to evaluate the Selective Serotonin Reuptake Inhibitors (SSRIs), the currently endorsed treatment for patients diagnosed as depressed. This chapter is devoted to evaluating the findings of this study in the context of the question just asked, "Do antidepressant drugs make us well?"

Over 4,000 patients who were being treated in clinics spread across the country were enrolled in the study. *At a cost of 35 million dollars, it was the largest study ever of the effectiveness of antidepressant drug treatment of depression.* It was also one of the most expensive studies ever conducted by the NIMH. For many in the field of mental health, it had great resonance. At the time, I was a professor and a practitioner.

This study's publication coincided with an important event in my life and I was eager to learn the results. In January of 2006, just prior to the publication of the first segment of the STAR*D study's results, I had a book published with Dr. Christopher Martell, "The Myth of Depression as Disease: Limitations and Alternatives to Drug Treatment." Dr. Martell is a clinical associate professor at the University of Washington in Seattle, where he was collaborating with others conducting research on depression. In this book we came to the conclusion that reliance on these drugs had little scientific justification.

My long teaching and practice reflected my conclusion that drugs were being favored, when I believed behavior therapy was the better treatment. It was my conviction, after decades of teaching and practice, that a great number of patients had been substantively and lastingly helped by behavioral techniques. We had evidence that met the rigorous requirements of scientific standards that our therapeutic procedures work and are more effective than antidepressant drugs.

Apart from scientific evidence, I could cite a plethora of personal anecdotal evidence as well. I successfully treated many patents using validated behavioral procedures. Some of these patients had sought my help after becoming disenchanted with psychiatric drugs. My therapy experiences were powerful and persuasive. I know that if I cited such cases as evidence this would appeal to many readers. *But this is a book that is dedicated to determining conclusions on scientific grounds; that is, empirically, not anecdotally.* Sound answers come from science, not personal impressions, including impressions derived from therapy, since, unfortunately, conclusions about the basis for that success are subjective. *Clinical conclusions are anecdotal evidence.* Frequently they are mistaken and all too easily they can be self-serving.

The STAR*D study, because of its design, size and sponsorship by the NIMH appeared to be a study that could challenge or confirm the conclusion that I and many of my colleagues had about the very questionable effectiveness of antidepressant drugs as treatments for depression. Clinical psychologists are educated and trained as scientist-practitioners. Fulfillment of these professional standards translates into an ethical obligation to find the most effective way to help people. The scientific method is the best route to such knowledge.

****

In order to understand the importance of the STAR*D study, we need to put it in historical context. The enormous growth in the number of people being diagnosed as depressed was alarming to me and to many of my colleagues. What was the justification for the great majority of these diagnoses or for the drug treatments that were being prescribed? The economic costs associated with the huge number of prescriptions being filled for antidepressant drugs were of concern as well. Was the field of mental health based on a scientific health and disorder model or on a product-driven, market-place model, exemplified by enormous public expenditures? Such swelling numbers and mushrooming costs required verification that drug treatment was warranted and worked.

We were not without medical precedents for our concern. Medical history is filled with stories of *medically endorsed, wrongful drug treatments*. Throughout the 19th century, parents dosed their children with morphine, codeine, heroin, and powdered opium in the form of soothing syrups. Doctors recommended these treatments, just as they recommended mercury, that highly toxic substance, for everything from cuts to constipation. Many of their patients swore by it. Some of these "cures" were standard treatments for decades, even longer.

It is easy to assume a superior stance and to convince ourselves that such things can't happen in these modern times of scientific methodology and advanced technology. But along with these advances in science has come the growth of industries related to these advances, most notably with regard to health care, the pharmaceutical industry. Herein lies the rub: To be viable, these industries *must* be profitable. In the mass markets that have evolved, profits hinge on the successful marketing of products. And the profits from antidepressant drugs have been enormous.

The pharmaceutical industry has become a prime example of commercial interests at work. The over-prescription of opioids is a far better-known example than antidepressant over-prescription. Abuse of opioids has been facilitated by some drug companies for profit despite the terrible toll of life and health that has ensued from their promiscuous prescription. The adverse effects of antidepressants are less dramatic, but they are significant and need to be understood.

Back to the STAR*D study, which made use of the Selective Serotonin Reuptake Inhibitors (SSRIs) to treat patients: Beginning with Prozac in 1987, doctors have been prescribing the SSRIs to treat depression. The SSRIs are the antidepressant drugs preferred by psychiatrists and they are the class of antidepressants that the STAR*D study was designed to investigate.

The Food and Drug Administration (FDA) approved the SSRIs as effective agents to treat depression. Given their approval by the FDA, their endorsement by the NIMH, and the psychiatric guidelines that specify the SSRIs as the treatment choice for depression, some regard any questioning of the value of these antidepressant drugs as an unwillingness to accept the results of scientific testing.

In fact, legitimate questions have been raised concerning whether the chemicals in the SSRIs and the other antidepressant drugs being prescribed to treat depression work as advertised. The indicative fact is that the FDA's approval of the SSRIs was based on *clinical trials carried out by the drug companies of diagnoses of depression that were based on interpretations of subjective reports, not verified biology*. As you saw in Chapter 3, DSM diagnoses of depression have failed to be found valid or reliable.

David Antonuccio is a clinical psychologist who is Professor Emeritus of Psychiatry and Behavioral Sciences at the University of Nevada. He is a respected scientist and academic, who has studied and critiqued the clinical trials that led to the FDA's approval of the prescription of the SSRIs as antidepressants. Dr. Antonuccio identified a number of defects in these trials *that biased the outcome in favor of the drugs.*

As a starter, the FDA's requirements for drug approval do not set a high bar. Only two positive trials are required for a drug to be approved. And here is the kicker: *It doesn't matter how many trials it takes to get those two.* With respect to the SSRIs, Prozac required *five* attempts by the drug companies to meet this excessively modest requirement; Celexa took *seven* trials to get those two; Paxil and Zoloft took *even more* trials before they got two favorable ones.

What should we make of drugs *that fail their tests more often than they pass them*? What other area of scientific testing sets such a low bar? Think about it practically. How willing would you or I be to set foot in an airplane that met such a standard of testing? Or a bus for that matter. These are not far-fetched examples. When a person takes an antidepressant, they are putting chemicals inside their bodies. If the chemicals don't do what they are supposed to do more times than not, you have to question the alleged value of the drug. What if the search for a vaccine against Covid-19 had been based on diagnoses of the virus that lacked validity and reliability? How likely is it that such a search would have resulted in an effective vaccine?

Dr. Antonuccio has described how the FDA allows drug companies to conduct drug trials. The drug companies advertise that they have developed a new drug to treat depression and they are seeking volunteers for clinical trials to test the drug. What does this mean in practical terms and why is it a problem? Quite simply, this means that those who volunteer may do so because they want to be treated with drugs.

In other words, the drug companies potentially produce a sample that is more favorably inclined to this form of treatment than others in the population would be. This means that the clinical trials may very well be based on a sample *biased in favor of drugs.* After all, how likely is it that someone who is leery of drug treatments or prefers to receive psychotherapy, not drugs, would volunteer for a study that will offer only drug treatments or placebo? Why wouldn't you expect that the volunteers largely represent those who favor drug treatment, which is one segment of the population, not the population as a whole. This is a structural problem that is anathema to good science since scientific studies by definition and by time honored tradition are designed to prevent biased samples. *Studies that fail to control for biases are likely to fail to deliver valid and reliable results.*

In addition, in these drug trials, doctors are required to tell volunteers that they will receive either a drug or a placebo. And they must inform the patients in advance about what side effects to expect from the drugs. *The presence or absence of the side effects alerts at least some of the volunteers as to whether they are on the drug or the placebo.* The expression used to describe those who realize that the lack of side effects means that they are on a placebo rather than on the drug itself is: "they become unblinded." Again, it is impossible to ensure that this knowledge will not influence how those who volunteered for the clinical trials respond to treatment. They volunteered for the study to get drug treatment, not a placebo, and many of them can guess what group they are in based on the presence or absence of the side effects. This in itself can and probably does affect the evaluations of those in both the drug and the placebo groups, potentially biasing the results in favor of the drug.

There is also the issue of the raters. Some clinical trials of antidepressants conducted by the drug companies assess improvement on the basis of ratings made by psychiatrists who favor drug treatment. This potentially *biases their ratings.* Because they interview patients about their experience, few psychiatrists are "blind" as to which patients are on which treatment.

Last but not least, *these studies are designed to last for a short period.* A strategy regularly employed by drug companies is to run studies for only two or three months of treatment before many of the adverse effects from the drugs have had time to occur. We know from studies lasting longer that many patients stop taking the drugs after a few months because of their noxious side effects or because they are not helpful. Running shorter trials under-represents the high attrition rates. *Attrition reflects drug failures,* so drug companies design their studies to be short-term studies, biasing the outcome in favor of the drugs.

Despite the flaws in the clinical trials, the FDA deemed pharmaceutical testing to have demonstrated that the SSRIs were superior to placebos in the treatment of depression and approved them to treat adults. How could any objective evaluating body not require correction of the flawed designs of these clinical trials?

As if this were not enough, examination of the clinical trials subsequent to approval has determined that the evaluations *significantly underestimated the size of the placebo effects.* Research related to the placebo effect is highly informative when evaluating drug effects and I will review the results of these studies in the next chapter. You will see how the placebo effect determined the outcome in the drug companies' clinical trials.

In summary, the objections that Dr. Antonuccio and a number of other reputable scientists have pointed out about the SSRI clinical trials, challenge the wisdom of the FDA's approval of the clinical trials of the antidepressant drugs. Tests conducted since the approval of the SSRIs have produced mixed results. Some studies have indicated antidepressant drugs to be more effective than placebos, while others have shown no difference. But appearances can be deceptive. Closer scrutiny of this research suggests the favorable evidence for the chemicals in these drugs to be weak. The studies are short term and many of the studies reporting positive results have been found to be misreports of results that actually were negative. Other research has disclosed that when studies that were supportive of these drugs were repeated with more rigorous designs, the advantage attributed to the drugs disappeared. Still other studies found the positive results for antidepressants disappeared within a year or less, challenging their value and meaning.

In 1989, in the early years after psychiatrists established prescription of antidepressant drugs as the treatment of choice for depression, the NIMH studied the effectiveness of several treatments for depression, including the antidepressant drugs being prescribed at that time. *The study found that the drugs were no more helpful than placebos.* A secondary measure for very severely depressed patients indicated superior results for the drugs.

A NIMH follow-up study published three years later, in 1992, found that this possible advantage for very severely depressed patients had disappeared. Moreover, a number of other measures having to do with long-term use of these drugs showed negative results. Compared with those given placebos, patients treated with antidepressants had higher relapse rates, a lower number of weeks being symptom free, and a high percentage seeking treatment 18 months later. Thus, *patients treated with sugar pills fared better than those prescribed antidepressant drugs*. Moreover, in June of 2018 an article published in the Journal of the American Medical Association reported that antidepressant drugs were one of the classes of drugs that *induced depression* in a significant number of those taking them.

Overall, the results suggest that the positive results reported for these drugs have been greatly exaggerated. When a benefit does occur, the results more likely are attributable to psychological factors (mainly a placebo effect) rather than to the chemicals in the drugs. I will be examining this psychological explanation of a placebo effect in detail in the next chapter.

****

The results of the STAR*D study were published in a series of nine reports spread over a year's time. The study sought to evaluate the effectiveness of the SSRIs in the treatment of seriously depressed patients. In particular, the study was aimed at testing the value of switching these patients from one antidepressant drug to another when the previous drug wasn't working. A common experience with these drugs is that the drug prescribed is not helpful. Psychiatrists believe this is because it is the wrong drug for this patient's depression, based on a theory that there are different biological forms of depression. The drug's failure triggers switching to another antidepressant with a different mechanism of action. The aim of the STAR*D study was to show that eventually psychiatrists will find the right drug for a patient's form of depression. Note that this theory prevails despite the fact that, as we saw in the last chapter, no theory of a biological basis for depression has been supported by science.

The study was well-designed in a number of respects, and its methodology seemed at first to meet the requirements for scientific testing. There was a glaring exception, however, that quickly became apparent: The researchers bypassed the sine qua non of drug studies. That is, *they did not assess the strength of drug treatment by means of a double-blind placebo control group.* To be clear, by double blind I am referring to studies that aim to disguise from the patients and from doctors who receive the sugar pill and who receives the drug (thus "double blinded").

The sugar pill test is time honored because it gives us a measure of the role of that important psychological element in healing, *belief.* The most significant question that has been raised about antidepressants is whether these drugs are any better than placebos. How could such a major treatment study ignore the importance of evaluating the placebo effect? Why weren't these researchers interested in evidence that whatever benefits they found for antidepressant drug treatment *went beyond a placebo effect?*

However, this was not my immediate concern. First, I sought to understand how the data were being analyzed. Immediately, I ran into problems that were disturbing. I began to discover what appeared to be discrepancies present in the first several reports of their results. At first, I presumed that the error must be mine. I puzzled over the publications for weeks, pouring over the numbers, but I couldn't make sense of them from one report to the next. At length, since I am accustomed to reading scientific studies and deciphering them, I began to wonder if perhaps it was the information rather than I am at fault.

To pursue this further, I turned to two colleagues, John Boren and Ed Pigott. Both Dr. Boren and Dr. Pigott are highly trained researchers with extensive statistical backgrounds. Dr. Boren is an experimental psychologist and is now a Professor Emeritus at American University. Dr. Pigott is a clinical psychologist who is a scientist and therapist, highly regarded for his research skills. Perhaps they could explain what I was missing. When they, too, had problems making the numbers cohere, we became determined to understand what was happening.

Thus began a year-long collaboration, led by Dr. Pigott, aimed at reviewing and deciphering the STAR*D study's results. During this time, we discovered to our astonishment that the results of the study, as they continued to be reported in subsequent STAR*D publications *were being misrepresented repeatedly.*

According to the authors of the study, the results resoundingly endorsed the effectiveness of the switching strategy for antidepressant drugs. They claimed that eventually a drug was found, with the right biological mechanism of action on the brain, to help most patients. Many newspapers and magazines, responding to NIMH press releases about the STAR*D study's allegedly favorable results, carried that story to their readers. The Harvard Mental Health Letter, taking them at their word, announced to its subscribers that the STAR* D results indicated that "with time and persistence nearly seven in 10 adults with major depression will eventually find a treatment that works."

Our review of their data disclosed that this is not at all what the STAR*D study's results show. *Analyzed properly, the results are highly unfavorable.* The study's reported positive findings for antidepressant drug treatment were the product of major deviations from their protocol.

What are *protocols*? Scientific studies have precise and detailed research designs, and these are called protocols. Any scientific grant funded by the federal government is required to have a protocol. Think of them like the rules of a game. They are predetermined procedures that you agree to abide by for the duration. Three strikes and you're out is a protocol in baseball. Protocols are essential to the design and implementation of all scientific experiments. You can no more change them in the middle of a study than you can change the number of strikes allowed in the middle of a baseball game.

A protocol specifies a study's objectives, experimental design, the selection and exclusion of subjects, the treatments to be assessed, what measures will be used to assess the results, the statistics to be used to analyze the data, safety issues to be addressed, and the publication plans. For a scientific study to be satisfactory, it must adhere absolutely to these specifications. You have to say in advance what it is that you are going to do and then you have to do it. Protocols are important because they maximize the likelihood the results will stand up, that they can be replicated by other researchers, that the science is sound.

This is not what transpired in the STAR*D study. As I take you through this, you will see how the researchers failed to adhere to their protocol. Understanding their infractions of the scientific method will not be difficult, and it will be clear that these infractions are as damning regarding antidepressant drug treatment as the absence of scientific justification for DSM diagnoses of depression (Chapter 3) and for the chemical imbalance theory (Chapter 4).

The purpose of the study was to assess the value of a drug switching strategy with patients who were regarded as *seriously depressed*; that is, patients who were diagnosed as being at least moderately or severely depressed, as opposed to being diagnosed as only mildly depressed.

Of the 4000 patients who entered the study, 931 were diagnosed as being only mildly depressed (23%; that is, about a quarter of the total). The psychiatrists had this information about the ratings of severity, the patients did not. The mildly depressed patients continued in the study and received drug treatments, but they were to be excluded from the calculations. Including them would be a violation of the protocol, since this was a study of patients who were diagnosed as being at least moderately depressed.

Studies that are designed to evaluate treatment effectiveness test patients before and after treatment to determine how much of a change, if any, has occurred that can be attributed to the treatment. Although the mildly depressed patients properly were excluded from the pre-treatment calculations, *they were included* in the post-treatment calculations. This violated the protocol and spuriously improved the apparent effectiveness of the drugs. After all, they were only mildly depressed before being given the drugs. They would have had to get worse to not have a positive effect on the results. This infraction is fully equal to changing the number of strikes allowed during a professional baseball game. In the world of science, it is unthinkable.

Let's look further. When making pre- and post-treatment calculations *the same scale has to be used for both measurements* so that any difference found between the pre and post measurements can be attributed to the treatment, not to the different measuring devices.

But in the STAR*D study, a use of different scales is exactly what happened. The protocol specified use of the Hamilton Depression Rating Scale as the measure of the severity of depression. Accordingly, this scale was administered pre and post treatment. The principal investigator of the STAR*D study had developed a depression questionnaire of his own that was similar to the Hamilton. The protocol specified this scale was to be used to track symptoms, not as an outcome measure. Their data showed this other scale *consistently gave less severe ratings for depression* than the Hamilton questionnaire.

When taking their measurements of the outcome of the drug treatments, the researchers properly used the Hamilton scale for their pre-measure, but instead of using it again as the post-measure to measure what improvement might have occurred, *they substituted the other questionnaire.* Even if the drugs had not been helpful, the lower scores on this scale would imply drug effectiveness. And no surprise, substituting this scale spuriously improved the reported outcome. It is another flagrant violation of their protocol and scientific standards.

Behind the study's drug switching design is psychiatry's unsubstantiated claim that depression is a biologically heterogeneous disorder. According to this theory, successful treatment is achieved when the right drug is found for each patient's form of depression. One of the goals of the study was to substantiate this claim. Contrary to their data, the authors of the STAR*D study inexplicably stated their results supported the switching strategy. *In fact, neither the theory nor the treatment strategy was supported by the study's results.*

Dr. Boren reviewed STAR*D's results with respect to this question of whether the different treatments with their differing biochemical actions met what was expected from the theory. In addition to being a Professor Emeritus at American University, Dr. Boren was employed by the National Institute on Drug Abuse (NIDA) to review drug research. He reported:

> The results from switching to the three different drugs were quite similar, in spite of dissimilar mechanisms of action . . .. There was no support for the theory that treating failed patients with drugs having a different mechanism of action would enhance the outcome.

In a separate publication, Dr. Pigott also summarized these results. He, too, pointed out that the results plainly contradicted the heterogeneity theory of depression, that the STAR*D researchers once again had misrepresented their results:

> The researchers claimed the switching strategy worked even though there were no significant differences in the comparisons of 11 pharmacologically distinct drug treatments. It did not matter what drugs were prescribed because every drug or drug combination yielded about the same effect as every other drug or combination.

So, the sequential treatment strategy failed: No drug worked any better than the others. Once again, these results should not be surprising. In Chapter 4, you learned that the serotonin theory has not been supported when tested and the same results were found for all the other neurotransmitter theories. The SSRIs are psychiatry's rain dances. Failure to report these negative findings and the negative implications of these findings, *which relate directly to current psychiatric treatment guidelines*, is another major violation of the protocol's requirements.

STAR*D study's most publicized claim was that almost 70% of the patients were treated successfully after up to four medications. The NIMH reported these results to the public. The claim was repeated in the Harvard Mental Health Letter and by many other newspapers. However, this conclusion, too, was based on a faulty statistical analysis. Statistical tests are based on a set of assumptions. For a statistical test to be valid, the data being tested must meet these requirements. STAR*D's researchers acknowledged that the statistical analysis used in calculating this reported finding of 70% success assumed either no dropouts or the same remission rate for continuing patients as those who dropped out. However, the data showed that *neither requirement was met*, disqualifying this analysis: With each successive drug treatment, the number of patients who dropped out increased and the number who remitted declined.

More patients dropped out of the study at each step than those who continued. The researchers did not count as failures the hundreds of patients who dropped out of the study soon after starting on the first drug. It was as if these patients had never been enrolled in the study. Many others dropped out later.

The prime reason patients drop out of drug studies is because they dislike the side effects of the drugs and see no benefit. By omitting the inclusion of these patients in their analyses they greatly reduced the number of reported failures. As for the second requirement, the absence of data from the dropouts made it impossible to compare their remission rates to continuing patients. *The claim that 70% of the patients were treated successfully by the SSRIs was spurious.*

Twelve months after treatment began, 1,410 (93%) of the 1,518 previously remitted patients *had dropped out* of the study. Take note: dropping out meant forfeiting getting free drugs. Only 108 (7%) were still in treatment. Not only did STAR*D's researchers fail to comment on these findings, they also did not follow up on them. Why carry out a study for 12 months and not pursue such provocative results? While we cannot know exactly what motivated this false reporting of the long-term results of antidepressant drug treatment, it is quite clear that false reporting abounded. In the face of such overwhelming evidence, it is difficult not to conclude that the authors of the study were determined to give an NIMH imprimatur to the standard psychiatric drug regimen for treating depression no matter what the results showed. In Chapter 12 I will review research results that corroborate that long-term use of antidepressant drugs is associated with continuous relapse, not recovery. Did these STAR*D patients drop out because they continue to relapse? Only follow up can answer this question.

Earlier in this chapter I reviewed Dr. Antonuccio's critique of the drug companies' clinical trials of antidepressant drugs as having falsely inflated the effectiveness of these drugs. He based this conclusion on research by Dr. Irving Kirsch, who obtained the data from these clinical trials through the Freedom of Information Act. Dr. Kirsch's analyses showed that the drug company reports of the clinical trials significantly exaggerated the effectiveness of antidepressant drug treatment.

In 2018, Dr. Kirsch once again made use of the Freedom of Information Act in order to obtain the STAR*D data from the NIMH. He found that the rates of improvement claimed for these patients had been inflated. They were *even lower* than what had been found on placebos in other studies. In Chapter 7 you will see an explanation provided by Giovanni Fava for why the results for these drugs were even poorer than for placebo. Dr. Fava's review of antidepressant research results has led him to warn that *the switching strategy can cause physical harm*.

The correct conclusion concerning the effectiveness of the SSRI antidepressants prescribed in this study is that *remission rates for these drug treatments, when calculated correctly from their data, were* at best *25–30%, not 70%* as reported by the STAR*D studies' authors and widely cited ever since. Numerous studies have found placebos help 25–30% of those taking them. Thus, the STAR*D results are fully in agreement with these studies, which include the previous NIMH studies which showed that the SSRIs are no more effective than placebos.

It is noteworthy that the high number of dropouts occurred even though doctors strongly counseled patients on the importance of continuing in treatment for the treatment to be effective. These were real patients, being treated in clinics across the country (not volunteers in drug trials), and they were told to persevere until a drug seemed to them to be effective and then to stay on it. A strength to the STAR*D study was that it lasted for a year, not just a few months as is most often the case. This enabled the opportunity to derive far better information about the effectiveness of the SSRIs.

However, contrary to the doctors' advice to persevere with their drug treatment, within that year the great majority of the patients dropped out of treatment, disappearing from the study without notifying the doctors or researchers—a critically important finding not discussed in the text that was buried in one of the tables of results required by the protocol.

Regardless of the erroneous interpreting of the results of the STAR*D's study, it is important to recognize that the data are there, ready to be analyzed and interpreted correctly. We can look at the data with an unbiased eye, with scientific detachment and in a true spirit of inquiry. As you have seen, when we do this, in stark contrast to the favorable reports of the study's outcome, the findings are so very substantial and so unfavorable in so many ways that the obvious conclusion is that *the study fails to support the prescription of antidepressant drugs as an effective treatment for people diagnosed as depressed.*

As I prefaced in my lead up to discussion of this study, previous results indicated that prescription of antidepressant drugs is not an effective treatment for depression. STAR*D, the most extensive test of these drugs, fully confirms this conclusion.

The British psychiatrist, Dr. Joanna Moncrieff, after reviewing the actual results of the STAR*D study concluded "... STAR*D suggests that in real life situations (which the STAR*D mimicked better than other trials) people taking antidepressants do not do very well. In fact, given that for the vast majority of people depression is a naturally remitting condition, it is difficult to believe that people treated with antidepressants do any better than people who are offered no treatment at all." I would amplify this by adding: Most people diagnosed as depressed and taking antidepressants are not depressed, they are sad, and these prescriptions not only are no more helpful than placebos, the drugs are potentially harmful.

Part Two

The STAR*D study is striking for several reasons. First, the study provides clear-cut empirical evidence that *antidepressant drugs are not very effective treatments for depression*. By comparing STAR* D's results with other research, we can infer that the SSRIs, just as was the case with previously prescribed antidepressants, are no better than sugar pills (placebos). Second, the study is another illustration of how *psychiatrists have misreported research results about drug effectiveness* when the findings have not been to their liking, with more examples to come in later chapters. Third, the *NIMH's silence on the actual results of the study* is a prime indication of how serious a problem we have in understanding and treating depression and other mental disorders.

The STAR*D study was conducted under the auspices of the NIMH, which is one of the institutes within the National Institute of Health (NIH), our acclaimed national research institution. This was not the usual NIMH grant. The study began seven years earlier, in 1999, as an NIMH conducted research contract, preceding the STAR*D grant. Three NIMH employees were co-authors of several of the STAR*D publications, two of them being branch chiefs. It is disheartening that the largest and most expensive study ever conducted on the effectiveness of the antidepressant drugs being prescribed to patients diagnosed as seriously depressed, a study carried out under the auspices of the NIMH, reported these chemicals were effective when this was not true. Our premier government mental health research organization has failed us.

How could this happen? How could the authors of a major study make so many false claims and have them accepted by NIMH reviewers and by reviewers at the psychiatric medical journal that published the results? The answer to these questions is not reassuring. Earlier I cited the fact that all the errors in the study worked to make antidepressants seem more effective. Equally as persuasive and equally damning is the fact that the evidence for these distortions was well hidden. I have since spoken with others in the field of mental health who are experienced at analyzing research results, who told me they suspected something was wrong with the study but had not been able to verify their concerns. There is, in these cases, no sword that can cut the Gordian knot in one fell swoop. It takes painstaking effort and time to unravel the relevant strands, and not many people have such time or are driven to make the effort. Nevertheless, the false claims should have been detected by expert reviewers at the NIMH and the medical journal that published STAR*D. After all, possession of this expertise qualified them for their positions. Up until recently we have operated on a system of trust; we extend our belief to the claims that qualified professionals make.

It is my sad contention that such *trust no longer is warranted.* Yet again, a "scientific" foundation stone for current psychiatric practice regarding depression is found to have been made up out of thin air. You have seen that psychiatric diagnoses clearly are not a product of medical science as claimed; that the scientific sounding claim for the chemical imbalance theory is devoid of science; and now we know that the well accepted rationale for prescribing and taking antidepressant drugs also has no science behind it. This is not a trustworthy system.

****

So, what happened to our critique of the STAR*D study? This, in itself, is a rather revealing story and let me present the negative before I come to the positive outcome.

As reputable scientists, my colleagues and I wrote up our findings in a carefully documented journal article. We then submitted the article to The American Journal of Psychiatry (AJP), the medical journal that had published the STAR*D articles so rampant with false analyses and claims. The AJP is the house journal of the American Psychiatric Association. The article we submitted met the expected requirements for consideration. We had the requisite credentials to be taken seriously.

There is a norm in professional journals for the way in which articles that meet requirements by credentialed authors are handled. It is customary under these circumstances for the editor to send submitted articles out for peer review by several expert reviewers before any decision has been made. The more controversial the claims of the article, the more important this process becomes. It takes weeks or longer to receive an answer under these circumstances.

This is not what happened in the case of our article. Our submission not only was rejected, we received the editor's rejection within days. We were faced with the inevitable suspicion that the editor did not follow the standard practice of submitting it to other professionals for review.

Wouldn't it have made sense, especially in a case where the results of a major study were being challenged, for the editor to request from the journal's scientific reviewers their opinion of our critique of the STAR*D study, especially since the AJP had published the STAR*D articles?

A recent article in the Scientific American cites Dr. John Ioannidis, an epidemiologist and professor at Stanford University's School of Medicine. He has been critical of the editors of journals, "the gatekeepers of scientific evidence

. . . who are responsible, both for looking into conflicts of interest and weeding out those studies whose conclusions do not match up with the supplied data." Dr. Ioannidis wrote that when contradictory evidence was submitted to journals "the reception was cold . . . and many of their editors have strong ties to the (pharmaceutical) industry." Does this last bit of information surprise any reader who has been following this book's revelations?

Fundamental to the scientific method is continued collection, analysis, and reporting of data to confirm or refute previously reported results, an iterative and corrective process that has proven essential to revealing Nature's stubbornly hidden truths. As Dr. Max Planck, the renowned physicist put it, "Science advances one funeral at a time." Also relevant is a famous story about the physicist, Dr. Richard Feynman. After publishing a ground-breaking paper on quantum mechanics that made him famous, he was found hard at work. When asked what he was doing, he replied he was attempting to disprove his theory. Drs. Planck and Feynman exemplify commitment to a scientific model. The abrupt rejection of our submission ran counter to this scientific tradition.

Now for something positive: Not all journals have fallen under the influence of business and career interests. Other journals have published our findings. The primary critique (the one rejected by the American Journal of Psychiatry) was published in 2009 in the journal Psychotherapy and Psychosomatics (Pigott, Leventhal, Alter, and Boren, "Efficacy and Effectiveness of Antidepressants: Current Status of Research," pages 267–279). It is available free of charge through the journal's website. References for the other two publications are given in the Notes for this chapter. Since our primary article was published, according to an organization that tracks research citations, it has been cited more than two hundred and fifty times in other journal articles pertaining to this area of research. This, in and of itself, is a statement of positive peer review.

Here is a final negative note. Prior to the STAR*D study the NIMH stated: "The NIMH will disseminate the results of STAR*D through a defined outreach to practitioners, the media, and the public." When the results were thought to be positive, that is what the NIMH did. As far as I know, there has not been one press release to practitioners, to the media, or to the public that the results have been deemed by trustworthy experts to be negative.

Nor has anyone at the NIMH given a TED talk on these very important results. Why would we not conclude that the NIMH has failed to give doctors and the public the truth about the absence of support found in this study (and others) for treating depression by prescription of antidepressant drugs? *False reporting of antidepressant effectiveness has a long shelf life.* The corrupted results keep getting reported as if they are true. Dissemination of the falsely reported results of the STAR*D study abound right up to the present time and they occur in well-respected publications.

Here are just three examples: The March 2018 issue of Scientific American carried an article on brain scans by Dr. John Gabrielli, a Professor in the Harvard-MIT program of Health Sciences and Technology. He cited the STAR*D study's fictitious results in illustrating his case. Richard Friedman is a professor of psychiatry at Weill Cornell Medical College. Dr. Friedman writes columns on mental health matters that regularly appear on the op-ed pages of The New York Times. In February of 2017, repeating the erroneous claims made for the STAR*D study's results, he wrote: "About one third of patients with major depression don't get better, even after several trials with antidepressant drugs." The implication is that two thirds *do* get better with the switching strategy. In fact, the result with these drugs was *significantly less than half that*, even worse or no better than those on placebo. These results align with the conclusion that whatever benefit exists is a psychological, not a chemical effect. His audience of millions of readers far outstrips the number of readers who have been informed about the actual results of the STAR*D study. After all, the number of those who read medical and psychological journals pales in comparison with those who read the New York Times.

This false narrative that antidepressants are effective for two thirds of those taking them is found even in stories directed at informing the public about the dangers of taking these drugs. Rachel Aviv, in an article published in the New Yorker in April 2019, recounts how a young woman's misery was worsened by the prescription of antidepressants (and other psychiatric drugs). But in the course of doing so, she cites these falsely reported claims for antidepressants as a justification for their prescription. The results, as we have seen, are the opposite.

The chemicals in these drugs have been found to be ineffective, but few know it. Dr. Thomas Insel, who resigned as the Director of the NIMH a few years ago, reported to researchers (not the public), that the primary antidepressant used in the STAR*D study yielded results no better than commonly found in other studies which included placebos. Our own re-analysis of STAR*D's results disclosed none of the other drugs prescribed in this study was any better. Dr. Insel went on to state, "the unfortunate truth is that current medications help too few people to get better and very few people to get well." These results are entirely consistent with the reports of the failed tests of brain theories cited by authorities in the previous chapter, who have no conflict of interest. Yet NIMH's research funding remains heavily focused on biomedical explanations for depression and psychiatric guidelines continue to recommend antidepressant drug treatments, producing 22 billion dollars in antidepressant drug prescriptions in the United States in 2013.

It is difficult not to be dismayed at how the NIMH has been silent about the dissemination of false and highly misleading information about the results of a major, very important and very expensive study funded by the NIMH. Reading this book has acquainted you with a number of examples of psychiatric researchers whose work is more reflective of financial interests than science. But this part of the story implicates the NIMH. The NIMH is supported by the public's money–your taxes and mine. The misreporting of the STAR*D study's results are of importance to millions of people. It was an expensive and extensive study whose results show that millions of people are spending a considerable amount of their assets on a treatment definitively found to be wanting. Yet the NIMH does not seem concerned about disseminating the actual results of the study.

The misrepresentation of STAR*D's results and the lack of interest psychiatric leaders have shown in acknowledging the actual results of the study are no surprise to those who have followed this subject without bias or a hidden agenda. This is not the first example of such misrepresentation, and it will not be the last as you will see later and read in the words of outstanding and objective scientists.

****

A review of this kind should not fail to mention, at least as a postscript, the curious issue of the drug companies' decision-making process. How do drug companies decide at what ailment a drug is to be directed? The popular understanding is that specific drugs are developed for specific treatments. Often, this is not the case. During drug development the effects of chemical compounds under study are assessed with respect to their economic as well as their healing value. The decision about what to call the "main effect" is a matter of choice, and that choice is made by the drug manufacturer. These judgments determine not only the drugs selected for manufacture but also to whom they will be marketed.

Drugs that might be beneficial in terms of health but are deemed to have too small a market are unlikely to be pursued. The manufacturer decides what effects are of interest based on which ones are likely to sell and that analysis determines what effects will be marketed as the drug's main effect. It's a business decision that may deviate from which effects are the most likely to be stimulated by the chemicals in the drug.

Psychiatric drugs provide particularly good examples. As I indicated in Chapter 4, the drug iproniazid was found to be useful as a drug to treat tuberculosis and was marketed with this being its main effect. However, it had only a meager clientele when it was prescribed for this purpose. It became a blockbuster in sales when its main effect was alleged to be a treatment for depression, marketed as Marsilid. The same story applies to another chemical that was being developed, this one as a preservative for penicillin, which was projected to provide not much of a financial return. Marketing it as an anti-anxiety drug transformed Miltown into a blockbuster, as well. Calling a drug an antidepressant doesn't make it so. Should sugar pills, as placebos which have the same level of success, thus be called antidepressants?

There are other effects, called the side effects of antidepressants, however, that can readily be discriminated against from placebo. We can make a convincing case that what are being called the side effects of antidepressant drugs are, in fact, its main effects. For example, whereas these drugs reliably lead to gaining weight (which is now called a side effect), placebos do not. These drugs could more truthfully be marketed for this purpose. Of course, then very few people would buy them.

In 2012, Dr. Antonnucio, who I cited earlier in this chapter, together with Dr. David Healy, a psychiatrist, psychopharmacologist, and former Secretary of the British Association of Psychopharmacology, wrote:

> . . . a true antidepressant should be clearly superior to placebo, should offer a risk/benefit balance that exceeds that of alternative treatments, should not increase suicidality, should not increase anxiety and agitation, should not interfere with sexual functioning, and should not increase depression chronicity. Unfortunately, these medications appear to fall short on all of these dimensions. Many of the "side effects" of these medications have larger effect sizes than the antidepressant effect size. To call these medications antidepressants may make sense from a marketing standpoint but may be misleading from a scientific perspective. Consumers deserve a label that more accurately reflects the data on the largest effects and helps them understand the range of effects from these medications.
>
> In other words, it may make just as much sense to call these medications anti-aphrodisiacs as antidepressants because the negative effects on the libido and sexual functioning are so common. It can be argued that a misleading label may interfere with our commitment to informed consent. Therefore, it may be time to stop calling these medications antidepressants.

Manipulations of this kind are likely to be more successful when applied to the treatment of mental disorders than is the case with physical illness. Whereas tuberculosis and the reactions targeted by various drugs can be objectively defined and reliably measured, when it comes to the diagnosis and treatment of depression and other mental disorders the sky is the limit as to who qualifies as a customer. Because of the faulty nature of these diagnoses, the door is open to drug manipulations to a much greater extent than is possible with physical illnesses.

6

Drug Effects and Placebo Effects

The association between side effects (of antidepressant drugs) and improvement is so strong as to be almost perfect.

—*Irving Kirsch, PhD*

Let's now discuss the placebo, a subject that is intriguing. It can also be, as we shall see, controversial because it is often misunderstood. First let us be certain that we have a clear understanding of the concept.

What is a placebo? *A placebo is a pill, a substance or a treatment that has no pharmacological value.* It has no active ingredient that can affect health. It is one that a patient assumes to be good medicine because a doctor recommends it. Doctors who practice medicine with individual patients are not supposed to prescribe placebos, but research doctors are allowed to do so when treating patients who have volunteered for drug trials. *The positive results generated by placebos are called the placebo effect.*

The placebo effect is a psychological effect. It is a well-known, important by-product of a good therapeutic relationship. In other words, the relationship itself generates a certain positive effect independently of the efficacy of the therapy. It can occur in addition to or in lieu of a drug effect. Unfortunately, and this is where "controversial" enters the picture, the placebo effect is sometimes seen as a weakness, as a susceptibility to suggestion and a lack of autonomy. The idea that one can be susceptible to manipulation can be, understandably, alarming. Unscrupulous individuals who try to gain power over others can give a bad name to something that is neutral in and of itself but that can lend itself to misuse. Some hypnotists, for example, have been unsavory examples of such misuse.

The placebo effect at its best is an example of the way that belief and trust can heighten openness and thus positive effects. At its worst, the placebo is an example of human vulnerability to abuse. When we think of a placebo, we think about all these things and we worry that the placebo may entail losing that precious sense of self, the inviolate "I" that allows us to decide what we will do at any given moment. It is as if acknowledging the placebo effect carries the heavy price of having bought into a lie, of having lost our dignity by allowing ourselves to be fooled. Our good sense rebels at this.

If, however, we understand the placebo effect as a reflection of trust in the doctor to whom we have turned in an hour of need; if we understand that it is associated with the hope that we will soon feel better with our doctor's help, then our perspective may shift. What is essential to understand is that when we believe in an expert helper and we put ourselves in that person's hands, it dispels fear. This enhances the healing process.

Our willingness to comply when a doctor offers us a pill stems to some degree from this receptivity to a helper's recommendations. In part it also represents a natural desire to solve problems in the easiest way possible. This is why many people are receptive to psychiatric drug treatments. It is tempting to believe we can swallow a pill which will mysteriously balance out the chemicals in our brain and make our unhappiness disappear–more than temporarily. We may be, as Dr. Arnold Relman, a former Editor-in-Chief of the New England Journal of Medicine wrote, a grossly over-prescribed nation. Nonetheless, it is easy to understand the attraction of being able to solve one's problems, whether physical or psychological, by taking a pill.

The fact is that humans can be very suggestible. If a doctor says that a certain medicine has the side effect of inducing tears, or if a hypnotist suggests to a subject that he or she is going to cry, an expectation is established, and the reality may soon follow.

Research has disclosed that the placebo effect plays a significant role in promoting a favorable response to the treatment of such diverse illnesses as headaches, gastric acid secretion, asthma, coughs and colds, seasickness, arthritis, and many other illnesses–even a favorable response to surgery. So the placebo effect applies to an enhanced response to treatments for physical illnesses as well as to the drugs prescribed by psychiatrists.

Research results demonstrate that the placebo effect is especially evident when it comes to *pain.* Our psychological state influences the degree to which we translate the body's warnings as pain. We all know that if we are more relaxed, we suffer less when we undergo even a minor medical procedure like getting an inoculation. It stands to reason that the placebo effect will come into play in relation to anxiety, fear, sadness, and depression, since these experiences are forms of pain. *Seen this way, we understand the placebo effect, not as a form of trickery, but as a dynamic expression of the connection between body and mind.* It tells us how essential faith, being a good listener, and having hope are to the healing process.

Studies have shown also that the doctor/patient relationship influences the placebo effects. These effects have been shown to depend heavily and quite specifically on the explanation that the doctor gives to the patient about why the treatment has value. In other words, *the effects of placebos are specific to the beliefs that people form about the drug they are taking.*

When doctors prescribe an antidepressant drug, they tell their patients these drugs correct a serotonin deficiency in the brain that is the cause of depression. Patients are told this pill, or perhaps another one like it, will enhance the amount of serotonin in their brain and by doing so, it will help them feel better. As we have shown in reviewing the data, this is false, but it sounds scientific, and many are impressed by this explanation. What then occurs is that this explanation can trigger a placebo effect.

In placebo-controlled studies, whether they are related to physical illnesses or mental disorders, where some patients receive a drug and others a placebo, we are able to measure how much of the effect comes from the drug and how much of the effect is contributed by psychological factors.

****

Irving Kirsch is a professor at Harvard Medical School, where he is Associate Director of the Program on Placebo Studies. Dr. Kirsch is professor emeritus at the Universities of Hull and Plymouth in Great Britain and the University of Connecticut in the United States. He is a psychologist and a first-rate scientist. His major area of research interest has been studying the placebo effect. When he entered this field in the 1990s, much less was understood about the issues than is the case today. He stated: "Although almost everyone controls for placebo effects, almost no one evaluates them." Many of the results I have cited above came from his research.

Dr. Kirsch decided to study the placebo effect associated with antidepressants. It is important to note that at that time he had no particular interest in investigating the effectiveness of antidepressant drugs, per se. His focus was the placebo effect, and he chose to study antidepressants because he knew that quite a number of researchers had found no difference in effectiveness between antidepressants and placebos. So this area of research was a good place to study a robust placebo effect. The question he sought to answer through his research was: *How much of the benefit derived from antidepressant drugs is a drug effect; that is, an effect that is due to the chemicals in the drugs, and how much is attributable to a placebo effect; that is, a psychological effect?*

He began by reviewing medical journal articles investigating the effectiveness of antidepressant drugs. He found 19 publications of placebo-controlled antidepressant drug studies, enrolling about 2,300 patients, which provided sufficient data for him to measure the relative weights of the drug effects and the placebo effects. He selected for his study all the publications he found that met the following criteria: a primary diagnosis of depression; sufficient data to do the calculations for the drug and placebo conditions; random assignment of participants to those conditions; and an age range of 18–75. These were the basic conditions that needed to be met.

In many of these studies, the patients were administered the Hamilton Rating Scale for Depression, which I discussed in the previous chapter on the STAR*D study as the measure designated to determine the severity of depression. The Hamilton or another scale was used to measure depression severity before and after treatment either by antidepressant drugs or by placebo.

Dr. Kirsch analyzed the data in these 19 studies of antidepressant drugs to measure both *the size of the drug effect and the size of the placebo effect.* He carefully spelled out the statistical method he used to make his calculations of the size of these effects. His method was straightforward and sound. Should you wish to know more regarding how he went about his calculations, go to the Notes for this chapter at the end of this book for the reference, Kirsch and Saperstein.

Dr. Kirsch and his psychology graduate student, Guy Saperstein, measured and compared the average improvement by the patients treated with drugs versus those treated with placebos for each drug that had been prescribed. By means of these calculations, they were able to determine the size of the drug effect, that is, the amount attributable to the chemicals in the drugs, and they could determine the size of the placebo effect, that is, the amount attributable to psychological factors, not chemical factors. Their procedure fully determined the amount attributable to the chemicals, but it did not account for all the psychological factors. Some of them might have occurred without the placebo, such as simply the passage of time or because of someone's help.

They found that *75% of the benefit* obtained from taking these drugs was obtained from placebo. That was a very large placebo effect and a very small drug effect. Dr. Kirsch expected to find a substantial placebo effect. He was surprised by the very small size of the drug effect since even just 25% is misleading. *Data analyses indicated that almost the entire therapeutic benefit attributed to the drug was a placebo effect.*

There was considerable variability in the response to the drugs. Some patients' responses were small, others moderate, others larger. However, the type of drug did not make a difference. Much later, Dr. Kirsch would investigate this variability in more detail and find that *the placebo response was consistent* across the full range. In fact, he would discover that the correlation between the drug response and the placebo response across this range was extraordinarily high, yielding a *correlation of .90.* Moreover, the placebo response as a percent of the drug response was highly consistent across drug types. This was true whether the drugs were the tricylics, the SSRIs, or other drugs (for example, lithium, which is not even an antidepressant).

This is not typical of drugs that work for physical illnesses. It is such a striking difference that after considerable later research Dr. Kirsch would come to an important conclusion. He believes that the 25% he had previously ascribed to a drug effect in his first round of research was not a response to the chemicals in these drugs. Rather, the drugs were functioning *as active placebos;* that is, as placebos that were induced not only by faith in the doctor, but also by the patient's response to the *side effects of these drugs.*

Side effects can enhance the drug effect because patients often interpret these effects as meaning the drug is working leading them to rate their experiences more highly. The thinking is, "I can feel the drug. It must be working." Feelings really matter to us, and we use them often as an index for judging the efficacy of a remedy. Dr. Kirsch had expected a robust placebo effect, but these results led him to understand more fully the power of this psychological effect.

There are two different kinds of placebos that have been used in double blind placebo-controlled studies: *inert* placebos and *active* placebos. Inert placebos have no side effects; active placebos do. They are sugar pills with a little extra something (for example, atropine) that induces a noticeable physical effect, such as nausea. This makes it difficult for patients to become "unblinded." In other words, it is harder for patients in a double-blind placebo-controlled study that uses active placebos to recognize the medication they are taking as a placebo if it produces side effects.

Surprisingly, despite their greater scientific value, only a small number of antidepressant research studies have used active placebos. The results of the studies that do so are revealing. When studies using inert placebos were repeated using active placebos, the previously found advantage for antidepressants disappeared. In most of these studies, patients responded equally to the drugs and to the placebo. No longer did the results point to the drugs being effective. As I indicated in the last chapter, the prime value attributed to the chemicals in a drug are called the *main effect*. It was the *side effects* of the chemicals in the drugs that accounted for improvement: an active placebo effect.

Dr. Kirsch would come to this very conclusion. He determined that the entirety of the patient response to the antidepressant drugs likely was due to the meaning attributed to the side effects of the chemicals. It was not because of any inherent chemical benefit. None of this research on the active placebo effect of the chemicals in the drugs would appear in his first round of published studies—not that this spared him the full strength of the psychiatric community's ire.

In fact, when Dr. Kirsch published his first round of findings, the outcry was immediate. Psychiatrists attacked him with fury. His critics accused him of being biased, of having cherry picked the studies he had analyzed. They even accused him of faulty math.

Now Dr. Kirsch is a professor and a research scientist with impeccable credentials. He has never been accused of any kind of academic impropriety. He knew he had chosen the studies objectively, not arbitrarily, that he had selected all the studies that met the sensible criteria he had established, and it is clear from all his previous work as well as from his present studies that his math was sound. That he subsequently was invited to join the faculty at Harvard Medical School to continue his studies of the placebo effect is all the affirmation needed.

Nonetheless as a good scientist, rather than simply seeking to defend himself, he responded to his critics by doing what good scientists do. He gathered more data, and it was even more decisive and more damning.

Making use of the Freedom of Information Act, he next examined the data that had been submitted by the drug companies to the Food and Drug Administration (FDA) that had gained approval of the SSRIs, the major antidepressant drugs being prescribed to treat depression (Prozac, Paxil, Zoloft, Effexor, Serzone, and Celexa). These are the drugs preferred by psychiatrists to treat depression that I discussed in the last chapter that were prescribed in the STAR*D study.

Dr. Kirsch hoped that by choosing to analyze the data from the clinical trials of the SSRIs, he would silence the accusations of bias. Surely, psychiatrists would not argue with the value of the studies that the drug companies used in their own clinical trials. Moreover, any bias was likely to be in favor of the drugs. And, indeed, he found that the drug companies' management of the data indicated industry-wide practices consistent with such a bias. (Recall Dr. Antonuccio's points that I covered in the last chapter). Nevertheless, *he found that the data from these clinical trials furnished even stronger evidence that the benefit attributed to antidepressants was a placebo effect (80–85%).*

One of Dr. Kirsch's colleagues in this research, Dr. Thomas Moore, at the George Washington University School of Public Health and Health Services, has written about the non-significant difference between Prozac and placebo:

> The most intriguing results were for Prozac, the bestseller that transformed how the nation thought about drugs and depression. Prozac patients improved about 8 points on a 0–50 scale of depression compared with 7 points for the patients who got a placebo.

A highly indicative aspect of the response to his work is what happened next: Psychiatrists were vocal in their opposition to the findings from Dr. Kirsch's first study, but when he reported the results of his study of the clinical trials of the SSRIs, results that confirmed all his prior findings and thus should have put their objections to rest, the psychiatric profession's response has been to continue to refuse to accept his findings. (A good example of this bias is what appears in Wikipedia, which cites a study that has statistical significance but falls far short of clinical significance, a well-recognized distinction in this area of research).

Dr. Kirsch's hopes that these data would lead his critics to acknowledge the strength of his research and the accuracy of his conclusions remains unfulfilled. To what must we attribute this refusal by a community that has been so vocal in proclaiming the science behind their drug treatments? It is difficult to see good faith in psychiatry's stance.

Ironically, Dr. Kirsch's discoveries were not news to those who have been engaged in this area of research. Unknown to many doctors and to the public, the researchers who conduct clinical trials and the FDA's reviewers of these trials have long referred to the small differences between the antidepressant drug response and the placebo response as the "dirty little secret." Why aren't those who know the most about the poor outcome with these drugs speaking out about it?

****

Let us return to the subject of the *side effects* and delve a little deeper. As I said above, Dr. Kirsch and others have directed attention to the important role that the side effects of antidepressant drugs play in how patients respond to antidepressants.

What are the side effects? Side effects vary from one patient to the next, but they are numerous and substantial: dry mouth, blurred vision, tremor, headaches, joint and muscle pain, nausea, weight gain, diarrhea or constipation, and sexual dysfunction. These are effects that can easily get one's attention. (Some drug effects are so disabling that they qualify as *adverse effects*, a subject I will discuss in the next chapter).

It doesn't matter how one generates side effects. Studies show that anti-anxiety drugs, sedatives, barbiturates, stimulants, antipsychotic drugs, opiates, and thyroid medications (all with side effects) produce side effects equal to antidepressants. Dr. Kirsch summarized the research results, stating:

> Drugs that increase, decrease, or have an effect on serotonin all relieve depression to about the same degree. But they all caused side effects and patients were informed to anticipate these effects in advance of taking the drugs.

Dr. Kirsch concluded, "The association between side effects and improvement is so strong as to be almost perfect." In other words, the positive effects attributed to the chemicals in the antidepressant drugs were not the result of some useful chemical effect but were attributable to how patients interpreted the side effects of the chemicals; in other words, they were *psychological, not physiological effects.*

This point is underlined by the results of some other studies conducted by Dr. Kirsch. In 2008, he studied the issue that had been raised after the first NIMH depression study in 1989 and was the focus in 2006 of the STAR*D Study; that is, the important question of the effectiveness of antidepressants with patients diagnosed as *severely depressed.* You will recall that in both instances research results failed to confirm the effectiveness of antidepressants as treatments for these patients.

Dr. Kirsch found that any comparative benefit for these seriously depressed patients that was derived from antidepressants was not due to an *increased response to the drug.* Instead, it was due to a *decreased response to the placebo.* In other words, it was how patients interpreted the side effects of the drugs that accounted for the results. This sounds complicated. In fact, it is simple. Severely depressed patients are more likely to be chronically depressed. Chronically depressed patients are more likely to have received prior treatment with antidepressant drugs. They are likely also to be prescribed higher doses of antidepressants with larger side effects. So, this group of patients is particularly aware of how the side effects of these drugs feel, fueling a response on this basis when the studies in which they participate administer inert placebos, which almost all of them do.

Also relevant to this issue are his findings with respect to studies he conducted on the *effectiveness of increasing drug dosage.* When antidepressant drugs don't work, psychiatrists and other doctors commonly increase the dosage. He found that higher doses were no more effective than lower doses. *There was no dose-response curve for antidepressants.* As I indicated earlier, this is out of keeping with what is found with drugs prescribed to treat physical illnesses that are known to be effective. This could not be said, for example, of insulin or of penicillin. However, it is in keeping with a psychological explanation of a placebo effect. *What higher doses of antidepressants do is cause more side effects.*

There is another issue. Psychiatrists have theorized about drugs that have different mechanisms of action. They explain drug failures by asserting there are different types of depression that require different drugs to address these different forms of the disorder. Identifying which drug is right for a given patient requires trial and error prescribing. In Chapter 5 I reviewed the STAR*D study's results for the different drugs that were prescribed. Drs. Boren and Pigott, whom I identified in Chapter 5, found that pharmacologically different drugs yielded the same results. And those results were equivalent to those found for placebo in other studies. Although their mechanisms differed, the common feature was they all had side effects, consistent with Dr. Kirsch's conclusions.

In summary, antidepressant drugs are prescribed for depression on the theory that they correct a deficiency of serotonin in the brain. But Dr. Kirsch found that *whether a drug increased, or decreased serotonin was not what mattered in the reporting of the outcome. The response was contingent on whether the drug produced side effects.* Dr. Kirsch's results indicate that when patients report improvement after taking an antidepressant drug, it is not a drug effect, it is a placebo effect that is manifested in two ways. In general, improvement occurs based on hope and belief in what one's doctor has said about a treatment. We see now that improvement also is based on how patients interpret the side effects of the drug they have taken in relation to what they have been told by their doctor. This magnifies the placebo effect. Just as Dr. Venstein had found in his research on serotonin and depression (Chapter 4), a drug's effect on serotonin is not the crucial issue.

Dr. Kirsch concluded, "Rather than comparing a placebo to a drug we have been comparing regular placebo to extra strength placebo." Those who benefit from antidepressant drugs do so on the basis of what they make of the drug's side effects, a psychological effect, not a chemical effect.

There is yet another ironic twist in this. Although the drug treatment regimen most often induces passivity, not problem solving, in some cases the placebo effect may prompt useful self-help behaviors. *The placebo effect can act as a catalyst, energizing patients to engage in positive behaviors that remedy depression.* It can act inadvertently, but helpfully, to jump start a beneficial outcome. For example, a patient who thinks that the antidepressant they are taking is providing some benefit might start to exercise or to engage in another self-helping behavior, which leads to improvement.

Some patients conclude it was the chemicals in the drug (rather than their own behavior) that proved to be helpful. So yes, in some instances, antidepressants can lead to positive changes. They do so in a roundabout way, however. It is rather like reaching over and around your head to scratch an ear with the opposite hand. What is needed is a treatment that promotes positive behaviors and eliminates dysfunctional behaviors. This can be accomplished effectively, reliably, safely, and inexpensively when it is designed as such and carried out deliberately and collaboratively.

A brief final comment is pertinent regarding psilocybin (mushrooms), a drug outside the mainstream that is sometimes touted as a treatment for depression. In 2021, Ezra Klein, the New York Times columnist, wrote about psyilocybin's potential benefits, including in the treatment of depression, anxiety, and drug addiction (others have touted it for PTSD), because of its alleged value in promoting openness to change. The research basis for this is weak. Conclusions based on only a brief follow-up (two months) are known to give unreliable results. Klein also acknowledges the adverse effects can be induced by psilocybin. However, his subject is the psychological effects associated with chemical effects, paralleling this process as it occurs in placebo-controlled studies. He makes a related point, warning that whatever value may be associated with the altered consciousness induced by psilocybin *is contingent upon acting on these experiences, stating that it was only by his acting on these experiences that he benefitted.*

Psychiatry's silence on the placebo issue means that primary care doctors are often unaware of how well-substantiated these results are in showing that antidepressants are nothing more than placebos. Some doctors along with psychiatrists are so enamored of drugs they simply refuse to believe these results. Patients may also strongly resist these findings when they are pointed out. Doctors in this country and elsewhere continue to prescribe antidepressants as the treatment of choice, catapulting the annual sales of these drugs into the many billions of dollars.

****

Let's review what we have covered so far. This is a book about the science related to depression. Psychiatrists have claimed that their medical practices are as sound scientifically as those by doctors who treat physical illnesses. In the opening paragraphs of this book I stated that this is false, that no good medical science supports how depression is diagnosed, explained, or treated. The research results we have reviewed regarding these basic issues reveals the following:

Diagnosis: For medical diagnoses to meet scientific standards they must be shown to be valid and reliable. Diagnoses of physical illnesses are based on objective data analyses that meet these scientific standards. Psychiatric diagnoses (the DSM) are based on subjective, unverified opinions of psychiatrists, not data, and they have failed to be shown to be valid or reliable. (See Chapter 3). With regard to depression, most diagnoses are mistaken because of a change first made to DSM-III and continuing in subsequent DSM manuals. It conflated sadness, a normal response to loss, with depression, a mental disorder. Since losses are common in life, the number of people who experience sadness far exceeds those who are depressed. As a result of this conflation of normality with abnormality, the number of people mis-diagnosed as depressed has skyrocketed. (See Chapter 1).

Explanation: Psychiatrists explain depression as resulting from a chemical imbalance of neurotransmitters in the brain. The theory is based on studies that violated basic scientific standards. Scientific tests of the theory have failed to corroborate the theory; in fact, the results contradict it. (See Chapter 4).

Treatment: The standard treatment for depression is prescription of antidepressant drugs. Numerous studies have found these drugs yield results equivalent to or worse than patients given placebo. (See Chapter 5).

Placebo effect: Whatever benefit is derived from antidepressant drugs is due to the placebo effect. Sound science is behind this conclusion. Thus, the positive effects of these drugs are psychological, not biological (medical). Billions of dollars are being mis-spent each year on pills that are placebos—expensive drugs with no medical value. (See Chapter 6).

To paraphrase Gertrude Stein, there is no there there. And yet this entire system remains firmly in place. *Psychiatry and Big Pharma are in complete control of the narrative.*

This is a scenario that could be the script for a TV comedy satire show if it were not real and disastrous. Millions of people are pinning their hopes on the value of this contrived, medicalized approach. They are pinning their hopes on a medicalized system that is wildly unscientific, one that can have seriously deleterious effects.

As Dr. Jerome Groopman, the Dina and Raphael Reconti Chair of Medicine at Harvard Medical School, has written in another context, "...in every era humanity wants to believe in its healers, who might be nothing more than salesmen with a good line." In the next chapter we shall see how dangerous these drugs can be.

****

As an addendum to place these issues in a broader context, let us take a moment to examine a discourse written by Sharon Begley that was published in Newsweek. Begley is an award-winning senior science correspondent for the Boston Globe who previously held the same position with Reuters. While her article doesn't add any new scientific information to the placebo discussion, it touches on the issues we have been reviewing and it is pertinent to our participation in a democratic society and to how we view our autonomy as individuals.

Begley has addressed a key aspect of this subject. She summarized for a general audience the findings on the effectiveness of antidepressant drugs, reporting that antidepressant drugs are like placebos in their helpfulness. But she cites concerns about "blowing the whistle on antidepressants." She reviews how Dr. Kirsch's research leads to the conclusion "that the lion's share of the drugs' effect comes from the fact that patients expect to be helped by them, and not from any direct chemical action on the brain, especially for anything short of very severe depression."

She reports on how psychiatry has mobilized against these findings, citing cases where scientists were warned not to collaborate in research with Dr. Kirsch if they expected grant support. She quotes friends "who believe Kirsch is right (but) ask why he doesn't just shut up, since publicizing the finding that the effectiveness of antidepressants is almost entirely due to people's hopes and expectations will undermine that effectiveness." In other words, the people she quotes are afraid this knowledge will spoil the placebo effect.

What Begley is really discussing is the issue of whether the population at large, or a segment of that population, can be treated like adults and whether they can behave as such. The population under discussion in this instance is made up of people who are seeking help. Can they be told the truth, or do they need to be infantilized?

As a general issue regarding truth telling in democracy, this has surfaced innumerable times in writing and even in film. It challenges, explicitly or implicitly, the meaning of democracy. From Emerson and Thoreau on, in writing, and from films like *Advice and Consent* to *One Flew Over the Cuckoo's Nest,* or to *The Manchurian Candidate* the underlying question is whether democracy is something for everyone, and under what circumstances is it justified to suspend the individual's right and ability to decide for him or herself. Both in film and on paper, the resounding majority vote has been resolved by democracy's champions *in favor of the truth.*

So, my question is the following: When it comes to addressing depression, should fake news trump factual news? Do we have the right to decide for others what truth should be told and what should be withheld? Is that kind of manipulation healthy or ethical? Doesn't it lead to layers of deception which the unscrupulous can use for their own self-interested purposes?

Begley writes that psychotherapy "is more effective than either pills or placebos, with lower relapse rates." She is right, yet she wonders if it isn't a "kindness" to keep patients "in the dark about the ineffectiveness of antidepressants" since there are not enough therapists, insurance plans discourage this form of treatment, and most patients are treated by primary care doctors. *Begley has identified precisely how things have been stood on their head by psychiatry's medicalization of mental disorder, by pharmaceutical industry power, and by the power of health insurance companies.* Psychotherapists are indeed in short supply. This is because insurance company reimbursement is directed against this more effective form of treatment.

Agency is essential; we own the consequences of our treatment choices. What if the treatment we are receiving is not helpful? Should one abandon observation to blind faith? We are the prime inheritors of the treatment choices we make, whether we choose to take advice to depend on drugs or psychotherapy, we are responsible when we maintain ineffective choices, regardless of what our doctor tells us. *The basic truth is that we must not absent ourselves from problem solving.*

The issue Begley has put in the forefront is what Dr. Kirsch has described as the story of the *Emperor Has No Clothes.* Doctors and patients have been led to believe in a failed theory. A highly orchestrated sales pitch has falsely promoted a poor treatment. Isn't it time to face up to what we know rather than choosing to believe in a naked emperor's non-existent clothing? This is the point that Dr. Kirsch makes when he asks, "Isn't it more important to know the truth?"

And yet, Begley has indirectly underlined, not a prescriptive, but a descriptive point. We see again and again that people can be resistant to the truth. Worse, they may resent those who make it difficult to maintain their mistaken beliefs. The town of Libby, Montana, illustrates this tragically.

Gayla Benefield told the inhabitants of Libby, Montana, the town she lived in, that people were being poisoned by a product from a nearby mine, vermiculite, which contained asbestos. It was used in everything from playgrounds for children to insulation for residential construction. No one believed her. According to the writer and lecturer, Margaret Heffernan, author of the book "Willful Blindness," they said things like, ". . . if it were really dangerous, someone would have told us;" or, ". . . if that was the reason that everyone was dying, the doctors would have told us," or again ". . . I can't be a victim and anyway, every industry has its accidents."

At length, a federal agency intervened, and it was discovered that Libby had a mortality rate 80 times higher than the rest of the United States. The town was drowning in a sea of asbestos. In a TED Talk she gave, Ms. Heffernan quotes studies indicating that in industry, 85% of employees know when something is wrong but will not speak out. In the story of the Emperor Has No Clothes, only a small child is willing to speak out.

For a very different response to the findings of Dr. Kirsch and the other scientists whose work I have been reviewing, consider the following report written by Benedict Carey of the New York Times in 2017,

> England is in the midst of a unique national experiment, the world's most ambitious effort to treat depression, anxiety, and other common mental illnesses. The rapidly growing initiative, which has gotten little publicity outside the country, offers virtually open-ended talk therapy free of charge at clinics throughout the country: in remote farming villages, industrial suburbs, isolated immigrant communities, and high-end enclaves. The goal is to eventually create a system of primary care for mental health not just in England but for all of Britain . . ..
>
> The demand in the first several years has been so strong it has strained the program's resources. According to the latest figures, the program now screens nearly a million people a year, and the number of adults with common mental disorders who have recently received some mental health treatment has jumped to one in three from one in four and is expected to continue to grow. Mental health professionals also say the program has gone a long way to shrink the stigma of psychotherapy in a nation culturally steeped in stoicism . . ..

> "It's not just that they're enhancing access to care, but that they're being accountable for the care that's delivered," said Karen Cohen, chief executive of the Canadian Psychological Association, which has been advocating a similar system in Canada:
>
> The program began . . . in 2008, with $40 million from Gordon Brown's Labor government. It set up 35 clinics covering about a fifth of England and trained 1,000 working therapists, social workers, graduates in psychology, and others. The program has continued to expand through three governments, both ideologically left and right leaning, with a current budget of about $500 million that is expected to double over the coming years . . ..
>
> The projected cost savings countrywide have been difficult to determine, given all the other economic factors in a $3 trillion, diversified economy, but the recovery numbers have given (the administrators) enough ammunition to argue for, and receive, funding from three governments in a row.

As a result of the research record, I have been reviewing in these chapters, unlike what is happening in the United States, Great Britain has decided to study in a major way the use of psychological treatments for mental disorders, including depression. The primary treatment the therapists in this program are being trained to offer is behavior therapy. Other psychological treatments are being tested as well. The final three chapters of this book will be about the scientific basis for behavior therapy for depression and other mental disorders and the advantages this form of treatment offers over drug treatment.

7

Antidepressant Drug Safety

As the psychopharmacology revolution has unfolded, the number of disabled mentally ill in the United States has skyrocketed.

—Robert Whitaker

Part One

The FDA has the task of balancing the economic benefits of the pharmaceutical industry against the health of patients. Doctors understand that all drugs have a range of effects, some positive and some negative. They believe that the drugs approved by the FDA are effective and safe. If the FDA maintains its commitment to scientific methodology, a small margin of error is regrettable but inevitable.

It is when boundaries erode and commitment to the scientific method weakens that a different order of problems sets in. This is precisely what has happened. Antidepressant drugs present us with a clear example of this different order of problem. In the interest of brevity, you will find validation for the adverse effects discussed in this chapter referenced in the Notes at the end of the book.

In the last chapter we discovered the delicate and complex role that side effects can play, a relationship that some doctors do not fully understand. Doctors know about the side effects of drugs, and they duly issue warnings about them when they prescribe drugs. Unfortunately, the term "*side effects*" can mask the serious physical harm caused by some of these drugs, which are then termed *adverse effects.*

What do we know about the safety of antidepressant drugs? It is easy to swallow a pill prescribed by a doctor and marketed by the televised and Internet hype that often goes with it, and many do so in full confidence that if the drug they are taking were not safe, the FDA would not have approved it and doctors would not be prescribing it. As you shall see, *there are reasons to question the safety of antidepressant drugs.*

Prescription drugs are not the same as other products and most countries have chosen to limit their demand. The United States and New Zealand are the only two countries that allow direct-to-consumer advertising of prescription drugs on television and the Internet. This form of advertising has been found to significantly influence patients and doctors. Patients regularly ask for specific drugs they have seen advertised, and a study found that when a patient inquires of his doctor about a drug, the doctor is likely to prescribe it.

The pharmaceutical industry lobbied Congress to pass legislation that permitted this form of advertising in 1997. The pharmaceutical industry's budget for direct-to-consumer advertising of prescription drugs *is almost twice the entire budget of the FDA*. Review of the truthfulness of these ads by the FDA is woefully poor. The quality of The FDA's oversight is revealed by a report that the FDA could afford only 59 employees to monitor 71,759 industry submissions of direct-to-consumer promotional materials. I shall examine this problem in Chapter 9.

In Chapter 5 I reviewed the evidence for calling into question the FDA's assessment of the *effectiveness* of antidepressant drugs. The FDA erred in approving the clinical trials of the SSRIs as demonstrating these drugs were more effective than placebos. A considerable research record also calls into question the FDA's assessment of the *safety* of antidepressant drugs, particularly with respect to their long-term use, which is the recommended treatment for many patients diagnosed as depressed.

When the benefit of a drug is attributable to the placebo effect, the cost/benefit analysis needs to be assessed by means of a different lens. After all, *if the value of a drug is psychological, why expose yourself to physical harm?*

Antidepressants have manifold adverse effects which take a while to occur. Some of these adverse effects are permanent. The adverse effects can be severe, and they can occur for all ages according to length of use, size of dosage, and whether combined with other drugs. To counter these reactions, doctors may prescribe additional drugs, and these have their own adverse effects.

This is not a new story. From their inception the record for the safety of antidepressant drugs has been questionable. This was true of the Tricyclics (TCAs) and the MAO Inhibitors, when they were the antidepressants of choice for treating depression. And it is true of the drugs evaluated in the STAR*D study, the Selective Serotonin Reuptake Inhibitors (SSRIs).

The Tricyclics (Elavil, Novartis, Pamelar, and Tofranil) induce serious adverse effects, including anxiety, confusion, weight gain, sexual dysfunction, sleep disturbance, constipation, and urinary retention. They are highly toxic if overdosed.

The MAO Inhibitors (Iproniazid, Marplan, Nardil, and Parnate) carry warnings as dangerous drugs. In addition to all of the above adverse effects, they interact with foods containing tyramine (cheeses, alcohol, some over the counter meds), which can cause stroke or cardiac arrest and can precipitate a psychosis. For a while they were taken off the market because they were found to be as dangerous as the anti-anxiety drugs, the highly addictive benzodiazepines, sold as tranquilizers and sleeping pills (Valium, Librium, Ativan, Restoril, Xanax, Dalmane, and Halcion). Despite these warnings, gradually psychiatrists began prescribing these anti-anxiety drugs and the MAO Inhibitors continue to be prescribed.

Today's most frequently prescribed antidepressants are the SSRIs, the Selective Serotonin Reuptake Inhibitors (Prozac, Paxil, Celexa, Zoloft, and Lexapro). The adverse effects of the SSRIs, which are claimed to be minimal, are underreported. The science journalist, Robert Whitaker, has reported that in the two years following the approval of Prozac, FDA's Medwatch program received more adverse event reports about Prozac than it had received in 20 years about the leading tricyclic antidepressant. Prescription of the SSRIs increased in 20 years by a factor of 40, from sales of $500 million to $20 billion. Medwatch estimated that 4 million people in the US, after taking Prozac, experienced one or more of the following adverse effects: mania, psychotic depression, anxiety, hallucinations, memory loss, tremors, impotence, convulsions, nausea, and insomnia. Similar results were found for the other SSRIs. By 1994, four SSRIs were among the top twenty most complained about drugs. Hospital admissions reflected these seriously adverse reactions: Eight percent of mental hospital admissions were diagnosed as SSRI-induced mania or psychotic episodes. The FDA's failure to alert the public to these adverse effects led Whitaker to describe the FDA as "lapdogs" of the drug companies, not "watchdogs."

****

Let's look at some risk factors associated with antidepressants with respect to gender, age, pregnancy, and socioeconomic status. There is considerable disparity in use with respect to gender. More than twice as many women as men take antidepressants. Almost a quarter of women in their 40s and 50s take antidepressants. Thus, women are at greater risk than men.

An important issue is the use of antidepressants during pregnancy. While many doctors do not recommend taking antidepressants during pregnancy, there are unfortunately too many who do. Pregnancy is a biological condition that can be challenging emotionally. Hormones increase, chiefly estrogen and progesterone, because they are important to development of the fetus, as well as preparing the mother's body to carry and deliver a baby.

Pregnancy is also a psychological condition–exciting and daunting. Many women find themselves emotionally reactive in ways that are disconcerting. Some find themselves more anxious and or irritable, some may take umbrage more easily, and the desire for surroundings that provide physical security can be very compelling. The physical changes can cause women to feel less attractive. Women may worry about losing the baby, about not being a good mother, about financial matters, about career concerns, etc. There are studies that indicate that postpartum depression, often mistakenly viewed as being hormonal, is more likely related to inadequate social and physical support following delivery.

Not all women experience all or indeed any of these physical or psychological symptoms, but enough women do that many have become part of a standard checklist of what to expect when pregnant. In grappling with these issues, women are well advised to avoid taking antidepressant drugs during pregnancy and to make use instead of psychological treatment if they need help.

Of particular concern are the adverse effects of antidepressant drugs on babies in utero. A comprehensive study published in 2010 reviewed the negative effects on babies of the dramatic increase over the previous decade in the number of pregnant women taking antidepressant drugs. The authors stated that researchers "have begun to openly question the safety of (antidepressant drugs) for maternal and pediatric populations." (See Notes for references on these risks). Most importantly, first trimester use of SSRIs is associated with risk of birth defects, primarily pulmonary and cardiovascular abnormalities. Benedict Carey, a science writer with the New York Times, reviewed a report by The World Health Organization, that warned infants whose mothers took antidepressants during pregnancy showed withdrawal symptoms, including convulsions. Researchers also have reported that exposure to antidepressants in utero is associated with increased risk of developmental defects. The negative effects on babies include irritability, weak crying, poor muscle tone, sleep disturbances, tremors, rapid respiration, and increased rates of admission to neonatal intensive care. Unfortunately, despite (and because of) the importance of this area of research, the studies lack rigor, limiting the certainty of the conclusions. There are no placebo-controlled studies or comparisons with psychological treatment.

Nevertheless, in this chapter I will review multiple well-documented adverse effects of antidepressant drugs on those taking them. Why would we not be concerned as well about the effects of these drugs on babies in utero? Since there is a superior treatment that poses no such risks (see Chapter 12), why would a woman take these drugs during pregnancy?

The point is that antidepressant drugs are not without *unintended effects* on the body. The most commonly occurring adverse effects are substantial weight gain; sleep disturbance; anxiety, and agitation; gastrointestinal disturbances; and adverse blood changes. Sexual dysfunction is common. Men stop taking these drugs because they induce erectile problems. Liver damage, facial tics and muscular rigidities can occur and can become permanent. Hospitalizations for adverse reactions to antidepressants occur with some frequency. The chemicals in these drugs have not been shown to be effective in treating depression, but don't think that this means they have no power. They are powerful and they pose risks.

There are adverse effects that I will review in more detail. They involve neurological damage, addiction, suicide, and violence. For the moment I will cite just a couple of adverse effects of particular concern to those at the other end of the spectrum: the elderly. Jane Brody, the Personal Health columnist for the New York Times, has warned of serotonin syndrome. Serotonin toxicity can result from the SSRIs when taken in combination with other drugs. This is not unusual, particularly in the elderly. The adverse effects of serotonin syndrome fall into three categories: cognitive dysfunction (confusion, agitation, disorientation), neuromuscular problems (rigidity, tremors, loss of coordination) and effects on the autonomic nervous system (fever, cardiac problems, profuse sweating). The condition can be life threatening for the elderly. In addition, a study published in the Archives of Internal Medicine of 5000 patients over a 5-year period found that those who took SSRIs had reduced bone density, were more likely to fall, and were twice as likely to have a broken bone–a risk factor of particular concern to older patients, even leading to their death.

Prescription of antidepressant drugs for children came later than for adults and has increased exponentially in the last 20 years. *Prescription of these drugs to children in this country increased from three to tenfold (depending on the source of the figures) between 1983 and 1996.* This shocking increase was followed by another 50% rise in the prescription of antidepressants to children between 1998 and 2002. These increases took place despite the very questionable evidence that these drugs are effective in treating children. They did so despite the evidence of their danger to adults.

Just as has been the case with adults, the failure of antidepressant drugs to be of help to children diagnosed as depressed has been followed by the prescription of even more powerful drugs to these children, *antipsychotic drugs* prescribed for bipolar disorder. The antipsychotic drugs block dopamine in the brain. The dopamine chemical imbalance theory, which has been advanced as the cause of schizophrenia (a psychosis), has failed, too, to be supported by research.

The antipsychotic drugs have not been shown to be effective with children diagnosed, likely misdiagnosed, as depressed and they can cause serious harm. It is illegal for drug companies to market any of these drugs for children because although they have been approved for adults, they cannot, by law, be marketed commercially to a different population (children) for which they have not been approved. Nevertheless, doctors are permitted to prescribe these drugs and some doctors do so.

This is called prescribing "off label." Despite the prohibition, the drug companies find ways to encourage doctors to make off-label prescriptions. They have been fined substantially for doing so, but that has not been much of a deterrent because the profits are so high. Between 1993 and 2009, the drug companies influenced doctors to prescribe these drugs off label. Prescription of antipsychotic drugs to children and adolescents in the US increased by a factor of five.

The adverse effects of prescribing these drugs to children are even worse than these effects on adults. Prescription of these drugs to children causes weight gains of 16 to 36 pounds (depending on which drug is prescribed), predisposing these children to type-2 diabetes. They increase blood glucose and cholesterol levels. Long-term use of these drugs is associated with Parkinsonism, diabetes, and pancreatic disorders. Some of the neurological side effects are irreversible, some even fatal. Unknown, are the negative effects these powerful drugs may have on brains that are still developing. The known and potential adverse effects of these drugs on children should be raising a red flag, but, oddly, this is not happening.

The record with respect to those diagnosed as depressed and prescribed antipsychotic drugs is not pretty. For example, just as is the case with antidepressant prescriptions to women, doctors are more likely to prescribe antipsychotic drugs to the elderly, the intellectually disabled, and the disadvantaged than they are to men. Foster children are four times more likely to be prescribed antipsychotic drugs than other children.

****

A subject deserving of meticulous attention is the relationship between antidepressant drugs and violence. *There is a documented association between antidepressants and suicide.* Therefore, the FDA requires a "black box" label for all SSRIs. Children, adolescents, and young adults in their 20s have been found to be at risk of suicide when taking these drugs, particularly if there had been a suicide attempt prior to taking antidepressant drugs.

The story of how the FDA came to put this black box warning on the SSRIs vividly illustrates the very serious adverse effects of these drugs, the steps the drug companies have taken to hide these dangers, and the weakness of the FDA's efforts to protect the public. Alison Bass, a science writer with the Boston Globe and Miami Herald, in her book, "Side Effects," tells this story. She describes how the drug companies hire psychiatric leaders to hawk falsifications about the safety and efficacy of psychiatric drugs with the compliance of the FDA. Chapter 8 explores how conflict of interest has influenced psychiatric leaders and researchers. Chapter 9 will give numerous examples of how the FDA has sided with the drug companies and failed to act in the public's interests.

Although the problem was known many years earlier, the FDA did not put the black box warning on the SSRIs regarding their association with suicide until 2004. But by 1991, the FDA had received 14,000 reports of adverse effects of these drugs, four times higher than any other medication. And the FDA knew from the clinical trials that these drugs were no better treatments for depression than placebos for children and adolescents. The FDA also knew that the drug companies had withheld information that the SSRIs were associated with increased suicidality. The public was unaware of these results because the drug companies only release clinical trial data when subpoenaed in civil or criminal cases. Public Citizen learned of these suppressed findings and they filed a petition in 1991 asking the FDA to put a black box warning on the SSRIs to warn of heightened suicidal behavior. The FDA did so thirteen years later.

David Healy, a British psychiatrist and psycho-pharmacologist, also knew of these findings because of his experience serving as an expert witness in lawsuits against drug companies, which gave him access to pharmaceutical industry records. It was not until 2003 that Dr. Healy succeeded in publishing his findings in a psychiatric journal. He has authored several books detailing how the pharmaceutical companies in their pursuit of profit hide results that show that the prescription of antidepressant drugs can be life threatening. He has documented suppression by the drug companies of antidepressant related suicides.

But in another illustration of how psychiatric publications of psychiatric research results mislead doctors and the public, a study was published in the American Journal of Psychiatry (AJP) in 2007 that purported to show that this black box warning was leading to more children committing suicide because they were denied these drugs. As was the case with the AJP's publications of the STAR*D study, the article received wide coverage in the media. Fortunately, this claim, too, did not go unchallenged.

Sidney Wolfe reviewed the AJP study in 2007. He was appointed by Ralph Nader as the head of Public Citizen's Health Research Group in 1971, holding that position until his retirement in 2013. This organization reviews scientific data on drugs and reports their results when they find evidence of drug effects having been misinterpreted and/or to be hazardous. They testify regularly before Congress about their findings. Ralph Nader has said of Dr. Wolfe, "He thinks doctors belong in areas that prevent patients from *becoming* patients."

Now back to the AJP article that claimed the black box label on the SSRIs, by discouraging the prescription of these drugs, was leading to more suicides. Dr. Wolfe pointed out that the data in the AJP study were much less trustworthy than those used by the FDA in coming to its ruling.

The FDA based their findings on meta-analyses of 24 randomized placebo-controlled studies (the "gold standard" in this kind of research). The data used in the AJP article were aggregate population rates, which is a discredited way of studying cause and effect relationships. Dr. Wolfe castigated the authors of the AJP article for writing it and the journal for printing it.

The March 2020 issue of Public Citizen's health newsletter gave the following warning:

> Antidepressants, including selective serotonin reuptake inhibitors (SSRIs), have been shown to increase the risk of suicidal thoughts and behavior in pediatric and young adult patients when used to treat major depressive disorder and other psychiatric disorders .... (P)atients should be monitored closely for worsening and for emergence of suicidal thoughts and behaviors. Families and caregivers also should be advised of the need for close observation and communication with the prescriber..

The size of the dosage of antidepressants is related to suicidal behavior in children and young adults. When comparing groups matched for depression severity, the rate of deliberate self-harm was found to be twice as high for those prescribed higher doses of antidepressants as those prescribed lower doses.

The relationship between the prescription of antidepressants and violence toward others has received less attention. This is unfortunate, given the level of violence in our society, particularly when there are reasons to look into this possible relationship. In 2010, a study by Thomas Moore and his colleagues examined the association between prescription drugs and violence. Violence has many causes, but they found twice as many acts of violence toward others for those on prescription drugs. Antidepressants were the drugs most implicated.

Mass shootings in this country, now occurring on a weekly basis, often are attributed to "mental illness," but violence toward others is an infrequent response in mental disorder. The mentally disordered are characterized by passivity, not violence. However, violence is not an unusual response to the abrupt withdrawal from these drugs. *When antidepressants are abandoned suddenly, hostility and aggression are common withdrawal reactions.* Thus, the explanation for the violence of "he went off his drugs" may have a very different meaning than what is implied. Since most likely the benefits of antidepressants are placebo effects, prescribing them to patients who may not follow a doctor's advice about how to stop taking them may more properly be seen not as an affirmation of their use, but an indictment of their prescription.

If you have been taking antidepressant drugs and are considering getting off them, you must be careful how you do it. Your body is likely to be physically addicted to them. To be safe, going off these drugs must be done under the guidance of a doctor. That's standard medical advice.

****

Part Two

Psychiatrists claim that the frequency of adverse effects caused by their drugs is very low. That's wrong. Psychiatry routinely under-estimates the harmfulness of antidepressant drugs.

Little attention is paid in psychiatric publications to the negative effects of these drugs even in those instances when their adverse effects have been reported by the FDA. In 2001, the Centers for Disease Control (CDC) learned there had been 26 million adverse reactions to psychiatric drugs, most commonly, antidepressants. Yet despite

> . . . this staggering number, there have been few reports of (these) errors . . .. Some prominent psychiatric journals have yet to include medical errors or adverse drug

> events as key word options for submitted manuscripts . . . . A similar search using (psychiatric) medication errors . . . yielded 69 citations. In contrast, a search of medication errors (associated with physical illnesses) in general yielded 4892 citations.

The FDA does not have complete and accurate reports of the adverse effects of antidepressant drugs. The FDA's adverse reporting system is called Medwatch, which keeps track of problems encountered after drugs enter the marketplace. Basic standards have been established by the FDA for the reporting of adverse effects, but the drug companies have been found to submit incomplete reports to the FDA. Only about half of reports of adverse effects submitted by the drug manufacturers met those standards. A senior scientist at the Institute for Safe Medication Practices reviewed 847,000 cases of reports to the FDA of adverse drug effects for drugs of all kinds over a 12-month period that ended in March 2014. The study found that the reporting of the adverse effects of prescription drugs is "deeply flawed." Medwatch identified mental health care patients as not having been systematically examined for such well-known problems as movement disorders, such as tardive dyskinesia; neurologic malignant syndrome; obesity; insulin resistance; serotonin syndrome; and the incidence and etiology or background of suicide.

The Centers for Disease Control (CDC) has reported that in 2017, 47,000 Americans died by suicide, a 50-year peak. They do not reveal the extent to which these deaths are attributable to the prescription of antidepressant drugs. Primary care doctors are the main prescribers of these drugs. Unfortunately, some of these doctors are contributors to the under-reporting of adverse drug effects because they do not follow up with their patients on their prescriptions of antidepressants. As we have seen, these are powerful drugs, and they can have big, unintended effects. When adverse effects occur, all too many doctors are unaware of them. Adverse events that are unknown go unreported to the FDA.

Like opiates and street drugs, *antidepressant drugs can be addictive.* This is a serious adverse effect that is often unacknowledged and unreported. The addictive properties of antidepressants have been well-documented (see Notes). As indicated, withdrawal effects from antidepressants can be severe. This leads many patients to stay on these drugs—a reaction that is at the heart of addiction. Often, being hooked is misinterpreted by the patient and the doctor as a recurrence of depression. Psychiatrists have denied that these drugs are addictive, inventing their own term for the addictive effect, "antidepressant discontinuation syndrome," as if this were a unique disorder, not a manifestation of an addiction. The evidence strongly suggests that the placebo effect and addiction explain why people take these drugs.

Psychiatrists argue that antidepressants are not addictive because they do not lead to craving higher doses. This defense is based on a very narrow definition of addiction. Cigarette smoking wouldn't fit under this definition, but any smoker who wishes to quit smoking knows very well the powerfully addictive properties of nicotine and the psychological dependencies that also occur with smoking.

The anti-anxiety drugs, the benzodiazepines (Xanax, Valium, Ativan, Klonipin) also are addictive. However, anti-anxiety drugs have *immediate effects* that can be helpful on a short-term basis. They differ from the antidepressants because, as we have discussed, the antidepressants have no such beneficial immediate chemical effect. For example, some people find anti-anxiety drugs appealing because they induce a temporary sedative effect that reduces a fear of flying, enabling traveling, even though they provide no enduring solution to the fear. The long-term effects of these drugs are something else entirely. Heather Ashton's book on the addictive properties of these drugs is a classic. She acknowledges the short-term value of the benzodiazepines but warns against taking them for more than a few weeks.

Psychiatry and the drug companies have taken lessons from the tobacco industry in fending off criticism leveled against the prescription of antidepressant drugs, especially when it comes to addiction. The terminology reminds one of an equivalent strategy that was developed successfully by the tobacco industry in the 1960s. The cigarette lobby convinced the U.S. Surgeon General that cigarette smoking should be defined as "habituation," rather than as an addiction. It was not until 1988 that the Surgeon General reversed that ruling and classified cigarette smoking as addictive.

We need to recognize just how effective language can be in re-casting reality, as any expert in propaganda understands. Drug marketers know the power of language in shaping beliefs. Another example is found in how psychiatrists account for drug failures. When a patient receives no benefit from a drug, the patient is described as being part of a class who are labeled as being "drug resistant." It's the patient's fault. Psychiatric denial of the negative reactions associated with prescription of antidepressants is a sad reminder of the Hippocratic oath, and of the maxim "first do no harm."

The rhetoric that accompanies the prescription of these drugs to children and adults has promoted self-medication, an increasingly serious public health issue as more young adults, raised on prescription drugs, take a benign attitude toward experimenting with prescription and nonprescription drugs. This is a societal issue that has become critical.

In 2018, the Journal of the American Medical Association (JAMA) published a study of 26,000 adults in the United States for the period of 2005 to 2014 that was designed to assess the adverse effects of a number of prescription drugs on depression. Several classes of drugs were assessed, including antidepressants and people taking multiple medications. *The study found that antidepressants were among the drugs that exacerbated depression by a factor of three.*

These findings are in line with the multiple adverse effects of antidepressant drugs that we have been reviewing. The authors of the JAMA study used the DSM criteria for depression, which confound sadness with depression so that patients who are sad are diagnosed as depressed. The negative implications can be and most likely are exacerbated for those who are put on multiple medications. In any case, the study found that the chemicals in these drugs *made these patients worse*, regardless of the true nature of their condition. Moreover, the negative effects of antidepressants found in this study have additional negative consequences: their worsening is interpreted by the patient and by the doctor *as a reason to continue taking these drugs*. Results such as these illustrate in various ways how antidepressant drugs are not remedying depression, they are *inducing it and contributing to it*, even propelling sadness into depression.

Many people ignore the risks associated with antidepressants. We are used to seeing information on possible adverse effects listed on the drugs that we are prescribed. Many have grown cavalier, as if the warnings apply only once in a great while. In the case of antibiotics, for example, the advantages of the drugs outweigh the risks, but then we do not take antibiotics on a regular basis. We take them only for a short time. Yet anyone who has had an adverse reaction to penicillin knows how important it is to take care even when the drug is used only occasionally.

Antidepressants are intended to be used daily and over a long period of time and the risks are endemic, with at least some of the adverse effects registered by most patients. Ignoring the risk does not make these drugs any less hazardous. We have a system that misdiagnoses many normal people as depressed, leading to the prescription of an antidepressant thereby exposing large numbers of people to this risk. Add to this, the fact that many ignore the danger of going off the drugs suddenly.

The SSRIs are presumed to be preferable to previous antidepressants because they have fewer side effects. In fact, if these drugs are taken for an extended period, adverse effects come into play. Remaining on these drugs long-term has been associated with a worsening of depression and a worsening of the prognosis of ever recovering from depression. Studies have found that patients on antidepressants are more likely to relapse than those on placebo. And the likelihood of relapse is significantly related to dose; that is, the higher the dose the greater the probability of relapse. Studies of hospitalized patients have found those not treated with drugs did better than those who were. Placebo-controlled studies have shown those on drugs experienced fewer good weeks after treatment ended. Results point to a conclusion that long-term use of antidepressants leads people to become chronically ill, an ominous, little-recognized issue I will get to shortly. Despite how alarming these findings are, psychiatrists continue to recommend long term use of these drugs.

****

Part Three

There are psychiatrists who have broken with psychiatric leaders and their colleagues and warned about the serious problems they have encountered in treating patients with antidepressants. One of the most outspoken is Joseph Glenmullen who teaches psychiatry at Harvard Medical School.

In two books on this subject, Dr. Glenmullen has expressed strong concerns about the adverse effects of antidepressants on the bodies of his patients. Dr. Glenmullen has observed *debilitating neurological effects* caused by antidepressant drugs: Parkinson's Disease, visual hallucinations, sexual dysfunction, agitation, dizziness, nausea, muscle spasms, tics, and withdrawal symptoms. These adverse reactions originate in the involuntary motor system, deep in the brain. They are the "brain's attempt to reverse the effects of (these) drugs." In looking into the research that has been done on these effects, he has grown concerned that exposure to antidepressant drugs causes brain damage and earlier aging.

Dr. Glenmullen believes that antidepressants don't correct an imbalance in the brain as is claimed, they do just the opposite. They create a chemical imbalance to which the brain must adjust. He cites research which suggests ". . . (the SSRIs) may affect a chemical lobotomy" by destroying the nerve endings that they target in the brain. Dr. Glenmullen is not alone in being concerned that these drugs are harming his patients. He cites researchers who provide evidence indicating that antidepressants inflict brain damage.

In 1996, Steven Hyman was the Director of the NIMH. Dr. Hyman is now the head of the Stanley Center at the Broad Institute, affiliated with Harvard and MIT, a biomedical research center engaged in research following up the Human Genome Project. When he was the NIMH Director, after reviewing the research results on antidepressants, he stated that antidepressants (and other psychiatric drugs) "create perturbations in neurotransmitter functions." In other words, they disturb the brain's functioning. Dr. Hyman concluded that the brain, on antidepressants, comes to function in a way that is "qualitatively as well as quantitatively different from the normal state (to compensate for this effect)." Simply put, *these drugs induce abnormality in the brain.* By what twisted logic would one assume causing abnormality in the brain is the way to produce normality?

Dr. Glenmullen argues for treating depression by psychotherapy except in the most serious cases. A number of psychiatrists agree with him. In a later chapter I will review the evidence that indicates behavior therapy is more effective than drugs regardless of severity level.

Robert Whitaker is a science journalist, not a medical doctor, but for many years he has been studying the untoward effects of the prolific prescription of psychiatric drugs. He is one of the most highly informed authorities on this subject. On the basis of very different data–*epidemiological data*–he has written about how psychiatry's medicalization has been associated with *a significant increase in mental disorder and mental disability.*

Epidemiology is the study of the causes and effects of illness. It is the cornerstone of public health. Whitaker points to epidemiological data that reveal a significant increase in the rates of *mental disability* since the advent of psychiatric drugs. *The number of people with a mental disorder who now qualify as mentally disabled has increased significantly with these prescriptions.* Whitaker makes his case on the basis of data from the Social Security Administration of those diagnosed with a mental disorder who qualify for federal disability payments because they are found to be too disabled by their mental disorder to function independently. Depression is one of his examples. In 1955, about 50,000 people were too disabled to function independently and were hospitalized as depressed. By 2010 an estimated 1.4 million adults were receiving a federal payment because they qualified as being too disabled by depression to function independently. Whitaker attributes this increase to the adverse effects of these drugs.

Whitaker discusses the changes that have occurred in the diagnosis and prognosis of depression since the medicalization of psychiatry. Textbooks for doctors in training to be psychiatrists that were written prior to this medicalization tell the story. In 1968, Dr. Charlotte Silverman at Johns Hopkins University, in her psychiatric text, "The Epidemiology of Depression," refers to the small number of people diagnosed as depressed, the low rate of hospitalization and rehospitalization for depression, and of depression being largely confined to older persons. Another psychiatric textbook published in 1974 by Dr. Dean Schuyler,

"The Depressive Spectrum," gives the same description of depression at that time, stating that "most depressive episodes will run their course and terminate with virtually complete recovery without a specific intervention."

These textbooks tell us that *prior to the medicalization of psychiatry, diagnoses of depression were rare and so were relapses.* Since DSM-III, there has been a huge increase in the number of people diagnosed as depressed and treated with antidepressant drugs. Relapse is frequent and the prognosis for these patients is far worse than was the case prior to the drug era. Patients who have been treated most intensively with psychiatric drugs show lower rates of recovery from their disorder than in the past and are hospitalized more frequently.

Again, we must ask ourselves why such alarming data concerning the adverse effects of these drugs is being ignored. In this context, Ms. Begley's speculations about the kindness of keeping the facts from people takes on a distinctly sinister cast. Rather than revolutionizing the care of depression, the most obvious conclusion is that *psychiatric drugs have created an unrecognized mental health crisis.*

Since diagnoses of depression are the most frequently made diagnoses of mental disorder, the conflation of sadness and depression comprises a large portion of the increase that Whitaker has identified. Apart from those few who are, in fact, clinically depressed, diagnoses of depression reflect two very large groups: *those who are sad and have been misdiagnosed as depressed and those who, after being misdiagnosed as depressed, are propelled into depression by the drug treatment regimen and the harmful chemicals in these drugs.*

Medical journals are the engines that drive health care. Doctors depend upon them to learn about the effectiveness and safety of available treatments. Editors-in-Chief of the prominent journals–and there are dozens and dozens of them–hold some of the most influential positions in healthcare.

As you would expect, the editors who are selected to fill these positions are representatives of the medical establishment. They are highly trained and experienced in their specialty and well trained in science. Often, they are believers in treatments that have become standard and resistant to challenges to the well-accepted treatments. Many have ties to drug companies. In the next chapter we will study the evidence that publications in medical journals on antidepressants are biased in favor of these drugs.

Occasionally editors are selected who are cut from a different cloth, who bring a different perspective to their positions, one that enables them to be more open to challenges to the status quo. Journal editors are uniquely in a position to be informed about entire bodies of research by virtue of the studies submitted to them for publication. The results of these studies, and the references cited in them that back up their conclusions, educate editors. Sometimes an editor sees in these articles vital information that challenges what is the accepted lore. Editors who are open to such challenges are extraordinary people. Established systems are highly resistant to change and those who support change may not be rewarded for their efforts. Yet their insight and independence make it possible, eventually, to set things right when few recognize and acknowledge how things have gone wrong.

As you also might expect, once an editor takes such a contrary stand there is the risk of being ignored, even shunned. Hence, the influence of these standouts is far from immediate. Dr. Glenmullen has written about how long it can take to set things straight. The history of psychiatric drugs has many instances of those in positions of responsibility offering false assurances about drugs being safe before their risks became clear. Prescription of cocaine and amphetamines are examples; in the 1960s and 1970s mental hospitals had many patients with amphetamine induced psychoses.

Dr. Glenmullen describes a 10–20–30 year cycle that characterizes prescription of psychiatric drugs. He describes an initial 10-year marketing period that establishes the belief they are revolutionary breakthroughs in treatment. During this time the drug in question comes to be prescribed regularly by primary care doctors for everyday maladies. This period is followed by 10 years when problems with their prescription become more apparent, followed by 10 years when these problems become undeniable, and alarms are raised about them.

Dr. Marcia Angell, the former Editor-in-Chief of the New England Journal of Medicine, and Dr. Richard Smith, the former Editor-in-Chief of the British Medical Journal, are such editors. They have written about how drug companies have corrupted the medical journals. They have warned that many influential medical publications have become purveyors of false information. The psychiatrist, Giovanni Fava, needs to be added to this list of courageous medical journal editors. His journal published our report of the true results of the STAR*D study and Dr. Healy's report of the suppression by the drug companies of the association of the SSRIs with suicide after other psychiatric journal editors had rejected publishing these findings.

Dr. Fava is a psychiatrist and Editor-in-Chief of the psychiatric journal Psychotherapy and Psychosomatics. He is also a professor in the Medical Schools at the University of Bologna in Italy and the State University of New York at Buffalo, as well as being President of the International College of Psychosomatic Medicine. For many years he has been studying research results bearing on the effects of antidepressant drugs taken long-term (more than 6 months). He has written of the substantial risks he believes are associated with what is today's standard treatment of depression: long-term prescription of antidepressants.

In the mid-1990s, based on his reading of antidepressant research results, Dr. Fava began raising questions about the likelihood that antidepressant drugs *worsened* depression, rather than alleviating the disorder. When he voiced his concerns, Dr. Donald Klein, now emeritus professor of psychiatry at Columbia University, commented, "The industry is not interested, the NIMH is not interested, and the FDA is not interested. Nobody is interested."

It is no surprise that Big Pharma would not be interested in these negative results. But surely, the NIMH and the FDA should be very interested indeed. These are federal agencies we expect to protect the public's interests regarding health care. Instead, they are significant contributors to what has gone wrong with mental health care. Again, this assertion, which may elicit skepticism in some readers, will be examined in the next two chapters.

Within the next ten years, after continuing to monitor research results, Dr. Fava found additional confirmation of his concerns that long-term use of antidepressant drugs can worsen the course of depression. *His review suggested to him that prolonged use of these drugs increases the likelihood of relapse and reduces the likelihood of ever recovering.* Dr. Fava suspects that long-term use of the SSRIs triggers changes in how signals and pathways related to serotonin receptors are damaged, thereby creating a greater vulnerability to relapse, an adverse and often permanent biochemical effect.

There is accumulating evidence that these drugs damage the brain. Dr. Fava has written that continued use of these drugs can increase the biochemical vulnerability to depression, worsen the course of depression, increase the likelihood of relapse, and generate bouts of "residual symptoms" of anxiety, insomnia, fatigue, cognitive impairment, and irritability. These are the very symptoms listed in the DSM to diagnose depression. *He also concluded that the common psychiatric treatment practice of switching from one drug to another to find a drug that works, that was the subject of the STAR*D study, propels patients into a "refractory phase" (resistant to treatment), characterized by low remission and high relapse. He cites evidence that patients who change antidepressants suffer from worsening withdrawal symptoms.* And he believes prolonged use of these drugs can precipitate bipolar disorders, which have been diagnosed more frequently with continued prescription of these drugs.

Dr. Fava has interpreted the results we reported in our critique of the STAR*D study's actual findings as being in line with his conclusions: remission rates decreased after each treatment step and rates of relapse increased after each treatment step. He concludes from STAR*D's results:

> Indeed, the indications are pretty clear: pharmacological manipulations, either by switching or augmentation may propel depressive illness into a refractory phase, characterized by low remission, high relapse, and high intolerance.

In other words, not only did STAR*D's results fail to corroborate the positive outcome that psychiatrists expected and claimed, but they also confirmed Dr. Fava's expectations of a negative outcome resulting from the standard psychiatric treatment prescribed for depression.

I have cited three (there are many others) experts in this field who warn that antidepressant drugs can be quite harmful. All three are highly informed and have substantial credentials for their opinions. Each of these authorities has come to the same concern that these drugs are harmful, and they came to this conclusion on the basis of different kinds of data: Robert Whitaker from his analyses of U. S. government publications of *epidemiological data*, Dr. Glenmullen from his *clinical observations* of his patients, and Dr. Fava from *outcome studies* of patients taking antidepressants long term. All three have arrived at the same conclusion: antidepressant drugs don't *reduce* mental disorder; they *induce* mental disorder. *They warn that these prescriptions are causing a significant number of patients to become worse.*

They are far from alone in raising alarm about the harmfulness of antidepressant drugs. Another reviewer cited earlier is the British psychiatrist, Joanna Moncrief, who is a practicing psychiatrist, researcher, and Senior Lecturer at University College London. Dr. Moncrief is another highly credentialed psychiatrist who has not bought into the pseudoscience that dominates mental health. She has written extensively about how drugs have turned depression, a disorder that previously was characterized by "short-term suffering, into long-term misery."

The risks associated with long-term use of antidepressant drugs appear to be analogous to the risks associated with cigarette smoking. Cigarette smoking is responsible for one in every five deaths in this country each year and reduces life expectancy by at least 10 years. We know how long it took for the public to accept its dangers, and indeed against all reason, large numbers of people remain in the thrall of addiction. More than that, many take up smoking every year. A contributor is that although cigarette smoking is dangerous, many smokers live to a ripe old age and die of something unrelated to smoking. Anomalies are present in all phenomena, and they should not influence our estimation of the dangers.

Antidepressant drugs appear to pose similarly dire risks to a significant number of long-term users. There are differences, however. Consider this: According to the Centers for Disease Control (CDC), quitting smoking before the age of 40 reduces the risk of dying from smoking-related disease by 90%. Taking antidepressants, however, can lead to *permanent brain damage.* For these patients there is no comparable safety net. And let's not forget the risks posed by long-term use of these drugs by children, which have increased dramatically and where the potential long-term consequences to still developing brains will last all the longer.

We do not have sufficient scientific corroboration to demonstrate conclusively that these drugs are so dangerous they should be suppressed immediately. But we do know enough to raise all the alarms. We know enough to determine that the effect of these drugs should be studied by scientists whose careers do not benefit from their use. We know that many researchers are intimidated; they depend on grants from psychiatrists on NIMH committees, whom they are fearful of alienating. Other scientists are in the employ of those who profit financially from the sale of these drugs. We know enough to know that the results of studies by scientists without these constraints should be publicized and not ignored and their independence fostered. And we certainly know enough to deter sensible people from blithely accepting this form of treatment for themselves. We have more than enough evidence to make loving parents think long and hard before allowing any doctor to prescribe these drugs for their children.

In a field that is rampant with *conflicts of interest,* which will be the subject of the next chapter, it behooves us to listen to the raised voices of highly regarded, objective scientists who have concluded, based on multiple analyses, that these drugs are more harmful than helpful.

Dr. Robert Berezin, who also has taught psychiatry at Harvard Medical School for many years, has traced the history of diagnoses and drug treatments for depression. He has written about how prior to the 1980s, diagnoses of depression and prescriptions of antidepressant drugs were very small in number compared with diagnoses of the anxiety disorders and prescriptions of anti-anxiety drugs (the benzodiazepines, chiefly Valium and Xanax). The anti-anxiety drugs proved to be so addictive and dangerous they led to congressional hearings (where they were labeled "the #1 drug problem in the US today"). That unfavorable publicity was one of the factors that led psychiatrists to shift away from diagnoses of anxiety and prescription of anti-anxiety drugs to diagnoses of depression and prescription of antidepressant drugs. But memories are short. As the bad publicity about the anti-anxiety drugs waned, the number of these prescriptions has risen. The American Journal of Public Health recently reported that in the last 20 years prescriptions of these anti-anxiety drugs have tripled and deaths from overdoses have quadrupled. Regarding biological psychiatry, Dr. Berezin, deplores "the excesses to which conventional psychiatric knowledge and practice can easily sink." He concludes, "The one thing we can learn from history is that we don't learn from history."

8

Conflict of Interest

Few psychiatrists are willing to admit that their specialty is out of control.
—Peter Gotzsche, MD

For a prescription drug to be profitable, doctors must prescribe the drug to patients. For doctors to prescribe a drug, research results must show the drug to be both effective and safe. But here lies the rub. Drug companies fund the majority of published drug research. Studies by independent investigators show that studies that are funded by drug companies are biased in favor of the drugs. As if this were not enough, other studies show that some doctors' prescription choices are biased by financial inducements from drug companies.

Melody Peterson, a former New York Times science journalist, has written:

> In the legal profession, lawyers cannot take cases in which they have a conflict that could compromise their work. But in medicine, scientists and physicians regularly perform work with which they have financial conflicts.

Conflicts of interest have become a major problem in health care. The drug companies funnel billions of dollars a year to researchers and healthcare practitioners. There is incontrovertible evidence that these payments profoundly influence what drug some doctors prescribe, how drug studies are reported in medical journals, and how the guidelines for drug prescriptions are written for doctors. This leads to many positive results being invented, and many negative results suppressed. Moreover, many journal articles appearing in medical journals are written by *ghostwriters* employed by the drug companies, not by the doctors whose names appear on them as the authors. Ghost writers slant the results in favor of the drugs.

This is less likely to be the case for those doctors who subscribe to or review research reports published by the *Cochrane Collaboration.* Cochrane conducts objective reviews of FDA approved drugs. Founded in 1993, this is a non-profit, non-governmental organization made up of 37,000 volunteers in 130 countries. The current head of the Nordic Cochrane Center and a co-founder of the Cochrane Collaboration, Peter Gotzsche, has written about the corruption that is endemic to how pharmaceutical companies pursue their business interests. Dr. Gotzsche has documented in detail the pro-drug bias that underlies drug prescriptions.

Before I continue, the following caveat must be established. Drugs have become essential to health care. There are drugs that are life savers for many people and that therefore should be prescribed. Nevertheless, Dr. Gotzsche reports that prescription drugs, taken as prescribed, cause 8 million adverse reactions annually and result in 2.7 million hospitalizations per year. Dr. Gotzsche cites data implicating drugs as one of the leading causes of death in the United States after heart attacks and cancer. Psychiatric drugs are particularly dangerous for people aged 65 and over. (See Chapter 7).

Dr. Gotzsche states that doctors "know little about drugs that haven't been carefully concocted and dressed up by the drug industry." But of particular concern to Dr. Gotzsche is that many of the abuses are not witless. At the heart of Dr. Gotzsche's thesis is the conflict of interest Melody Peterson has written about that applies to doctors. Dr. Gotzsche warns that some doctors have "self-serving motives for choosing certain drugs" and that the excesses of the drug companies would not be possible without this physician collaboration.

In an effort to counteract what more and more professional and governmental entities have recognized as the *purchasing of bias* by the drug companies, a number of states have passed Sunshine Acts. These acts require the drug companies to report promotional gifts and payments to individual doctors in the hope that making such conflicts of interest public will deter unethical practices. Vermont, Massachusetts, Minnesota, West Virginia, DC, California, and

Nevada have passed such laws. Unfortunately, few people are aware of the availability of this information.

An issue of critical importance is how conflicts of interest have affected publications in medical journals. Dr. Richard Smith, the former Editor-in-Chief of the British Medical Journal, has extolled the role played by medical journals in the dissemination of medical science. In an article published in 2006 in the Journal of the Royal Society of Medicine, he wrote about landmark studies published in medical journals "that changed medicine," such as the first studies of anesthesia and the reporting of the cause of malaria. But Dr. Smith felt compelled to register his concern that the growth of conflicts of interest has led to questionable science in many articles now being published in medical journals:

> . . . medical journals have failed to effectively manage conflicts of interest(. . ..) Most authors in medical journals do have financial conflicts of interest, particularly in their relations with pharmaceutical companies. These undeclared conflicts of interest can have profound effects on the studies undertaken and the conclusions they reach(. . ..)Most journals also face an ethical problem in being so closely associated with pharmaceutical companies(. . ..)

Other doctors who have taken on the task of monitoring research have condemned the false representation of the effectiveness of drugs in medical journal articles. Dr. Marcia Angell, who is one of today's most respected medical experts, has written about this. She has condemned the misreporting of research results as signaling an alarmingly "corrupt" alliance that has developed between doctors (including researchers) and drug companies, such that "it is simply no longer possible to believe much of the clinical research that is published, or to rely on the judgment of trusted physicians or authoritative guidelines."

Medical journal editors recognized that this bias afflicts the research they publish. Richard Horton, Editor-in-Chief of the Lancet, one of the most highly regarded medical journals in the world, put it succinctly: "Journals have devolved into information laundering operations for the pharmaceutical industry." Several of these editors sought to do something about it. The first rule they adopted was to disqualify any article by an author who had a financial connection to the drug under study. *That proved unworkable because it disqualified just about everyone!* So, they came up with a default position. Authors of journal articles accepted for publication must disclose all their financial arrangements with drug companies. These connections are printed at the beginning of published articles. The intent is to inform readers when skepticism is warranted.

A study by Kristin Rising, published in 2008 in the medical journal PLOS Medicine, focused on how publications assessing the effectiveness of *drugs for physical illnesses* were contrived to make the drugs look better than they are. Dr. Rising and several colleagues analyzed reports published five years later of the effectiveness of the drugs approved by the FDA from 2001 to 2002. They found that *five times as many studies with favorable results were published as studies with unfavorable results.* Many of the studies with negative results were not submitted for publication. *Of those with negative results that were published, almost half of them failed to report that the results did not support their conclusions.* They had substituted for their negative findings the positive results from secondary measures as if they were the measures that had been specified in their protocols (See Chapter 5 for details on protocols).

Dr. Rising's study is an illustration of the unfortunate fact that not all researchers report their findings fully and objectively. Science does not exist in a vacuum. Drug prescription is a lucrative marketplace and researchers can be swayed by considerations other than their data. Corruption of scientific data occurs all too frequently because of the financial rewards.

In Chapter 5 you saw that while antidepressants are not very effective treatments, they are the most highly prescribed drugs of any kind to young adults in this country. Those who medicalize psychiatry are richly rewarded. *Psychiatric researchers have been identified by science reviewers as the readiest to promote false claims about their drugs, principally the antidepressants.* Dr. Angell found psychiatric drug research to be "the most florid example of the problem." She has written,

> I have spent most of my professional life evaluating the quality of clinical research, and I believe it is especially poor in psychiatry. The industry-sponsored studies(. . .)are selectively published, tend to be short-term, designed to favor the drug, and show benefits so small that they are unlikely to outweigh the long-term harms.

Dr. Angell goes on to write that practices such as these affect "the results of research, how medicine is practiced, and even the definition of what constitutes a disease."

Gardner Harris, a New York Times science journalist, has come to the same conclusion about psychiatry. He wrote,

> . . . the intersection of money and medicine and its effects on the well-being of patients has become one of the most contentious issues in health care. Nowhere is this more true than in psychiatry.

Dr. Gotzsche also has identified psychiatrists as the most culpable doctors with respect to conflicts of interest, reporting that psychiatrists collect more money from the drug companies than any other medical specialty. He refers to psychiatry as "the drug industry's paradise." He identified conflict of interest as associated with the misreporting of the effectiveness of antidepressants.

The New York Times was incredulous about an article printed in the Journal of the American Medical Association (JAMA) that urged pregnant women to continue taking antidepressant medication lest they fall back into depression. Recall that in Chapter 7 you saw that pregnant women taking these drugs put themselves and their babies at risk. The Times editorial stated,

> Hidden from view was the fact that most of the 13 authors had been paid as consultants or lecturers by the makers of antidepressants. Their financial ties were not disclosed to JAMA on the preposterous grounds that the authors did not deem them relevant.

Dr. Rising's study described how the effectiveness of drugs prescribed for physical illnesses has been corrupted by conflicts of interest. Erick Turner conducted a similar analysis in a 2008 study *aimed at evaluating whether the reporting of the effectiveness of antidepressant drugs is biased.* As Dr. Rising had found, Dr. Turner discovered that positive results for these psychiatric drugs are more likely to be published. Many studies assessing antidepressant drugs falsely reported positive outcomes. *The reporting of the results for antidepressant drugs was even more biased in favor of the drugs* than Dr. Rising had found for drugs prescribed for physical illnesses.

Dr. Turner and his colleagues obtained the FDA's reviews of 74 trials of 12 antidepressant drugs prescribed to 12,564 patients between 1987 and 2004. They then compared the FDA's conclusions about the effectiveness of these drugs with the results that were reported for these drugs in the medical journal articles. Now, as I pointed out, there is considerable reason to view the FDA's positive valuations of these drugs as overly generous. But for this discussion, let's accept their conclusions.

The FDA concluded about half (54%) of the 74 trials had positive results for the drugs vs. placebos. By contrast, the publications in medical journals of these results indicated that almost all of the studies (94%) had positive results. In addition, all but one of the studies identified by the FDA as positive were published in medical journals, whereas of those with negative results, all but three were either not published or published spuriously as if the outcome had been positive.

As Dr. Turner and his colleagues wrote, "the negative results were 'spun' to make them look positive." In other words, Dr. Turner found that the STAR*D study's misreporting has many companions.

Dr. Turner discovered that the journal articles had reported the helpfulness of the drugs to be significantly greater than what had been calculated by the FDA. Not just somewhat greater. The false reports did not consist of minor rounding errors. *The fabrications ranged from boosts of 11% to 69%, inflating the value of these drugs by an average of 31%.* These are truly significant misrepresentations of the results, further invalidating the favorable outcome reported for antidepressant drugs.

Falsification of the value of antidepressants has been highly successful *because the absence of science behind psychiatric practice simplifies manipulations that impute undeserved value to psychiatric drugs.* A medical profession offering diagnoses and treatments that are based on ideology, corrupted science, and financial gain presents endless opportunities for chicanery. Elsewhere in medical practice, scientific knowledge of physical illnesses constitutes a safeguard.

This corruption is not, of course, limited to antidepressants. Gardner Harris examined the record with regard to psychiatry's antipsychotic drugs. He cites a number of cases of highly questionable prescriptions of antipsychotic drugs, such as Risperdal, being written for problems such as eating disorders. In Minnesota, from 2000–2005, drug makers *paid psychiatrists to prescribe Risperdal to children.* Their prescriptions increased nine-fold. Those psychiatrists who received more money wrote more than three times as many of these prescriptions as other psychiatrists. The drug produced serious, debilitating side effects, creating far more problems than it allegedly remedied. The statistics regarding prescription practices in Minnesota are sadly illustrative and there is good reason to believe this is not specific to Minnesota.

Ray Moynihan, an award-winning health journalist, has written about this partnership: "Psychiatry's intimate relationship with the pharmaceutical industry has become notorious." In an article published in 2011 in the British Medical Journal, he described the corrupt collaboration that exists between psychiatry and Big Pharma. It is instructive and alarming, since it lists many of the ways that Big Pharma, with the collaboration of psychiatry, is able to exercise an unwarranted influence over doctors and the public:

> Psychiatry has become pharma's goldmine, with a simple business plan. Seek a small group of specialists from a prestigious institution. Pharma becomes the professional kingmaker, funding research for these specialists. Research always

reports under diagnosis and under treatment, never the opposite. Control all data and make the study duration short. Use the media, plant news stories, and bankroll patient support groups. Pay your specialists large advisory fees. Lobby government. Get your pharma sponsored specialists to advise the government. So now the world view is dominated by a tiny group of specialists with vested interests. Use celebrity endorsements to sprinkle on the marketing magic of emotion. Expand the market by promoting online questionnaires that loosen the diagnostic criteria further. Make the illegitimate legitimate.

In Chapter 4, we saw that claims for the chemical imbalance theory and for antidepressant drugs restoring balance were unsupported. Massive marketing of this disinformation has persuaded doctors to believe in the value of these drugs. Indeed, it is no simple matter to see through this onslaught of propaganda.

You are familiar with the saying, "follow the money." In this book, I have cited reputable, highly credentialed authority after authority, who have done just that. They all agree that many, if not most, psychiatric publications in medical journals on the effectiveness and safety of antidepressant drugs are not to be trusted. *Conflict of interest, spawned by a multi-billion-dollar drug industry, not science, is governing how depression is being diagnosed, explained, and treated.*

****

Conflicts of interest are not confined to the biased reporting in medical journals of drug effectiveness and safety. This source of falsification can be found throughout psychiatric practice. Drug companies hire doctors to promote their products as part of "drug education programs." And doctors are misled by an army of sales reps, with their gifting of trinkets that apparently are trivial but turn out to have inordinate influence on prescribing practices.

In 2009, the journal Psychotherapy and Psychosomatics reported on *conflicts of interest for the authors of the clinical guidelines that are established for the treatment of psychiatric diagnoses.*

Guidelines give the criteria for doctors to follow when making a diagnosis and they direct the treatment to be provided for that diagnosis. Guidelines determine the treatments doctors recommend to their patients. They are created usually by groups of doctors who have been appointed for this purpose. They are supposed to be evidence-based and free of bias. Yet studies reveal that as many as 90% of the authors of clinical guidelines had at least one financial tie to the pharmaceutical industry, all of them with the companies whose products were being reviewed. Why would we assume their opinions were uninfluenced by their compensation? Why condone this practice?

David Henry is a Professor in the School of Medicine and Public Health at the University of New Castle in Australia who specializes in evidence-based medicine and clinical pharmacology. Ray Moynihan is a science journalist who has been a visiting editor at the British Medical Journal. They have named a trend that started in the 1980s *"disease mongering."* They define it as the practice of expanding the definition of illness to increase markets for those who sell or offer treatments. Commonly occurring human experiences are egregiously diagnosed as mental disorders. The conflation of sadness and depression is a glaring example of conflict of interest but far from an isolated one.

As far back as 1976, Henry Gadsden announced this goal in an interview with Fortune magazine. The dynamic CEO of Merck & Company, whose revenues quadrupled under his leadership, declared that his dream was to make drugs for healthy people. He said that he wanted Merck to be like Wrigley's chewing gum, with drugs for everyone. This strategy has led to the creation of questionable psychiatric diagnoses.

In 2006, an entire issue of the medical journal PLOS Medicine was devoted to the topic of *disease mongering*, which "... turns healthy people into patients, wastes precious resources, and causes iatrogenic harm" (that is, an illness caused by a medical treatment). A CDC report released ten years later stated that up to one in five children suffers from a mental disorder. This is an example of disease mongering engineered by psychiatry in collaboration with the drug companies.

Of interest in this context are two descriptions of disruptive behaviors given by the CDC in the report, *Mental Health Surveillance Among Children—United States, 2005–2011.* These are the diagnosis of Oppositional Defiant Disorder and Conduct Disorder. While there are children who need help for problems related to acting out, most of these diagnoses are of dubious validity and set dangerous precedents. At what point do these encroaching diagnoses turn a high-spirited thrust for intellectual autonomy into a disease? It is easy to write guidelines that attribute problems in the classroom to mental disorders that are rightfully the result of normal variations in development, stress at home, misguided classroom requirements, and poor teaching skills or conduct. Sensible parents need to see the danger in this over-medicalizing of a child's behavior.

You saw that Dr. Spitzer had second thoughts about his medicalizing of DSM-III. Allen Frances headed up the construction of DSM-IV, and he, too, has written about this issue, deploring how disease mongering based on the lost distinction between sadness and depression has afflicted primary care doctors. Dr. Frances attributes this effect to direct-to-consumer advertising by drug companies:

> Antidepressants are often prescribed loosely. Fewer than one third of antidepressant users have consulted a mental health professional in the past year. Most of the prescriptions are written by primary care doctors, with little training in psychiatric diagnosis and treatment, after very brief visits and under the influence of drug salesmanship. How did we get into this mess? There is no mystery. The massive overuse of antidepressants (and also antipsychotics) began about fifteen years ago when drug companies in the US were given a precious and unprecedented privilege—one that is appropriately denied them in the rest of the world. They were suddenly free to advertise directly to their potential customers on TV, in magazines, and on the Internet. The companies also aggressively built up their marketing to doctors, especially primary care physicians who were "educated" into the notion that depression was being frequently missed in their practices and that it is a simple "chemical imbalance" easily corrected by a pill. The consequent casual medicalization of normality mislabeled as sick many people with nothing more than the expectable symptoms of everyday life.

Many mental health professionals and primary care physicians are unaware of or ignore these realities. These doctors are poorly informed about the defectiveness of the DSM, the absence of a scientific basis for the chemical imbalance theory, and the poor outcome from antidepressant drug prescriptions. They trust psychiatric claims, the FDA, the NIMH, and medical journal publications reporting on antidepressant drug effectiveness.

The truth of Dr. Frances's commentary is that Big Pharma has been a huge promoter of this medicalization. But the *profession of psychiatry must accept the first and professional responsibility*, not drug company ads, despite their reprehensible influence. We have seen the central role played by the DSM. Each edition of the manual, beginning with DSM-III, advanced by DSM-IV, and continuing with DSM-V, was directed and produced by psychiatry. Primary care doctors base their misdiagnoses and ensuing prescriptions on the DSM's conflation of sadness and depression. Psychiatrists take the Hippocratic oath, that supreme expression again maleficence: *first do no harm.* Employees, even CEOs of pharmaceutical companies have not taken such an oath, and they are expected to turn a profit. While we deplore their lax standards and their dishonesty, they have not sworn to an oath to do no harm.

****

An example of psychiatric conflict of interest that was widely publicized is found in the psychiatric diagnosis of bipolar disorder in children, a DSM depressive disorder whose diagnosis has increased enormously with little scientific justification.

In 1994, psychiatrists changed the Diagnostic and Statistical Manual of Mental Disorders (DSM-IV) to diagnose emotional swings in children as bipolar disorder. Between 1994 and 2003, *diagnosis of bipolar disorder in children increased by a factor of 40.* Children were diagnosed as bipolar on what serious scientists view as inadequate grounds. Moreover, the therapeutic effect of these drugs was not demonstrated and many of these children diagnosed as bipolar experienced serious adverse effects from the drugs (see Notes).

Joseph Biederman is the psychiatrist regarded as most responsible for this explosion in the diagnoses and prescriptions written for children alleged to have bipolar disorder. Dr. Biederman is Chief of Clinical and Research Programs in Pediatric Psychopharmacology at Massachusetts General Hospital and is a Professor of Psychiatry at Harvard Medical School. He was at the forefront of the research, the advocacy, and the implementation of the increased diagnosis and treatment of bipolar disorder in children, advocating prescription of the drug Risperdal. Gardner Harris, the New York Times science writer, has written of how Dr. Biederman "helped to fuel" the dramatic 40-fold increase in prescriptions of bipolar drugs to children.

Dr. Angell, who as a former Editor-in-Chief of the New England Journal of Medicine, is no slouch at evaluating research, has written of Dr. Biederman's studies,

> Dr. Biederman's own studies of the drugs he advocates to treat childhood bipolar disorder were so small and loosely designed that they were largely inconclusive .... Thanks to Dr. Biederman, children as young as two years old are now being diagnosed as bipolar and treated with a cocktail of drugs, many of which were not approved by the FDA for that purpose, and none of which were approved for children below ten years of age.

In 2008, Dr. Biederman became a person of interest to Senator Charles Grassley of Iowa, as chairman of the Senate Finance Committee. Senator Grassley was concerned about conflicts of interest of psychiatrists doing the bidding of drug companies and held Senate hearings on the issue. A problem must be viewed as quite serious nationally for the Senate to hold such hearings.

Drug companies recruit psychiatrists with reputations in the field as spokespersons to influence the prescribing practices of psychiatrists and primary care doctors. Since knowledge of the existence of a conflict of interest can adversely affect that expert's power, psychiatrist's reports of the income they receive from the drug companies can be important public information.

Senator Grassley was investigating whether Dr. Biederman had violated federal, Harvard Medical School, and Massachusetts General Hospital regulations having to do with the reporting of income. Dr. Biederman had failed to report on a disclosure report filed with his university that he had received income from the drug company Johnson & Johnson. Senator Grassley knew from Johnson & Johnson that the drug company had paid Dr. Biederman $58,169 during the year in question. Senator Grassley also discovered Dr. Biederman had received almost two million dollars over eight years from other pharmaceutical companies which he did not report properly.

Dr. Biederman is just one of a number of prominent psychiatrists holding prestigious positions who were investigated by Senator Grassley. They all had failed to report to their employers income from drug companies related to their advancement of the prescription of psychiatric drugs.

Another case investigated by Senator Grassley was that of Dr. Frederick K. Goodwin. Dr. Goodwin, also a psychiatrist, was a former Director of the NIMH. He was the host of a satellite radio channel programmed by National Public Radio (NPR), "The Infinite Mind." As Gardner Harris, of the New York Times, has reported, Dr. Goodwin earned at least $1.3 million from 2000–2007 giving marketing lectures for drug companies, income not mentioned on the program or to his employers.

In 2005, he made a number of scientifically unsupported comments about bipolar disorder. He warned that children with bipolar disorder who were left untreated could suffer brain damage. He went on to declare, "But as we'll be hearing today, modern treatments, mood stabilizers in particular, have been proven safe and effective in bipolar children." At the same time, GlaxoSmithKline paid Dr. Goodwin $2,500 to give a promotional lecture for its mood stabilizer drug, Lamictal, at the Ritz Carlton Golf Resort in Naples, Florida. Records given to the Congressional investigators show that GlaxoSmithKline paid him more than $329,000 that year for promoting Lamictal.

On another program Dr. Goodwin said, "As you will hear today, there is no credible evidence linking antidepressants to violence or suicide." Dr. Goodwin was paid around $20,000 by GlaxoSmithKline, which failed to publicly disclose studies showing that its antidepressant, Paxil, increased suicidal behaviors. Margaret Low Smith, vice president of NPR, stated that if she had been aware of this conflict of interest, NPR would not have broadcast these programs.

In a sweeping confirmation of the concerns that psychiatry had become too cozy with the pharmaceutical companies, Senator Grassley not only found reason to go after these individual psychiatrists, but also to direct his attention to the

American Psychiatric Association (APA). He was concerned that the APA was financially dependent on the pharmaceutical industry. In 2000, the American Psychiatric Association received $13 million from the pharmaceutical industry compared with $10 million from dues-paying members. Benedict Carey and Gardner Harris, science writers for the New York Times, reported, "In 2006, the latest year for which numbers are available, the drug industry accounted for 30% of the association's $62.5 million in financing." In response to the pressure over conflict of interest, in 2009, the APA announced that it would "phase out pharmaceutical funding of continuing medical education seminars and meals at its conventions." Two months later it accepted $1.7 million from the drug companies for the APA's annual convention in San Francisco.

****

The National Institutes of Health (NIH) is our country's medical research agency. It rightly has enjoyed a sterling reputation for research world-wide. The NIH comprises 27 Institutes and Centers, among them being the National Cancer Institute, the National Eye Institute, the National Heart, Lung, and Blood Institute, and the National Institute of Allergy and Infectious Diseases. The National Institute of Mental Health (NIMH) is another of these institutes.

Nowhere is the profession of psychiatry's conflict of interest more influential or problematic than at the NIMH. Much of the corrupted research I have cited has been supported and approved by the NIMH. The NIMH is led by psychiatrists and they have made certain that the profession's interests are well served. Psychiatry's private interests appear to dominate how the NIMH supports research and how it communicates with the public about depression and other mental disorders. The sad truth is that this agency appears to have fallen prey to a professional bias.

The NIMH is the bulwark of the medicalization of mental disorders. Support for research into psychological factors, of how these disorders are products of learning and experience, has been minimal by comparison. The single mindedness of the psychiatric leadership on the issue should be troubling to anyone concerned about health care. Why are we short-changing substantial psychological research that has led to better outcomes and shows such promise?

The NIMH is in a different place scientifically from the other institutes at the NIH. It is the only institute that relies on and promotes diagnoses and treatments that are so unsubstantiated in their validity and reliability. It is the only institute that has defined the disorders it studies as of biological origin when there is abundant evidence that favors the conclusion that the great majority of mental disorders are psychologically determined.

As Dr. Jerome Wakefield, whose work was cited in an earlier chapter, has written,

> We've thrown tens of billions of dollars into trying to identify biomarkers and biological substrates for mental disorders. The fact is we've gotten very little out of all that(. . .)By over-focusing on the biological, we are doing patients a disservice.

Interestingly, Dr. Thomas Insel, who was Director of the NIMH from 2002 until 2015 agrees with much of Dr. Wakefield's point. During his tenure Dr. Insel oversaw the spending of 20 *billion dollars on neuroscience and genetics research*, much of it related to depression. After his departure from the NIMH, he lamented that this enormous expenditure *has neither improved the success of drug treatments for mental disorder nor reduced the debilitating effects of mental disorder.* His remarks did not reference the ominous research results I reviewed in the last chapter, which indicate that *not only has the medicalization of psychiatry failed to remedy mental disorder, it has contributed to it.* Dr. Insel's summation, after he left his position of power, of the failure of drug treatment has informed few of the truth about the errant nature of this spending of the public's money in pursuit of a justification for the medicalization of psychiatry. Nothing has changed at the NIMH. Since his departure these expenditures have continued. But as the old saying goes, to get out of a hole you have to stop digging.

Psychological research based on a behavioral model has produced far more valuable results than has biological research. Why are we not investing more heavily in treatments that are known to be effective than in treatments that are not? What if even half of the billions of dollars the NIMH spent on neuroscience had been invested instead on behavioral research? We don't know for certain what the returns would have been since there is no data to verify the counterfactual. But there is strong evidence that investments in behavioral research offer the likelihood of providing significant *immediate* benefit to current patients, and greatly advancing our proficiency in providing more effective treatments in the future. This surely holds true as well for improving our effectiveness in addressing disordered behavior that does not qualify as mentally disordered.

Even so, behavior therapy's superior results and safety in the treatment of depression have led to it being increasingly recommended to patients. The treatment often is presented as if it were an adjunct to the overarching view that depression is a brain disease requiring medical care. This is false. The empirical basis for the development of behavior therapy, along with the treatment's greater success, constitute a direct challenge to psychiatry's medical stance. The two therapies exist in diametric opposition. One predicates a brain disease explanation for which there is no satisfactory scientific evidence; the other is based on substantial research results that indicate that the great bulk of human behavior, both normal and disordered, is a product of positive and negative experiences, not a broken brain.

This is a matter of common sense. As you shall see in Chapter 10, behavioral principles are so well established and accepted that people hardly recognize or think about their use (and usefulness) in everyday life. Psychiatry's absence of interest in these principles as they apply to treatment and Big Pharma's reliance on these principles as they apply to sales is one of the great absurdities of our current system of mental health "care."

It is demonstrably the case that failure to prioritize behavioral research, which offers so much greater promise of a pay-off, has sabotaged our understanding of the basics of mental health and mental disorder. There are substantial reasons to challenge the idea that our incomplete understanding of the chemistry of the brain is more important to an understanding of mental disorder than is the knowledge that exists of psychological factors. It is why mental health care lags behind the care of physical illnesses. For mental health care to measure up to our understanding and treatment of physical illnesses, the NIMH must change its priorities. And for that to happen, mental health care must be governed by science, not by ideology and conflict of interest.

9

Big Pharma and the FDA

The incongruence between the scientific literature and the claims made in FDA-regulated SSRI advertisements is remarkable and possibly unparalleled.

—*Jeffrey Lacasse, PhD and Jonathon Leo, PhD*

The Food and Drug Administration (FDA) is responsible for monitoring the effectiveness and safety of prescription drugs and medical devices. The scientists at the FDA have a record worthy of respect. However, award-winning science journalists who have reported for the New York Times, have identified lapses in the FDA's detection of drug company practices. Doug Critser in "Generation Rx," and Melody Petersen in "Our Daily Meds," documented instances of unsatisfactory FDA regulatory oversight for drugs of questionable effectiveness and safety. Alison Bass, who teaches at Brandeis, and is also an award-winning health/science journalist, has done this documentation specifically for psychiatric drugs in her book, "Side Effects," with particular reference to the FDA's approval of antidepressants.

In Chapters 5, 6, 7, and 8 I reviewed falsified or mistaken reports of the science related to *antidepressant drug effectiveness and drug safety*. This chapter will examine government oversight of the *truthfulness of drug companies marketing of their drugs* to the public. I will begin not by examining the quality of the FDA's detection of fraudulent claims by the drug companies, but by citing legal actions taken by the Department of Justice, which is under the U.S. Attorney General. The Department of Justice investigates and prosecutes false claims.

In 2010, *the pharmaceutical industry in the United States became the biggest defrauder of the federal government*, as determined by payments made for violations of the False Claims Act (FCA). The payments surpassed those made by the defense industry, which had been the leading defrauder before this.

The False Claims Act was passed under the administration of President Abraham Lincoln to prevent goods suppliers from defrauding the Union army. Hence, it is called the "Lincoln Law." Over the intervening century and a half, the act has been amended and its terms have been more clearly defined. Supplying a false claim does not in itself qualify as a violation. There must be either *knowledge that the claim is false, willful ignorance, or reckless disregard of the knowledge.* So, let's be quite clear about this: the actions of the drug companies were determined to be planned business practices.

Pharmaceutical company cases accounted for 25% of all federal FCA payouts compared with 11% by the defense industry, that is, by the industry in second place. There have been 165 pharmaceutical industry settlements, comprising $19.8 billion in penalties for marketing schemes that violate the FCA. Many of the infractions were for illegal marketing of drugs for uses not approved by the FDA, such as promoting unauthorized prescription of drugs to children. The drug companies also were caught engaging in widespread bribing of doctors to prescribe their drugs. Purposely overcharging federal programs for drugs was another major infraction.

Here are some examples of the offenses and penalties. Take note: if you only look at the size of the fines the drug companies are paying, you might conclude that our regulators are doing their job quite well. At first glance, it seems that justice is being done since these fines are enormous in the aggregate. It is easy, however, to misread the picture that they present. Look closely and a picture emerges that is disturbing.

In the early 2000s, Merck's COX-2 pain reliever, Vioxx, was highly marketed and widely prescribed, with sales of $2.5 billion just in 2003. Merck was fined $950 million after it was revealed the company had suppressed studies showing Vioxx was dangerous. So they knew this and still continued marketing the drug. Estimates of the number who died from heart attacks and strokes after taking the drug vary from 30,000 to 90,000. Such an elevated number of casualties are what might be expected as the tragic consequences of a war zone—not as the result of prescribed medicines.

Forest Pharmaceuticals was fined for marketing the antidepressants Celexa and Lexapro to children and adolescents. These drugs, both with blockbuster sales (more than a billion dollars annually), were never approved by the FDA for children or adolescents, only for adults. Their off-label promotion included sales pitches to doctors to promote pediatric use and hiring doctors for the same purpose at psychiatric meetings. In 2010, Forest settled with the U.S. Department of Justice under the False Claims Act and to resolve criminal charges for a fine of $313 million.

In 2012, GlaxoSmithKline pleaded guilty to criminal charges under the False Claims Act. They paid a $3 billion settlement, which included a criminal fine of $1 billion for having marketed the antidepressants Paxil and Wellbutrin to children, for whom these drugs were not approved. They had withheld, as well, data bearing on the safety of a diabetes drug, Avandia. They were giving kickbacks to physicians for prescribing this drug, including trips to Jamaica and Bermuda, spa treatments, and hunting excursions. Gardner Harris of the New York Times reported the FDA estimated that Avandia was causing hundreds of heart attacks and instances of heart failure each month. During the period cited, GlaxoSmithKline had sales of Paxil amounting to $11.6 billion, of Wellbutrin of $5.9 billion, and of Avandia, of $10.4 billion. A penalty of $3 billion hardly measures against these earnings. For the drug companies such fines are so small that they do not act as deterrents. Quite clearly, *these crimes pay*, and fines are just the cost of doing business.

Nicholas Kristof, The New York Times columnist, has written about Risperdal. This was the antipsychotic drug Gardner Harris cited that Johnson & Johnson had paid Minnesota psychiatrists to prescribe. Johnson & Johnson marketed the drug to children and adolescents diagnosed as bipolar, choosing not to reveal they knew that the drug caused breast development in boys. Johnson & Johnson also successfully lobbied the state of Texas to prescribe Risperdal, not generics. The state paid $3000 a year for each Medicaid patient rather than the $250 generic cost. *In 2013, Johnson & Johnson paid 2 billion dollars in penalties for suppression of the negative effects of Risperdal against 30 billion dollars in sales.* Again, it is the cost of doing business. Nor did the adverse effects of this drug stop Johnson & Johnson from marketing it. Johnson & Johnson later promoted the person in charge of marketing the drug to the position of CEO. Kristof ends his column by calling for "tougher enforcement of safety regulations . . . and white-collar criminals need to be prosecuted."

During the early 2000s, a period of record fraud, the compensation for the CEOs of the 11 largest drug companies rose from an average of $6.8 million per CEO in 2003 to an average of $18 million per CEO in 2012. While many economic factors fueled this bounty, it is nevertheless striking since we hold dear in our culture the basic concept of rewarding beneficial activities and punishing harmful ones. *Instead, we find CEO compensation increased dramatically in an era of flourishing illegal activity.* This is the reverse of what Kristof called for. When it comes to doling out rewards to CEOs, the financial well-being of a company and its stockholders apparently override the physical and financial harm done to patients.

It bears repeating: the chemicals in these drugs are powerful and they were falsely and knowingly being vigorously marketed as medicines to those for whom they had not been found to be safe or effective, inflicting harm to their health and wallet.

****

Inadequate monitoring of drug company ads is far from the only problem faced by the FDA. Drug companies fund the majority of the biomedical research reported in this country. As I reviewed in previous chapters, much of this research is being misreported. Dr. Sidney Wolfe, the former head of the health care division of Public Citizen, has reported "growing evidence" of a "systematic bias" in medical research. Dr. Wolfe pointed out that research carried out by the drug companies is far more likely to find favorable results for their products than research carried out by researchers who have no financial relationship with the pharmaceutical industry.

The FDA knows this and more. A senior regulator at the FDA, Thomas Marciniak, expressed dismay at what has happened to the drug companies. In 2013, he wrote:

> Drug companies have turned into marketing machines. They've kind of lost sight of the fact that they're actually doing something which involves your health.

Dr. Richard Smith, the former Editor-in-Chief of the British Medical Journal, has described how the drug companies deceive the FDA and the medical profession about the effectiveness of drugs coming to market. He has detailed how the companies achieve this deception by manipulating the design of their studies. For example, a trial is conducted against a treatment the company in question knows to be inferior; a drug is tested against other drugs administered at too low a dose to be effective or at too high a dose to show their drug to be less toxic; trials are conducted that are too small to show differences; they use multiple end points in the trial and select for publication only those that give favorable results. Dr. Smith points out that these actions, taken by many different companies, serve the purpose of hiding significant problems with the drugs whose trials are being manipulated. Patients are likely to suffer when the FDA fails to recognize these manipulations and doesn't act.

The problem has evolved invasively. Lewis Hunter, the former CEO of Cambridge Associates, a global investment firm, has written several books on the degrading of FDA oversight. He is a representative of the financial world rather than that of health care, but he warns that this country has devolved into a system whereby the success of the pharmaceutical industry is fostered by a relationship between business and government to the detriment of health care. He writes of how the drug companies hire former FDA experts to assist them in getting drugs onto the market that should not be approved. Mr. Hunter writes, "All these financial ties encourage a 'wink and a nod' relationship between researchers working for the drug companies and regulators, who are often the same people, thanks to the revolving door."

Some years ago, the Associate Director of the FDA, David J. Graham, was critical of how the leadership of the FDA was going about doing their job. Dr. Graham spoke out about the FDA's role in the following terms:

> FDA is inherently biased in favor of the pharmaceutical industry. It views industry as its client, whose interests it must represent and advance. It views its primary mission as approving as many drugs it can, regardless of whether the drugs are safe or needed.

Since then, the problem has worsened. A number of years ago *the pharmaceutical industry was permitted to begin funding the FDA approval process*, according to an arrangement whereby the drug companies fund acceleration of drug approvals. This arrangement is neither a matter of good practice nor of safeguarding the public. As science reporter Melody Peterson has pointed out, this has placed the FDA in the ridiculous and ethically compromised position of having the drug companies *fund their own regulation.* *The fox has been invited into the chicken coop.* A stipulation in this agreement, modified only slightly since its inception, is that the FDA cannot use these funds to evaluate the safety of drugs once they have been approved. The drug companies themselves are expected to fulfill this role. Thus, the underfunded FDA gets more drugs onto the market sooner and is even less capable of subsequently monitoring the drugs.

Part of this arrangement allows the drug companies more leeway to promote their drugs for off label uses. Public Citizen's Health Research Group looked into this arrangement by conducting a survey of the FDA's reviewers, who responded (anonymously) that many of the drugs they had recommended against had been approved by their bosses. The FDA reviewers believed that FDA standards had been dangerously lowered.

The drug companies had argued successfully that the acceleration of drug approvals was imperative to get needed drugs approved more quickly. So, what has this acceleration and liberalization of drug approval produced? The Edmond J. Safra Center for Ethics at Harvard University investigates "widespread ethics lapses of leaders in government, business and other professions." They evaluated 979 drugs that had been approved by the FDA over a 10-year span. Two of the 979 were judged to be "break through advances." More than 90% were "me-too" drugs. "Me-too" drugs are drugs, whose structure is very similar to already known drugs, that add no therapeutic value. Twenty percent of the approved drugs produced enough harm to cause FDA regulators to "add a serious warning or have them withdrawn." The Safra Center wrote,

> Flooding the market with hundreds of minor variations on existing drugs and technically innovative but clinically inconsequential new drugs, appears to be the de facto hidden business model of drug companies. In spite of its primary charge to protect the public, the FDA criteria for approval encourage that business model .... The business model works. Despite producing drugs with few clinical advantages and significant health risks, industry sales and profits have grown substantially at public expense.

Dr. Marcia Angell, writes that "the pharmaceutical industry is not especially innovative." She decries the great prevalence of FDA-approved "me-too" drugs that are no more effective than the drugs they replace. She adds that the drug industry is the most profitable industry in this country and that drug prices have little relationship to the costs of making them. Dr. Angell wrote,

> Over the past two decades the pharmaceutical industry has moved very far from its original high purpose of discovering and producing useful new drugs. Now primarily a marketing machine to sell drugs of dubious benefit, this industry uses its wealth and power to co-opt every institution that might stand in its way, including the US Congress, the FDA, academic medical centers, and the medical profession itself.

Dr. Joseph Stiglitz, the Nobel prize winner for economics and former World Bank Chief Economist, has added,

> (. . .)Drug companies spend more on advertising and marketing than on research, more on research on lifestyle drugs than on life saving drugs, and almost nothing on diseases that affect developing countries only. This is not surprising. Poor countries cannot afford drugs, and drug companies make investments that yield the highest returns.

The New York Times recently described FDA regulations as a hybrid of political interests, special interests, and science. They did so after the FDA, in response to former President Trump's pressure, approved "convalescent plasma" to treat Covid-19 patients even though the data did not support approval. The editors at the New York Times wrote: "Special interests have played as much of a role as actual data in the approval of questionable cancer drugs and faulty medical devices for almost as long as the agency has existed." In this book I have documented the case for antidepressant drugs being entitled to full membership on a list of drug approvals based on pressure, not science. The Times editorial went on to state: "This makes it hard to trust the regulators to do their jobs . . .."

Dr. Peter Gotzsche, of the Cochrane Collaboration, *has singled out psychiatry as a major player in FDA/drug company malfeasance.* He faults psychiatry's alliance with the drug companies as having led to practices that are deviations from science. The standards Dr. Gotzsche applied in coming to this conclusion are those governing science and good health care which, as one of the founders of Cochrane, he understands very well. As we have seen, psychiatric leaders have claimed fidelity to scientific standards, but their actions are far more in alignment with their own ambition to be recognized as legitimate medical experts, their business interests, and the financial interests of the drug companies.

****

The preceding four chapters provide strong evidence that the FDA's approval of antidepressant drugs is a blemish on its record as a regulatory agency. Some of the FDA's failure to identify and eliminate these prescriptions can be explained by the budgeting insufficiency mentioned previously: the FDA has too few employees to monitor drug company ads and claims. *An effective FDA is essential to health care.* The FDA needs better funding to conduct its oversight mandate and the pharmaceutical industry cannot be described as supportive when Congress debates the FDA's budget allocation. Instead, as a prime example of the problem, the FDA now has some employees whose salaries are dependent on drug company money, not government money. This is not a satisfactory way for the FDA to conduct oversight of drugs.

This brings us to examining one of the prime contributors to the FDA's failed monitoring of the effectiveness and safety of antidepressant drugs: *ghost writing.* Ghost writing is a significant issue because it is a major contributor to false beliefs about the effectiveness and safety of antidepressant drugs. As I stated previously, many articles published in medical journals are not written by the doctors whose names are on them, although those doctors may review or even contribute to the articles. Instead, they are comprehensively composed by ghost writers who are employed by the drug companies and who remain anonymous. Publications on the effectiveness and safety of antidepressant drugs in psychiatric journals are noteworthy examples. *Ghost written articles commonly misrepresent a study's findings to favor the interests of the drug companies, yet the FDA has ignored this deception.*

Ben Goldacre is a British doctor whose first book, Bad Science, was an international best seller. In Dr. Goldacre's latest book, "Bad Pharma: How Drug Companies Mislead Doctors and Harm Patients," he discusses ghost writing. He points out that college students are given dire warnings against plagiarism, but:

> . . . to the best of my knowledge, no academic anywhere in the world has ever been punished for putting their name on a ghostwritten academic paper . . .. Often these academics have had little or no involvement in collecting the data or drafting the paper . . .. While the publication might look like a spontaneous project from an independent academic, it's generally part of a carefully choreographed timetable of publications, all running to the marketing schedule of one company's product.

A report by Public Citizen, in May 2017, gives a snapshot picture of why ghost writing is a serious problem. The example is the antidepressant Celexa. Here is an abbreviated reproduction of their report that describes how ghost written articles are spun. This is long, but I believe it is so expressive of the problem that I am quoting it at length:

> The Wagner paper described what appeared to be an objective double-blind, randomized controlled trial, the gold standard of drug research. It was one of the first published studies documenting an effective treatment for childhood and adolescent depression, and it reported only mild adverse effects with use of citalopram.

Although citalopram was not then (and never has been) approved by the Food and Drug Administration (FDA) for use in children or adolescents, Wagner and her colleagues concluded that their eight-week study "further support(ed) the use of citalopram in children and adolescents suffering from major depression."

Eager to promote the use of citalopram for treatment of these younger patients, Forrest aggressively publicized the Wagner paper, presenting it to professional societies, pitching it to various media outlets and arranging for Dr. Wagner to chair a continuing medical education program to educate doctors about the study(. . ..)

Pharmaceutical manufacturers have historically maintained tight control over data from their drug studies(. . ..) Only in rare cases are these secret documents revealed to the public. This happened in a lawsuit against Forest that was settled in part in 2014, when patients' attorneys fought successfully to have some of the confidential corporate documents related to the Wagner paper unsealed(. . ..) The unsealed documents describe how Dr. Karen Wagner and the other authors listed on the citalopram publication did not draft the original manuscript. Instead, the paper was ghostwritten by Natasha Mitchner, a contractor hired by Forest's marketing department. This allowed the company to maintain control over content(. . ..)

Ghostwriting was a common practice at Forest at the time when the citalopram paper was written . . .. Maintaining control of the trial data and manuscript drafting allowed Forest to selectively spin the results presented in the Wagner paper to favor citalopram. Had they reported only the results based on the protocol that had been developed before the study began, the drug would not have appeared more effective than placebo.

The ghostwriting team modified these results by including data from eight subjects who became aware that they were taking citalopram due to a packaging error during the study . . .. Indeed, when these subjects were removed from the results, citalopram no longer appeared to be more effective than placebo. The inclusion of these eight "unblinded" subjects, a violation of the study protocol, was not reported in the Wagner paper. And although the Wagner paper described only mild side effects, such as nausea and fatigue, troubling signs of agitation went unreported. In fact, eight subjects taking citalopram displayed signs of agitation, hypomania (unusual gaiety, excitement, or irritability), anxiety or other states of emotional arousal, whereas only one subject taking placebo experienced such psychiatric symptoms.

> Worst of all, while Forest swiftly published and aggressively publicized the Wagner paper, the company sat on results of a second study in adolescents that had provided much more negative results. In that second study, which was not published until 2006, citalopram had not even come close to proving more effective than placebo. Moreover, twice as many subjects taking citalopram displayed suicidal thoughts or behavior than those taking placebo(. . ..)
>
> The APA is unlikely to retract the ghostwritten Wagner article in response to the letter sent last August, as the American Journal of Psychiatry's editor-in-chief had already curtly rejected a similar request for a retraction earlier in 2016 . . .. Even if the Wagner paper is retracted, it may be impossible to fully reverse the impact the study has had on prescribing practices. The study has now been cited in multiple systematic reviews(. . ..)

How representative is this case? According to the following medical journal article, there is a condoned, institutionalized slanting of antidepressant drug research in favor of the drugs by ghost writers and by researchers with conflicts of interest. The Journal of Clinical Epidemiology published a study in 2015 that reported on 185 meta-analyses of the effectiveness of antidepressant drugs (meta-analyses are a collection of similar studies on a particular subject). The study found that *one third of these medical journal articles had been ghost written by employees of the drug companies and of the other two thirds, more than three quarters of them were written by researchers who had a conflict of interest* (they were being paid by the drug companies). Studies by those with industry ties were significantly more likely to report favorable results for antidepressants versus placebo than by researchers who had no such ties. As Dr. Goldacre wrote, *why is the FDA not regulating ghost writing*?

In the early 2000s, the FDA's failure to regulate antidepressant drugs adequately did not go unnoticed by some other public servants charged with protection of the public. When a state entity intervenes to take on the role of a national watchdog agency, the implicit criticism of that federal agency is stinging. This is precisely what happened in New York. Because of poor regulation by the FDA, the state of New York took legal action against GlaxoSmithKline (GSK) for a national, not just a state problem. In 2004, the Attorney General of New York filed a lawsuit for fraud against GSK for the marketing of the antidepressant, Paxil, to teenagers. GSK had failed to publish four studies of this antidepressant with alarmingly negative results. They had evidence that twice as many on Paxil as on placebo considered suicide after taking the drug.

A settlement was reached requiring that this information be reported. Another part of the agreement *was the establishment in New York of a drug registry* requiring that all trials submitted for listing must have been registered when they were initiated. *Otherwise, the results of the trials could not be published.* This was an effort to prevent the drug companies from hiding negative results. For years, the FDA had failed to adopt this regulation nationally and it was not for another three years that the FDA did so, in 2007.

Why is this registry so important? One unfavorable outcome and one favorable indicates that the outcome is 50% favorable. Eliminate reporting the unfavorable and suddenly the outcome is 100% favorable. Finally, the FDA acted to require that all trials that were later to be submitted for FDA approval *must be pre-registered.* This action is what made possible the studies I cited in the last chapter by Dr. Rising and Dr. Turner, documenting the misrepresentation of the effectiveness of drug treatments in publications in medical journals.

Despite this important step, Public Citizen has raised strong concerns that in the past two decades oversight by the FDA of the pharmaceutical industry has *worsened.* They are critical of the FDA for having developed a "distorted mindset" with the industry it regulates. In 2014, Margaret Hamburg, FDA Commissioner from 2009 until 2015, speaking to a group of more than 300 drug company executives, "called for more *regulatory flexibility* and a new era of partnership with the biopharmaceutical industry." Public Citizen has charged that the FDA's desire for "regulatory flexibility" is a euphemism for a lowering of standards that has led to "approval of products that are unsafe, ineffective, or both."

Public Citizen reported that the FDA proposed a guidance that would *allow the drug companies to tell doctors a medication is less dangerous than the FDA had concluded.* (See Notes). If this guidance is approved, the drug companies will be permitted "through medical journal articles and discussions with doctors (to claim) that the FDA-approved labelling overstates a medication's risks . . . (and) the FDA will not object to this misrepresentation of a drug's safety."

This preposterous guidance was opened for public comment. Here are a few of the comments Public Citizen cites: From a *physician*: "I am appalled at the prospect of allowing drug companies to tell me a drug is safer than the FDA's assessment and expert committee analysis determines." From a *pharmacist*: "It is time for the FDA to step up and do its job . . . I no longer trust pharmaceutical companies to give me accurate information on drugs or the FDA to guarantee a proper drug." From a *consumer*: "It is unbelievable that consumers have to ask the FDA to prohibit pharmaceutical companies from telling my physician that drugs are safer than the FDA says they are." Public Citizen urged the secretary of Health and Human Services to reject the guidance.

In the last chapter I discussed the FDA Medwatch program. Once the FDA approves a drug, the drug companies are required to report to the FDA any adverse events they have been informed about. FDA epidemiologists and safety evaluators review and analyze these reports to assess the frequency and seriousness of the adverse events. Gardner Harris, of the New York Times, investigated how well this is being handled.

He found that FDA assessments had been undertaken on only 35% of the drugs that had gained approval. In many cases these tests had been pending for over a decade. Harris reported that the FDA never required a timeline for the tests. When questioned about it, the FDA official in charge of reviewing this oversight told Harris he believed the drug companies "are taking that commitment very seriously." One might ask, how would they behave if they were not taking that commitment very seriously?

Public Citizen also cited Dr. Mitchel Mathis, director of the FDA's Division of Psychiatry Products, for writing on the homepage of the FDA an endorsement for prescribing the antidepressants Prozac and Lexapro to children. Public Citizen pointed out that the FDA should not be endorsing products it regulates. Dr. Mathis's broad statement greatly exaggerated the value of antidepressant drugs for children, many of whom I would add are mis-diagnosed as depressed. Had the claim been made by the companies that sell these drugs it would qualify for consideration by the FDA as a violation of advertising regulations.

A number of other egregious examples illustrate how the FDA has been more supportive of business interests than the science related to antidepressant drugs. The FDA adopted a policy of withholding negative information from the labels on antidepressants. The FDA even reversed a manufacturer's decision to amend its drug label to say that the drug was associated with increased hostility and suicidal ideation among children. Last , it took the astonishing step of urging drug companies to withhold from doctors and the public the results of studies in the clinical trials that showed these psychiatric drugs were no better than placebos on the grounds that this *might scare people away*.

Suicide related to antidepressant prescriptions is under-reported. Dr. Gotzsche has cited the troubling case of a college student who committed suicide after volunteering for a clinical trial conducted by Lilly of their antidepressant, Cymbalta. The FDA, the regulatory agency responsible to the people it is supposed to protect, refused to respond to the press and researchers who requested the data, stating, "Some clinical trial data are considered trade secrets, or commercially protected information." Dr. Gotzsche reports that when data ultimately were revealed through the Freedom of Information Act, 41 deaths and 13 suicides were discovered to have occurred during this clinical trial. (the college student's death was not one of them; four other known suicides among volunteers also were not included).

There was a time when the FDA was doing a much better job protecting the public in their monitoring of the big drug companies. There are those who have stood up against the erosion of standards. I have already cited the exceptional case of David J. Graham, but there are others. Dr. David Kessler, a pediatrician, also deserves praise for his actions when he was FDA commissioner from 1990–1997. In 2021, President Biden appointed Dr. Kessler to oversee the manufacture and distribution of coronavirus vaccines to the American public.

When Dr. Kessler headed up the FDA, he took his mandate seriously and was instrumental in the actions taken to combat the dangers of smoking cigarettes. Dr. Kessler was awarded the Public Health Hero Award from the University of California Berkeley School of Public Health for his efforts to regulate tobacco. Because of his efforts to strengthen regulations to address abuses by industry, much of his term as FDA commissioner was spent defending himself against attacks. Industries have powerful friends.

Dr. Kessler also raised concerns about misleading drug company claims, citing the inaccuracy of information conveyed by pharmaceutical ads in medical journals. Two of the drugs of concern to him were the antidepressants, Paxil and Zoloft, about which he wrote, "A disturbingly high proportion of these advertisements contains misleading information and many appear to violate existing FDA regulations governing the accuracy and balance of prescription drug advertising." Within a year of leaving his post, the FDA loosened its restrictions on drug marketing, including allowing *direct-to-consumer advertising* of prescription drugs. As I have indicated, this made it much harder for the FDA to control the accuracy of the content of the marketing of Zoloft, Paxil and every other drug. The great value of this loosened marketing to the drug companies is clear, its value to the public is quite dubious. In 2005, an article reviewing these ads was published in PLOS Medicine by Drs. Lacasse and Leo, which concluded, "The incongruence between the scientific literature and the claims made in FDA-regulated advertisements is remarkable and possibly unparalleled."

We have established as national goals a healthy (profitable) pharmaceutical industry and a healthy (physically and psychologically) public. It is inevitable that the FDA, in fulfilling its mandate, will lean one way or the other in balancing these sometimes divergent interests. However, the record I have cited leads to the conclusion that the FDA is leaning too much toward satisfying the interests of the drug industry. The FDA's inept handling of antidepressant drugs is a prime example of this bias. It is time for the public to be better served.

FDA regulations determine how doctors practice medicine. Medical regulations are supposed to be based on tests that determine objectively what drugs are approved for different diagnoses. The quality of medical care depends on the quality of these regulations. The drug companies have the same imperatives for growth and profit and the same pressures from their stockholders and boards of directors as other industries. Everyone is responsible to someone else and in this intricate chain of business commands, the last link is the one with the least knowledge about the details of the business—the stockholder. The need to satisfy the requirement for profit can obscure what should be the primary goal of those in charge: the safety and care of the patient. It is up to the FDA to ride herd on drug company infractions.

Drug companies exert their power at high levels of influence. Drug company lobbying of Congress plays an important role in compromising adequate regulation by the FDA of prescription drugs. The pharmaceutical industry spends more money lobbying Congress than any other lobby in this country, to the tune of more than $250,000 per senator and member of Congress annually. This vast outpouring of capital has limited government efforts to regulate and control how pharmaceuticals go about their marketing. We need to pay better attention to our elected and appointed representatives if public interests are to be better served.

****

Weak government oversight is not new, nor is it unique to the pharmaceutical industry. Historically, the government has failed to exercise proper oversight of a number of industries with tragic results. Years ago, Ralph Nader uncovered how the Department of Transportation had failed in its oversight of the automobile industry, causing Americans to die because they were driving unsafe vehicles. Hurricane Katrina revealed how the Army Corps of Engineers had failed to protect New Orleans from great damage from floods. Collapse of the housing market has been traced to the government's laxity in regulating Wall Street. Pollution of the drinking water in Flint, Michigan, and elsewhere was due to elected officials failing to abide by proper standards, standards that still appear to be ignored when it comes to Native American reservations. Dupont, a member of the chemical industry, was found to have polluted the ground water and drinking water in West Virginia for decades. Volkswagen, a member of the automobile industry, was caught having devised software specifically engineered to deceive emissions inspections while they actually blasted the environment with pollution.

Industrial harm is deplorable wherever it originates, but *when the damage done to health comes from chemicals sold as healing medications the violation is even more profound.* It is personal. Our families and friends suffer, and we see that suffering. Our children and parents can suffer or die. You and I can die. And all because we did as we were advised and took a substance into our bodies prescribed by those we are supposed to trust. Therefore, it is imperative that the individuals or groups who work to maintain our health meet a high standard. As we have seen, too often this is not the case. Business interests have trumped public interests.

Commentators have common themes in detailing these problems: The FDA is seriously underfunded to do its job and in an important sense has been captured by the industry it is mandated to regulate. As a result, the FDA has failed in too many instances to act against the prescription of drugs that have been shown to be unsafe and ineffective. Antidepressants are a prime example. Congress has been compromised by the big drug companies and it is up to the public to make certain that the FDA is led by a commissioner who regards duty to the public as the primary task. The FDA must hold the drug companies accountable if healthcare is to be delivered in a form that serves the public's best interests.

Let us move now to the heart of this presentation. *What I have said up to now is widely known among serious scientists, but it has not been propounded satisfactorily to the general population.* Many are persuaded that the brain disease theory is as solidly based as any other medical explanation for disease and that antidepressant drugs are the treatment of choice for depression. Those who have read this book will understand that when it comes to mental disorders, neuro causality is a theory that has repeatedly failed scientific testing, yet this failed theory continues on because it is an economic bonanza for the drug companies and bolsters psychiatric practices. You have seen as well that the effectiveness claimed for antidepressant drugs is unproven. The application of this failed theory with antidepressant drugs only improves the quality of life for those who take them because of a placebo effect—*a psychological effect.* And the chemicals in these drugs have the powerful potential to wreak serious and even irreversible physical harm.

There is a better and safer way. Let us instead, in the chapters that follow, examine some *psychological principles derived from good science* that provide an accounting of the origin of normal and abnormal behavior. Unlike psychiatry's medicalization, these principles do, in fact, have the power to change human action and experience for better. Behavioral treatment of depression, based on these psychological principles, is more effective than antidepressant drugs and behavior therapy is safe. This is the subject of the final three chapters of this book. An attentive reader will be both surprised and reassured by the degree to which he or she is able to follow and understand the principles of psychological science that govern our behavior. You will find out how these principles have produced an understanding of the cause of depression and how to treat depression effectively and safely. And you will see the data which shows convincingly that behavior therapy should be the treatment of choice for depression.

10

Behavioral Science

The science of nature has been already too long made only a work of the brain and the fancy. It is now high time that it should return to the plainness and soundness of observations on material and obvious thing."

—Robert Hooke, 1665

The pharmaceutical industry has spent billions of dollars to promote psychiatry's brain-based explanations for mental disorders. The media have joined in by enthusiastically creating a bandwagon effect, playing up neurological explanations for all sorts of things in addition to mental disorder. Newspapers are filled with stories of "new discoveries" about the brain that are largely speculative. Whatever behavior is under discussion, reference to the brain appears to be mandatory. Often, little or nothing new has been added that is of substance. Louis Menand, the essayist and critic, made this point when he reviewed a book on the supposed neuroscience behind interest in sports. He wrote,

> . . . (this) is a book for people who think that if, instead of saying that people are happy when their team wins, you say, "Activity increased in a region called the ventral striatum," or instead of talking about stress, you talk about "a surge of cortisol," then you are onto something. Substituting such language gives

> the appearance of a higher order of explanation, when nothing of value has been added.

Here is an example from the New York Times. In August 2018, an article by Claudia Dreyfuss carried the following headline, "Rewiring Her Brain to Win at Poker." It is about Maria Konnikova, an experimental psychologist who is a science writer at the New Yorker. Dr. Konnikova taught herself to play poker from scratch, earning $200,000 in poker tournaments. There is not a word in the article about any rewiring of her brain. No such data was available. The article is all about how by studying the game of poker Dr. Konikova became highly proficient at it, also coming to understand the social conditions she faced playing poker with men, some of whom are con men. It is about how studying the game enabled her success. It is about the benefits of *effort and learning*, yet the headline implies it is about the brain's "rewiring."

This has reached such a pass that the English journalist and critic Stephen Poole wrote an article in 2014 called "Neurobollocks," in which he said that adding the prefix "neur" was often part of a rhetorical attempt to turn "dismal" science into "hard" science.

Poole cites Paul Fletcher, professor of health neuroscience at the University of Cambridge who told Poole he was exasperated by much of the coverage of neuro-imaging research that alleges that some brain activity that has been detected is the answer to profound questions about psychological processes.

Poole writes of Dr. Fletcher's comments about these attributions:

> This is very hard to justify given how little we currently know about what different regions of the brain actually do. Too often, a popular writer will opt for some sort of neuro-flapdoodle in which a highly simplistic and questionable point is accompanied by a suitably grand-sounding neural term and thus acquires a weightiness that it really doesn't deserve. (T)his is no different to some mountebank selling quack salves by talking about the physics of water molecules' memories(. . ..)

The psychiatrist and psychopharmacologist, Dr. David Healy, has referred to psychiatry's use of neurologically tinged language as having replaced psychoanalytic "psychobabble" with biological "biobabble:"

> (Psychobabble) was not a harmless development. It had incalculable consequences for how we view ourselves, how we bring up our children, and how we view issues such as moral and criminal culpability. Now this psychobabble has been all but replaced by an equally vacuous biobabble, which in turn has consequences for

how we view ourselves, how we view the turmoil of adolescence or school underachievement or, finally, moral and criminal culpability.

In his book, "Outliers: The Story of Success," Malcolm Gladwell followed up on psychologist Anders Erickson's research on musicians. Gladwell explains success less in terms of an inherited special musical ability than on well-timed effort. He describes a variety of noteworthy outcomes as products of effortful behaviors occurring under favorable conditions. *His explanations are based on behavioral/environmental interactions, not biology.* He shows how *interest and effort produce success when timed to take advantage of opportunities offered by one's circumstances.* He gives examples as diverse as the prowess of professional hockey players, how middle school students were helped to learn and to like math, and he explains the entrepreneurial success of Bill Gates. For a negative example he recounts how South Korean airplane crashes resulted from behaviors pilots had learned naturally in their culture that were disastrous when flying airplanes. And he explains how these pilots were "cured" (and the lives of their passengers saved) by identifying the social determinants of the pilots' dysfunctional behavior and teaching them to behave more effectively. *His examples are behavioral explanations of success and disorder.* Most importantly, Gladwell's book tells the story of mankind's advancement as having been determined by effort, problem solving, and learning. It is a story of psychology, not of biology.

Behavioral science has led to an understanding of the principles governing how learning takes place. Its methodology stands in sharp contrast to the overblown and unverified biological theories. *Behavioral research is empirical*; that is, entirely data based. It is critical to understand that the success of the advertising industry has been built on these verified behavioral principles. Daily, applications of behavioral research enhance the sales and profits of the industries it serves. Although the public still needs to be educated about the value of a learning (behavioral) viewpoint, industry got the message long ago and behavioral science has been used routinely in the service of profit.

Industries have learned from this psychological research how to influence consumer behavior and they capitalize on this knowledge every day. Corporate America also routinely uses behavioral principles to enhance effective and efficient human relations. Leadership skills, teamwork, negotiation techniques, and conflict management fall under the aegis of behavioral principles.

Many of the most successful and highest paid athletes hire sports psychologists to help them to improve their performance, cope with the pressures of the intense competition they face regularly, and to continue to enjoy playing their sport when it requires such hard work. Sports psychologists are experts in several fields related to physical performance and their knowledge of behavioral principles guides much of the help they provide to athletes.

Your interest in the products you want to buy and to use is largely instigated by marketers who employ behavioral principles. The financing of television programs is built on an understanding of these principles. The commercials you see on television and the Internet, the naming rights for stadiums and the billboards inside them, even how and where products are displayed in grocery stores, what colors are used to attract or repel people (ever wondered about those garish colors in fast food restaurants?), how advertising for men differs from advertising for women, how cars are sold, to name but a few things. All of these are examples of the application of behavioral principles that originated in psychology laboratories.

Psychological principles derived from empirical research have guided marketers in how to influence what you believe and how you behave in relation to their products. They systematically associate their products with activities you enjoy. Drug commercials on TV and the internet are prime examples of the application of behavioral principles. They are designed according to the behavioral principles of *classical and operant conditioning.* These principles will be explained in the next chapter.

These industries are not interested in pursuing brain research in the hope that this will provide them with an accounting of the brain's electrical and chemical functioning as it relates to consumer behavior. They are quite happy to spend enormous sums applying psychological principles that they know will pay off by influencing your behavior. The pharmaceutical industry, which is intent on promoting unsubstantiated brain-based claims for human behavior, spends far more money on the marketing of its products and on lobbying (putting psychological principles into action) than it does on brain research. *When it comes to the bottom line, the pharmaceutical industry concentrates its spending on psychological knowledge as the dependable way to sell their products.*

The computer industry is another prime example of an industry that knows the value of behavioral principles and has put this knowledge to use. You've seen how prominent a place these devices have taken on in people's lives. People's behavior with their smartphones provides an excellent example of behavioral principles in action.

In April 2017, Anderson Cooper, on 60 Minutes, presented a story about how smartphones are designed to control the behavior of the user. A former Google product manager and other computer experts who were interviewed cast the design of these phones in terms of brain mechanisms. But their references to the brain were superficial and largely inaccurate. The engineering of these phones employed behavioral science, not neuroscience.

Dr. B. J. Fogg, who is a professor at Stanford University, teaches his students behavioral principles. He teaches them "how behavior works so they can create products and services that benefit everyday people around the world." One of his doctoral students, Tristan Harris, took these lessons to Google. Google has paid attention to behavior principles in how they design their apps. Nir Eyal's book, "Hooked," is about how web designers capitalize on their knowledge of behavioral principles in their designs for the operation of smart phones. Their methods apply lessons learned from Dr. B. F. Skinner's behavioral research on what are called variable reinforcement schedules.

Industries spend lots of money to hire lobbyists, who help elected officials write the bills they will submit for legislation. Elected officials know that how they write the bills determines financial contributions important to their re-election. How they do so and how they vote on legislation are highly influenced by positive reinforcers that support the mutual interests of both parties. The tax-cut bill passed under former President Trump is a good example. Vast sums of money (a powerful positive reinforcer) are involved because industries know how to employ positive reinforcement to their advantage.

Positive reinforcement is only the beginning of the story. Because our reactions are made up of both *likes* and *dislikes that influence our behavior*, industry has turned to other behavioral principles as well. You value your TV remote because it includes a mute button that allows you to escape from commercials that you would rather not listen to. Designing the device with this feature is an example of the application of the principle of *negative reinforcement*, the special importance of which I will discuss in the next chapter. TiVo operates in the same way because it, too, is designed to spare you from commercials and other breaks that you would prefer to skip watching. *Our behavior is governed by what we like and by avoiding what we dislike.* We operate on the basis of both principles, often to our advantage, but not always.

However, behaviorally based explanations are far less popular in the media than stories that allege some basis in brain mechanisms. The fact is that behavioral scientists have produced the body of knowledge that is being applied.

It is not unusual for behavioral principles to be denigrated. David Brooks, the New York Times op-ed columnist, wrote in November of 2017 that electronic devices are "causing . . . addiction on purpose to make money." He writes, "Most social media sites create irregularly timed rewards; you have to check your device compulsively because you never know when a burst of social affirmation from a Facebook like may come." Laboratory science in behavioral psychology provides the research underpinning for these behaviors and effects.

Noam Schreiber is a writer for the New York Times and a former senior editor of The New Republic. In April 2017, he had a page one story in the New York Times about how Uber uses behavioral principles to exploit its drivers by leading them to work in places and at times that are of greater value to Uber than to the drivers. He cites how Uber has learned techniques from the design of video games (Lyft operates in the same way). In fact, these video games were designed according to these same behavioral principles. Schreiber makes the point that although the principles being used are no different from those used by other companies and industries cited above, when they are directed at employees instead of customers a moral issue arises. This is because employers are in a far stronger position to control employees' behavior than customers' behavior. He, too, is right.

Facebook has been in the news recently in this regard. Jaron Lanier is a computer scientist and computer philosophy writer, who works at Microsoft Research. He has written that Facebook has "served to elevate the role of the con artist to be central in society." The Internet is well known to include programs that promote beliefs in falsehoods that benefit special interests. The internet traffic in transmitting anecdotal information, much of which is not factual or scientifically valid. Such transmissions reinforce erroneous beliefs. As the subsequent investigations of Russian interference in the 2016 presidential election have indicated, sometimes the information that is disseminated is designed precisely for this purpose (for example, the special counsel's investigation into Facebook/Cambridge Analytica). The data collected on the internet may be used not to inform or educate, but to manipulate people to the advantage of special interests or for profit.

Freedom of speech is an important issue. These behavioral principles are powerfully effective, and there clearly are instances where they are being used in a way that do raise critical ethical issues. The fundamental issues inherent in this problem need to be reconciled in ways that prevent these principles from being mis-applied to our detriment.

Individuals, companies, and governments are applying these principles in various ways to their benefit, financially or politically. Their use needs to be regulated or otherwise controlled and industry has resisted such efforts. But let's be clear about this: *these behavioral principles are there for the taking.* They exist in the same way gravity exists. Gravity also has effects we do not like. The principle of gravity exists whether you are applying it to the design of a guillotine, or a roller coaster, or a parachute. Principles based on our understanding of nature are open to a range of uses. They are just as available to be used for the benefit of the public as they are for the benefit of business. *But doing so requires public understanding of their existence and potential value, and controlling their application instead of ignoring their ubiquity and denigrating their importance.*

In behavior therapy it is the individual with a behavior therapist who decides the purpose to be served by the application of these principles. Psychiatry is unique in its resistance to this knowledge when conceptualizing and remedying mental disorders. Whereas behavior therapists and many businesses have concluded it is in their interest to use behavioral principles to be of use to their clients, psychiatry has concluded that it is in its interests *not* to use them. Psychiatrists are adamant in their allegiance to medicalization, despite the greater benefit of a behavioral approach. Patients suffer as a result.

In October of 2020, the New York Times reported research findings that the most effective treatment for cocaine and amphetamine addiction (the most commonly abused stimulants) was behavioral, using a treatment called *contingency management*. The Times asked why this treatment is so underused? Why indeed? As you shall see, *behavioral treatments are superior to drug treatments for all of the common mental disorders, including depression.*

****

Behavioral researchers have focused on *learning experiences as basic to mental disorder* rather than on very poorly understood and unsoundly based neurological explanations. There is an abundance of evidence that *human behavior is largely a matter of learning, which includes the learning of the dysfunctional behaviors that characterize the mental disorders.* The variables that govern the learning process are far more available for study and far less complex than the chemical and electrical actions of the brain. This is no small thing. Discovery in science lies in our ability to define and measure events. As a result, we know a lot more about the psychological factors that influence how people behave than we do about tracing behavior to brain functions.

By the same means, behavioral researchers have demonstrated how *these disorders can be corrected by psychological methods.* Their research has paid off clinically: therapies that direct attention toward reversing the negative effects of behavioral/environmental contingencies have proven to be more helpful than psychiatric drugs. Patients are all too readily enticed by the immediate appeal of the fictions of a brain disease explanation and the idea that a pill is the remedy. Health care is too important to be ceded to such manipulation. Like it or not, real help requires a patient's knowledge and effort. What is surprising about that? It is one of life's basic lessons.

Discovery of the learning principles that underlie the treatment practices of behavioral psychologists can be traced to the history of the development of the scientific method. The empirical model on which behavioral psychology is based goes back to the objective methods employed by Charles Darwin and Gregor Mendel. Darwin was a biologist and a geologist, who created a revolution in biology by explaining how organisms evolved over eons of time. In 1859 he published "On the Origin of Species," in which he classified organisms and described how species survived. Building upon painstaking data collection he came to understand how hereditary accidents (mutations) conferred advantages to some organisms in coping with their environment, leading to "natural selection."

At around the same time, Gregor Mendel, a botanist and Augustan Friar, was studying pea plants. When his studies came to light some thirty years later, they furnished the genetic explanation for what Darwin had discovered. Mendel identified the basic unit of heredity, which has since been given the name "gene." By the beginning of the 20th century, the findings of these two researchers led to the explanation for evolution: Genetic changes are selected automatically when an organism's offspring carry a gene that enables a new behavior that enhances the likelihood of their survival.

Richard Dawkins, the evolutionary biologist and an emeritus fellow at Oxford, in his book, "The Selfish Gene." added to this theory. Dawkins pointed out how animals evolved by selection of "the trick of rapid movement." He explained how muscles are the mechanisms that make such movements possible. He wrote,

> . . . the main way in which brains actually contribute to the success of survival machines is by controlling and coordinating the contraction of muscles, but this leads to efficient preservation of genes only if the timing of muscle contractions bears some relation to the timing of events in the outside world.

Thus, gene survival depends upon *behaviors that capitalize on what the environment has to offer*. This principle has also been verified as governing the process of learning and its effects can be measured daily, not by eons. *Behaviors that are synchronized with what the environment has to offer are reinforced.* Mammals, a small group within the animal kingdom, evolved with larger brains and an expansion of this potentiality for learning. No longer was behavior predominantly instinctual. The effects of this interactive "education" *based on the consequences of behavior* are profound. This learning process leads to individuality, improved communication, and empathy. Dolphins and whales in the ocean; wolves, elephants, and the great apes on land; and parrots in the sky, all behave in ways reflective of these learning capabilities.

John Colapinto, in his book, "This is the Voice," explains how our superiority among mammals owes much to our far greater capability to communicate with one another. Speech is enabled by our vocal cords. With evolution and upright locomotion, our larynx—the human voice box—descended from the back of the mouth, where it resides in lower animals, down in the throat, thus expanding our capability for making different sounds. Language became possible and it evolved on the basis of learning principles.

The great potential of human behavior is shaped by learning. Advances in the development of the human brain, with such structures as the cerebral cortex and hippocampus, enabled humans to engage in more complex *voluntary* activities than was possible for our nearest relatives in the animal kingdom, producing results that paid off. Humans came to dominate the world, becoming the ultimate predators. Far more effectively than any other animal, we learned what behaviors worked under different circumstances, we remembered those behaviors, and we communicated this information to others of our kind.

The primatologist, Richard Wrangham, is a professor of biological anthropology at Harvard. He traces a developmental process related to the brain's development as an organ for learning that has thrown light on why other animals have not developed brain power comparable to that of human beings. Neurons require unusual energy to function. Our brain weighs just three pounds, but the neurons in our brain fully require 25% of the energy that is consumed by our body. Dr. Wrangham believes that our ability to supply our bodies with the energy these neurons need comes from a surprising source. A million and a half years ago, our ancestors overcame their fear and learned to tame fire. Our distant ancestors learned to use fire to cook food. Cooking releases far more energy from food than eating food raw. Without that extra energy there would not be enough hours in the day to supply from raw food the energy needed to support the 86 billion neurons that came to populate the human brain.

The energy derived from cooked food led in turn to the growth of more neurons, producing additional capability for learning how to manage environmental opportunities and challenges. Even more complex behaviors evolved. A progressive, reciprocal process took place in neuron development and in behavioral interactions with our surroundings. Increasing potentiality produced more and more benefits by means of trial-and-error behavior, a process that continued until we reached the physiological limit of neuron support that can be derived from the additional energy supplied by cooking food.

However, the physiological limit on neuron development did not set a limit on the benefits to be derived from the opportunities found in our environment. *Learning continued to expand; behavior increased in complexity.* Learning experiences facilitated the vital activities of language development, socialization, and problem solving. *These capabilities were made possible by our neurons, but they are significantly under the control of learning derived from behavioral/environmental interactions.* The experiences of the last 50,000 to 100,000 years, when humans first began using language and gathering into large groups, have changed him drastically. *While we have not changed genetically since then, our way of life has been transformed by what we learned from our experiences.* Over these thousands of years, we have learned how to organize societies, feed ourselves reliably, teach our children, create inventions, and set up institutions to greatly facilitate our goal-directed behavior.

Dr. Hal Whitehead, a psychologist who studies animal culture, points out that learning has great advantages over genetics. Genetic transmission only is vertical: parent to offspring. *Learning, by contrast, is transmitted vertically and horizontally: parent to offspring, young to old, and creature to creature.*

Over the centuries, our circumstances have changed enormously as our understanding of the world around us has increased and our behaviors have been shaped to take advantage of this knowledge. We no longer fear mastodons and plan how to bring them down; instead, we look both ways before crossing the street on our way to the grocery store and we pay attention to the grocery store hours to make certain we have milk in our refrigerator. The inescapable conclusion is that our ability to learn from our actions and to make use of this capability is the central determinant shaping our behavior. Learning is the key to our success as individuals and as societies. *Understanding the learning process is crucial to understanding human behavior—our weaknesses as well as our strengths.*

If we extrapolate from the Darwinian/Mendelian theory of evolution by natural selection, we can identify three entities: There is the world, with that part of it that constitutes the environment that surrounds us. There is our body, with our brain and the body parts connected to it. And there is our behavior, how we engage with our environment. These are, of course, parts of a whole, which we have divided conceptually into three separate entities. As such, they have been subjected to independent scientific study since progress in science depends upon circumscribing an entity for study in order to come to an understanding of its operations and relationships.

Attempts to understand both our environment and our brain go back many centuries, and we have made considerable progress in our study of both. Scientists have greatly expanded our knowledge of the world we live in. Use of the scientific method as it applies to the sciences of biology, chemistry, and physics exemplifies this great growth. Although we can go back to Galen's dissections of the brains of goats in the 1st century, understanding of the brain has grown considerably in the last 100 years and particularly in the last several decades. The brain is extraordinarily complex, involving biochemical systems, neural regulatory circuits, and endocrine, immune, and autonomic neural components. Scientists agree that there is nothing in the known universe as complicated as the human brain.

Our third entity, the study of *human behavior*, is much younger, dating back a little over a hundred years. Nonetheless, because this subject is less complex than the other two, our knowledge of the learning process has grown considerably, particularly in the last half century. Scientists know a great deal about how learning takes place and by taking behavior as the subject matter, our understanding of mental disorders has grown considerably. We now have a good grasp of human development and the causative psychological factors leading to many mental disorders.

We are far more informed about the principles that govern learning than we are about the brain's physiological operations. Importantly, we have discovered that *mental disorders arise in the same way and according to the same principles as the learning of behaviors that we value;* that is, through interactions with our environment. *Studies have shown that dysfunctional behaviors can be learned because of their immediate positive effects even though the long-term effects are decidedly negative.* These findings are highly significant. They tell us that behavioral research can give us the answers we seek to our most important questions about mental health and mental disorder.

****

Behavioral psychology can be said to have begun with Ivan Pavlov's publication in 1897 of his study of the conditioning of a dog to salivate to a sound by pairing that sound with food. This learning is based on the principle of *contiguity* (they occur together). A few years later, Edward Thorndike presented his Law of Effect as a determinant of learning, identifying a different principle of learning from that demonstrated by Dr. Pavlov. In the 1930s, B. F. Skinner published his extensive research on what he called *operant conditioning*, demonstrating in more detail how this second principle controls much of human behavior. Drs. Thorndike and Skinner had identified how behavior also is controlled by its *effects*. Favorable effects increase the likelihood the behavior will be repeated, unfavorable effects reduce the likelihood a behavior will be repeated. In this regard we are not so different from other animals.

How we respond to others and the world, behaviorally and emotionally, is shaped by our circumstances, our actions, and the consequences of our actions. The process is dynamic. If the effect of our behavior is favorable, we are inclined to repeat it. If it is not, we must adapt by initiating new behaviors. Effective, lasting change does not take place by inactivity and the tuning out of experience. This principle is fundamental to why behavior therapy is more helpful than drug treatment. Beyond the bogus science and beyond even the adverse side effects and harmful long-term effects of many psychiatric medications, this is, in the final analysis, the most persuasive argument against drug therapy. It is by examining and being guided by our experience that we are able to make use of our unique capabilities as human beings *to problem solve.*

Behavioral research not only explains how ordinary behavior is acquired, it sets the stage for studies of the behaviors that characterize mental disorder. And that research in turn led to the development of treatments to remedy mental disorders by applying these principles, first in laboratory studies and then clinically.

By the 1960s, research in *cognitive psychology* had developed to the point that Dr. Albert Bandura, professor of psychology at Stanford University, was able to explain that cognitive research *demonstrated how man's cognitive abilities played an important role in the etiology of disordered behavior.*

Much of our behavior is under the control of language. Our language and cognitive abilities are what distinguish us as human beings. Language is composed of words and we use words to represent and guide our experience. Based on what we detect through our senses we make guesses about what is out there. These are *cognitions,* in the form of appraisals, expectations, and beliefs. They are mental representations of our situation, and these mental constructions create choices as to what actions to take that go beyond simple assessments of friend or foe, edible or inedible. This capacity to devise mental representations of what we see, hear, and touch has enabled us to be creatures who are far superior at the conceptualizations necessary for problem solving.

Nevertheless, our capability to learn from our experience does not guarantee we will always take the right lessons. Our use of language is a great facilitator of understanding, but words can carry different meanings. Katy Waldman, a writer for Slate, has written, ". . .words can illuminate and obscure and hoodwink and rescue." We know that lapses and errors can and do occur. All too often, empirical evidence is trumped by anecdote. Sometimes words even belie actions that are inconsistent with them. Words can be more influential in shaping and maintaining beliefs than actions and evidence. This can sometimes lead to serious trouble. For example, people can adopt false negative beliefs about themselves, others, and the world around them that have negative consequences for their mental and physical health.

Although we are highly social, our behavior also is highly individualized and can be antisocial in nature. As the ultimate predators, we have found ways to prey on one another like no other animals. People not only learn to cooperate to achieve common ends, they also learn to cheat one another for personal gain. There is, of course, a genetic component to our predation. But our behavior is learned from experience because successful behaviors are reinforced behaviors.

Because learning is specific as well as varied, the expression of classes of behavior, known as traits, is far from consistent. Research has disclosed that honesty, for example, is not a unitary trait. People who cheat in one area of their lives may be quite moral in their behavior in other areas. Our language can rationalize behaviors that express self-interest at the expense of others. Even within the boundaries of their own moral convictions, people find reasons to betray their deepest values in the face of opportunity or pressure. The story I have told in this book is filled with examples of this truth. We have all observed from watching public figures and possibly our own behavior that when payoffs become outsized, our moral compass may lapse.

Even though our behavior is plastic and that we are quite capable of trial-and-error behavior to problem solve, studies show that *once a response has been learned it is resistant to change.* Resistance to change is an important contributor to our vulnerability because after taking the wrong lesson from our experiences we can settle on the wrong behavior and blind ourselves to the more rational conclusion.

People hold onto their mental representations; they do not give up their opinions easily. We take comfort in having arrived at an explanation, particularly when it is an explanation given to us by an authority, such as a doctor or political leader we trust. This is often the case with anecdotal evidence when people close themselves off to objective evidence that is contradictory to false beliefs. We resist any suggestion that the commitment we have made is wrong.

Avoidance of change is common and takes on special importance because it is associated with dysfunctional behaviors. In economics, avoidance behavior has been given a name, the Sunk Cost Fallacy. This refers to the tendency people have to continue spending on a bad investment rather than facing up to having made a bad decision. Cost aversion is not confined to financial decisions. People sometimes stay in unsuccessful and unhappy relationships for the same reason and most of us are familiar with the persistence of unpromising behaviors. As you shall see, behavioral research has provided an explanation for such dysfunctional behavior. This is not to say that people are incapable of change; quite the opposite is true, as this line of research has helped to combat.

Our experiences have taught us the value of knowing facts, about preservation of beliefs and practices, and about the importance of knowing how things work. Thus, we have created school systems to educate our children. Nevertheless, being educated doesn't ensure that we will not be exploited. There are people and groups, who encourage us to believe in falsehoods and to behave in ways that redound to their benefit, not ours. Even when we realize that we are being duped, we often resist change. Some people are more vulnerable to being exploited. We see this in cults where members will sacrifice their autonomy for a leader who has bilked them materially and emotionally with very little return. And we are seeing it in relation to Covid-19.

No one likes the idea of having been taken in. It is embarrassing to feel like a fool, difficult to admit to oneself, let alone someone else. This happens to people all the time. For many marketers and politicians (who are masters of persuasion) this is the name of the game. The internet is loaded with clever charlatans. Modern life is full of its own brand of predators who are skilled at taking advantage of people's gullibility, as is typified in the expression "dupers' delight." Being taken in is human. The shame should be the dupers, not ours, but it is often the one deceived who feels embarrassed. Nevertheless, we are responsible for our behavior and suffer the consequences of our errors.

****

This brings me to the important and often misunderstood subject of *feelings* and what to make of them. I first touched on this subject in Chapter 1 in the discussion of sadness and depression. Feelings play an important role in influencing human behavior. Positive feelings often have to do with bonding with others and they are related to what works for us in our interactions with others and the world we live in. Negative feelings arise in relation to what doesn't work. Hope and fear are the emotions that anticipate pleasurable and painful experiences, respectively, and these feelings are elicited by events that have been associated with these favorable and unfavorable experiences. Fear is a particularly powerful instigator of behavior.

Many experiments have demonstrated that fears are learned readily when an individual is subjected to adverse conditions. Previously neutral stimuli that are repeatedly paired with aversive stimuli lose their neutrality and acquire anxiety-provoking properties. The process is automatic and the learning that ensues is subject to error. One can take many wrong lessons from fears. All animals respond with fear to perceived threat, but in humans, because of our cognitive abilities, the response is more complex. As important as feelings are to us, they can be, and often are, unreliable guides. *Negative feelings are poor references for what is governing our behavior that needs to be remedied.* Some people fear taking elevators or riding escalators and avoid taking them. Since elevators and escalators are quite safe, this fear is not grounded in reality. We can feel we are in danger when we are not.

Dr. David Barlow, Professor of Psychology at the State University of New York at Albany, has studied and described the various physiological, cognitive, and behavioral properties associated with fear and anxiety. Not only is fear or anxiety a common experience in life and in mental disorder, so is *avoidance behavior* in reaction to fear. *Avoidance behavior is learned because it quickly relieves distress, whether or not the perceived source of that stress is rational.*

Some avoidance behaviors are functional. When driving an automobile, we stop at red traffic lights to avoid accidents. We avoid coming in contact with others when we are ill so as not to transmit our germs to them. We avoid looking directly at the sun to prevent harm to our eyes. When the actions being avoided are dangerous, avoidance behavior is functional and valuable.

Avoidance behavior is dysfunctional when it is misguided. In mental disorder, this takes on particular importance when avoidance behavior blocks our discovery that what is being avoided is not dangerous. Importantly, avoidance behavior prevents the learning of functional behavior. Phobias are the best illustration of this. Take the example of a person who has had negative experiences in social situations. By declining invitations, he escapes from his anxiety. He feels relieved despite missing out on what he might have gained from the experience. As you shall see, in other cases, when avoidance behavior occurs in relation to loss, depression can result. Avoidance behaviors are dysfunctional because they serve to perpetuate a problem by blocking behavior that would eliminate it. A valuable finding clinically is that when avoidance behavior is corrected, the feeling of anxiety with which it is associated is relieved along with it.

In behavior therapy, once avoidance behavior is identified and targeted for change, it is replaced by problem solving behavior. The important point is that while the negative feelings of anxiety, sadness, and depression are very compelling, behavioral psychology has learned that *the remedy for these negative feelings comes from targeting the crucial behaviors responsible for them, not from directing the treatment at reducing the feelings themselves.*

Studies have shown that much of our learning is automatic, including the learning of problematic avoidance behaviors. Often how we acquired our behavior lies outside our awareness. Fortunately, this does not mean we cannot determine what has gone wrong and how to remedy it. A behavior therapist works with his patient to identify the actions and behavioral mechanisms that are responsible for the negative feelings of fear and depression. These observations are the basis for diagnosing, designing, and implementing the treatment.

To be clear, a behavior therapist does not ignore a patient's negative feelings. The therapist offers help to reduce distress (for example, by providing relaxation training), but takes aim at correcting the behavior that has led to the problem and is interfering with a solution. There is nothing unusual about such an approach to healing pain. A doctor treating a painful laceration stitches the wound together rather than prescribing an anti-anxiety pill.

****

In a profound irony, some popular images of the two forms of therapy, behavior therapy and drug prescription, have been reversed. In the popular imagination behavioral approaches are dismissed sometimes as mechanistic, as mind control, a kind of induced robotic behavior. Behavioral treatments are even confused with brainwashing. Those unfamiliar with the science behind these treatments fear they will be subjected to an involuntary re-alignment of their most profound beliefs and values and that their autonomy will be compromised.

Movies like "The Manchurian Candidate" (both versions) in which the protagonist does not even remember being programmed confirm such fears. In another movie, "A Clockwork Orange," the main character is subjected to painful experiences to "cure" him of his pathological behavior. More recently, in the Jason Bourne movies, the main character has been programmed by the Central Intelligence Agency, using behavior modification techniques, to have such astonishing mental and physical abilities that he is able to overcome dozens of determined operatives pursuing him. Unfortunately, his superiority comes at the expense of having no memory of his previous life.

These Hollywood fantasies should not be confused with behavior therapy. Behavior therapy is dependent upon a close, continuous collaboration between the therapist and the patient. They engage to discover the cause-and-effect relationships that are governing the patient's problems. The goal of the treatment is to heighten the patient's awareness of the behavioral contingencies governing the problem, not to obliterate his will. A plan is devised for the patient to engage in behaviors that will overcome the problem as it is now understood. It is drug treatment that is mechanistic since the treatment assumes (falsely) a drug will mindlessly trigger a chemical reaction in the brain that transforms sickness into health.

11

Mental Disorder as Learned Behavior

Environmental stimuli rather than an underlying illness (.).determine and maintain what is labeled as deviant behavior.

—*Charles Ferster, PhD and Mary Carol Perrott*

I have commented on some popular misconceptions about behavior therapy. For example, I cited movies that gave the impression that behavioral techniques were developed and used to deconstruct the will and destroy autonomy. Much of the resistance to the use of behavioral principles to remedy mental disorder is based on a misunderstanding of the practices developed from them. This is not to say that psychologists have never misused the instrument. In fact, there was a fairly recent incident in which behavioral research was applied to the use of torture in the interrogation of Al Qaeda suspects, a grotesque development that has been condemned by behaviorists as well as by many of our nation's leaders and much of the public.

The two CIA psychologists who directed the torture of prisoners are not identifiable as members of the behavioral community. They misused research on animals that had been conducted by Martin Seligman in the 1960s and 1970s. In these studies, an animal after repeatedly being subjected to aversive conditions from which there was no escape, gave up trying. Dr. Seligman referred to this outcome as "learned helplessness." These CIA psychologists re-ignited the kind of criticism that followed the studies of Dr. John B. Watson and Dr. Mary Cover Jones of "Little Albert" in the 1920s. Fear of animals was induced in a child who previously had no such fear and then the child's fears were extinguished. The studies should not have been allowed and no longer would be permitted. Behavioral psychology was in its infancy and the rules governing the boundaries of what is permissible were much less clearly identified.

In Chapter 10 you saw how behavioral research has been applied by industry to enhance the bottom line and you saw examples of inappropriate use. Behavioral research should not be mischaracterized because of the bad behavior of those who violate our country's values in pursuit of profit. Nor should it be dismissed because of poorly informed criticisms of what behavioral psychology stands for and promotes. The record shows that behavioral research in pursuit of the science governing human behavior has been conducted responsibly, according to high ethical standards.

B. F. Skinner's book, "Walden Two," a utopian novel of an ideal society, contributed to this negative opinion of behavioral psychology. This book came to be viewed, much to Dr. Skinner's dismay (since he had a decidedly non-authoritarian social system in mind), as in the same genre as George Orwell's, "1984" and Aldous Huxley's "Brave New World." It is a book about an ideal society where children were taught systematically to value their community and grew up experiencing personal satisfaction within a vibrant, mutually reinforcing environment. Certainly, these are worthy values. Dr. Skinner made the mistake of calling this "behavioral engineering," which did not have a reassuring sound to it. He was a strict determinist, who believed free will is an illusion, and he was a declared atheist. This, too, did not go over well with many people. Nevertheless, he had many followers and his book led to the creation of several communities that sought to put his views into practice.

Dr. Skinner's personal beliefs were in no way prerequisites for or results of his science, which was based on objective procedures and data driven. The results were not a product of his societal views. In fact, they have been repeatedly verified by other scientists who come from a wide variety of religious traditions and have yielded highly significant results. These studies have been valuable sources of information about the conditions that govern learning.

****

The physiological mechanisms that support our behavior exist in our brain and nervous system. But, and this is essential, even if we knew more about the brain's chemical and electrical operations, this knowledge would supply only a limited explanation for the cause of behavior. *Our actions are governed far more by learning than by instinct.* This basic truth goes a long way toward explaining the failure of psychiatry's brain-based explanations for depression.

We are well informed about the learning processes that govern behavior because they are so available for study. Drs. Darwin and Dawkins observed that our bodies are built genetically for responses to be learned when they are advantageously synchronized with environmental events. *Our behavior is shaped by our environment and the consequences of our actions.* We are goal directed to pursue energy and to avoid harm. In the simplest of examples, a child who out of curiosity touches a hot radiator learns not to touch it again. We can explain and predict the course of our behavior without reference to neurology.

Psychologists have been studying the relationship between behavior and its consequences for more than a hundred years. Since the middle of the 20th century these studies have produced a vast body of verified findings. Their findings have enabled the formulation of hypotheses about the causes of ordinary and disordered behavior that are testable. *Unlike the results of tests of brain theories, this testing has confirmed cause and effect hypotheses and led to the development of useful principles of behavior.*

There is a principle in science known as the Law of Parsimony or Occam's Razor: When there are different explanations for a problem, the simplest theory that fits the data should be selected. In this case, the record shows that psychological theory is simpler and it fits the data; biological theory is more complex and does not.

Conditioning studies have demonstrated that behavior is learned because it has consequences. *Behavior is learned, maintained, and changed by its consequences.* These consequences are called *reinforcers*. Research results reveal what constitutes a reinforcer in these systems, demonstrating that *reinforcers are not identified subjectively (anecdotally), but by their predictable effects on behavior (that is, by the data).*

Research has been conducted using *natural reinforcers* (for example, food) and *social reinforcers* (for example, approval), leading to an understanding of how behavior is governed in the real world. Researchers have investigated the effects of different *ratios of reinforcement* (the percentage of times a behavior is reinforced), *delays in reinforcement* (how soon the reinforcer follows the behavior), and *differing amounts of reinforcement.* These studies have revealed the etiology and plasticity of our behavior. Moreover, because they identified the cause of the behavior, they set the stage for other studies exploring how to modify behavior, since the researchers were informed as to how the behavior came to be present. Other studies demonstrated *that the dysfunctional behaviors that characterize the mental disorders are established and changed in the same way as normal behaviors.*

This formulation makes no reference to a disease process in accounting for mental disorder. In the learning of deviant behaviors, the brain is functioning normally. It is performing its basic functions, but it is doing so in response to conditions that lead to the learning of dysfunctional rather than functional behaviors. Unlike physical illnesses, no foreign element is responsible for the great majority of mental disorders. The lessons learned from this research have led to studies exploring how to promote the behavioral changes that are needed to *remedy* the various expressions of mental disorder. The remedy does not come from medicine, but from an understanding of the circumstances that surround and prompt disordered behaviors. This understanding facilitates learning more effective behaviors.

In this chapter, I will confine myself to a brief review of some basic behavioral principles. I will give some examples of how they apply to the *learning* of normal and abnormal behavior and to the *correction* (unlearning) of abnormal behavior. These findings substantiate the conclusion that the appropriate model for mental disorder is not a *medical model.* It is a *behavioral model,* which is educational in nature, not medical. The majority of disorders in the DSM are better understood and remedied if cast in behavioral terms.

Behavioral researchers do not regard biological factors to be irrelevant. Biology sets parameters. Our brain and nervous system provide the physiological basis for sensory and motor functions and cognitions. Some biological factors are well verified and comprise basic components of behavioral principles. Clearly, the reinforcement system that underlies the environmental/behavioral contingencies that govern learning is hard wired as are the memory functions involved. Thus, the behavioral model I am describing is predicated on biology that has been verified. It stands out distinctly from those biological theories which have not been verified scientifically, such as the chemical imbalance theory.

In Chapter 4, I examined the failed biological theories that are claimed to explain mental disorder, principally the chemical imbalance theory and genetic explanations. Some theorists have proposed a theoretical model for mental disorder that is a combination of biological and psychological explanations–called a *diathesis.* Within a diathesis model, a genetic vulnerability is not regarded as sufficient to cause mental disorder. Stress (a psychological factor) is required for the disorder to be instigated. According to this conceptualization, people have different biologically determined thresholds for being disrupted by stress; for some, manifesting a disorder requires a lot of stress, for others, not so much.

This theory is plausible. However, as you have seen, any contribution from genetics is small relative to the influence of learning. Most importantly, the diathesis explanation suffers from the same absence of scientific corroboration as the genetic explanations. There are no medical tests or laboratory results relating biological factors to mental disorders as there are with physical illnesses. Since such vulnerabilities cannot be detected directly, this idea, true or not, cannot help in an individual case. The basic fact remains that all that we have to go on, objectively, is a person's behavior and the person's environmental conditions. Fortunately, *research results indicate that identifying behaviors and their context is sufficient to arrive at the cause-and-effect relationships that govern human behavior, including disordered behavior.*

To summarize, the behavioral potentialities of our biology are open to study in a way that the physiological functioning of the wiring and the chemistry of the brain and nervous system are not. Being observable, various behaviors have been studied extensively and have revealed how animals (humans included) are equipped by their brain and nervous system to benefit from two kinds of learning processes I mentioned in the last chapter: classical conditioning (Pavlov) and operant conditioning (Thorndike, Skinner).

These conditioning (learning) principles explain how our behavior often is determined automatically and mindlessly, since it is governed by the *immediate* effects of our experience. Although we have the mental ability to supplement and to override the immediate effects of our experience, it remains true that much of our behavior is governed like that of other animals. As you shall see, *this principle applies not only to motor behaviors but to physiological reactions.*

At the same time, we know that our *cognitive* abilities separate us from other animals. We are far more advanced in our use of language, enabling us to routinely make use of our language capability to make assessments and to problem solve. Although other animals vocalize, our abilities far exceed theirs. Unlike other animals, much of our behavior is under the control of cognitive representations of our experience. We add up our experiences mentally and decide what matters to us, making choices benefitting from our uniquely high intelligence.

However, as I have indicated, it is well known that we can be wrong about what we make of our experiences and what we expect from our actions. Research on the causes and effects of mental disorders points to contributions from *cognitive errors*, from misinterpretations of our experiences, leading to dysfunctional behaviors derived from our most valued asset as human beings; that is, our cognitive ability.

Lives include varying amounts of negative circumstances with differing negative consequences. *We know that poverty, trauma, victimization, social isolation, and other such painful occurrences not only lead to sadness, these experiences and how we respond to them, can cause depression and other mental disorders.* A large factor determining the seriousness of the outcome of these negative experiences is attributable to the ways we cope with trauma, as many authors of fiction and non-fiction have described. As we have seen, they wrote stories predicated on a model that assumes that life experiences shape behavior and happiness. They wrote about how differences in experiences, and individual reactions to them, define many lives. Many aspects of these accountings have been research tested.

****

Beginning with our earliest days in infancy as we emit behaviors, motor and vocal, there are consequences of these behaviors. When we are hungry, we learn to respond in ways that lead to our getting fed. We learn how to be rescued from the discomfort of a wet diaper. Later, we learn to point to what we want and then we learn to use language to ask for things. We learn to avoid what we fear or do not want. Many years of research in psychology laboratories has led to the development of verified principles that explain the origin and maintenance of these behaviors.

Let's begin this description of behavioral principles by describing the difference between *classical conditioning* and *operant conditioning.* In classical conditioning, a stimulus *precedes and comes to elicit a response,* often as a reflex. This is learning by association. In Pavlov's famous experiment, a hungry dog, which naturally (biologically) salivates at the sight of food but not to the sound of a buzzer, learned to salivate to the buzzer because the buzzer was repeatedly sounded immediately before presenting the food (a learning or "conditioning" process). *An environmental event altered the physiological state of the animal.* Similarly, when someone gets sick after eating a particular food, the sight or smell of that food can induce nausea. *These are learned, involuntary, classically conditioned responses. Our physiology is subject to conditioning: a psychological, learning process.*

Classical conditioning has been demonstrated to occur regularly in a large number of organ systems in the body, producing measurable changes in the person's physiological state. As examples of classically conditioned responses, various influences on our interactions with the environment can come to produce blushing, dry mouth, changes in heart rate, arterial constriction and dilation, and changes in the stomach lining. Note that their occurrence is not evidence of a disease. These are all normal, involuntary, physiological reactions that are learned responses to particular circumstances.

Classical conditioning also contributes to *voluntary* responses. Take the example of a child going to a doctor's office for the first time who shows no distress. After a painful injection, on subsequent visits the child becomes tearfully resistant. This negative behavioral reaction was learned by experience. *Positive* physiological and psychological responses also are learned the same way.

Learning that occurs by means of classical conditioning can be unlearned; that is, *extinguished.* When Pavlov changed the arrangements of the experiment by no longer following the buzzer with food, the conditioned response of salivation gradually dropped off until the response was gone. It was extinguished. This, too, is an expression of *a physiological change determined by an environmental change.*

Clinical predictions have followed from this research. Behavior therapists teach their patients how to behave in ways to unlearn classically conditioned fears. The best treatment we have for phobias is based on the application of this principle. The therapist arranges for the patient to make contact with the feared stimulus under conditions that lead to extinction of the fear and the learning of functional behavior in its place. This becomes a useful skill that patients carry away with them after therapy ends. They learn how to remain normal.

A second form of learning was first identified by Dr. Edward Thorndike, then later studied intensively by Dr. B. F. Skinner. It is called *operant conditioning.* A new response is learned because of its *consequences.* Favorable consequences increase the likelihood that behavior will be repeated. A child learns all sorts of self-help behaviors because they are expedient. Unlike classical conditioning, operant conditioning is not a function of what immediately *precedes* a response, like the buzzer being sounded just before a dog receives food that elicits salivation. Operant conditioning occurs because of what immediately *follows* a response.

A favorable outcome increases the likelihood the response will be repeated. This reliable and validated finding is known as *positive reinforcement.* As an example, young children learn to speak words because their vocalizations get positive attention. We learn behaviors that pay off, just as a dog returns to the bowl where it previously found food. A child learns to say "please" and "thank you" because of parental praise, a powerful positive reinforcer.

Events associated with a *decrease in an aversive state,* such as pain or fear, are called *negative reinforcers.* Take note that the definition of negative reinforcement *is not the infliction of pain* (punishment) as many people think, it refers to behaviors that are learned because they are associated with *pain reduction.*

Interestingly, a child can be taught to say "please" and "thank you" by punishment as well as by positive reinforcement, but behaviors established based on punishment have been found to be accompanied by distinct disadvantages. Compliance learned through punishment induces aggressive behavior. It is likely to lead to the establishment of the behavior along with negative baggage. Behaviorists have learned that punishment is a less effective way to promote behavior than using positive reinforcement.

When our ancestors came face to face with a dangerous animal, they experienced fear. When they fled from that objective danger their fear dissipated. Today, many of us experience the same effect when we wear a mask, social distance, and wash our hands to protect ourselves from Covid-19. A similar process occurs when a person who is afraid of elevators decides to take the stairs instead. That choice, too, is reinforced by a reduction in fear. These are examples of behaviors instigated by fear–one normal (functional, because the fear is realistic), the other abnormal (dysfunctional, because the fear is not realistic). Both illustrate the operation of n*egative reinforcement.* Learning occurs because a response is followed by *fear reduction*. This principle has considerable value in accounting for both normal and abnormal behavior.

Much human behavior is a product of operant conditioning, which is associated with voluntary musculature, but classical conditioning, which is associated with involuntary musculature and physiological responses, also plays an important role. Moreover, when associated with emotional responses, classical conditioning can be more salient. Negative emotions get our attention. We are inclined to act on them, sometimes to our detriment. As an example, among the mental disorders, panic attacks often are instigated by harmless classically conditioned increases in heart rate that the person misinterprets as signaling a heart attack being imminent. Conditioned fears that develop in humans can be more resistant to extinction because of our cognitive ability. We can attribute significance to non-significant events. We can invent reasons to justify our fears.

Extinction of operant behavior follows the same basic principle I described for behaviors learned based on classical conditioning: In this case, extinction occurs if the reinforcing consequences of behavior lapse. Pavlov extinguished a classically conditioned response by breaking the connection between the associated elements. The same principle holds true for operant conditioning. Once we have identified the reinforcer, we are able to extinguish the behavior by withdrawing it. This understanding is important to experimenters because it provides a means of verifying that the reinforcer for a behavior has been correctly identified. It also has proven very useful clinically in assessing whether the target of therapy is on the right track. A parent who dislikes listening to her child's whining can stop attending to whining to find out if her lack of reaction reduces the frequency of this behavior.

For scientific purposes and for discussion we separate classical and operant conditioning to understand how they originate and operate differently. But most often they occur together and are interrelated. A child who is punished for lying (an operant behavior) also experiences a wide range of reflex responses to the punishment, such as changes in heart rate, blood pressure, and hormone secretions (classically conditioned). These conditioned responses can promote other behaviors, some helpful, some not. A great deal of research has been directed at sorting this out. More research is needed to advance the effectiveness of our treatments.

As we develop in our lives, the behavior of another person often constitutes our most important reinforcer. For young children, parents determine almost all the important environmental consequences for their behavior, so they supply most of the reinforcers for the child's learning. Later, other significant people, friends, peers, and spouses, become reinforcers. For all of us, life involves challenges that must be mastered. *Sometimes, the "solutions" we adopt are problematic because dysfunctional behaviors are reinforced.*

Another behavioral principle that deserves to be mentioned is *generalization.* A behavior conditioned to a stimulus is elicited by similar stimuli. A child, after being bitten by a dog, may be afraid of all furry animals. Generalization means not having to learn every lesson as if for the first time, but sometimes it goes wrong, and fears are spread. *Behavior therapists work to limit problematic generalizations.*

Evolution conferred on the human brain a tendency toward over-reaction to threat, probably because of the survival value of this direction of misjudgment. Not infrequently, this leads to avoidance behavior. *Understanding how to identify and eliminate various forms of avoidance behavior is basic to behavioral treatments.* And because avoidance behaviors can be subtle, not infrequently the therapist must be astute in identifying them.

****

Medical and psychological researchers usually begin their studies by doing experiments with animals. You may have read about how our efforts to find a vaccine for Covid-19 began this way. *Of particular interest to behavioral psychologists has been the study of fear induction and extinction because mental disorder is so associated with fear (anxiety).* These studies indicate how learning principles explain the learning of behaviors that are dysfunctional. As I have indicated, much of our behavior is governed by its immediate consequences, not the long-term consequences. This is true even though the positive effects of the immediate consequences can be outweighed by the negative longer-term effects. This principle is key to understanding many mental disorders.

Here is an example of some experiments conducted years ago by Neal Miller, an experimental psychologist at Yale University. These studies by Dr. Miller revealed the process by which fears are learned, how dysfunctional behaviors result, and how such fears and behaviors can be unlearned (treated successfully).

Rats were put in a maze made up of two compartments, one white and one black, that were joined together and separated by an open doorway. At the beginning of the experiment the rats showed no fear in either of the compartments, moving about freely.

When a mild electric shock (harmless, but painful) was delivered through a grid on the floor of the white compartment, the animals escaped from the shock by running out of the white compartment into the black compartment, which had no grid. This phase of the experiment illustrated that rats learned to escape physical pain by running into the black compartment. *Their behavior was reinforced by their escape from a painful electrical shock.*

Then the conditions were changed. The shock apparatus was disconnected; no shock was delivered through the grid. Nevertheless, when the animals were placed in the white compartment, they still ran out of it. There was no longer any physical pain motivating their running into the black compartment, but *fear* had been conditioned to aspects of the white compartment (for example, its color and the appearance and feel of the grid). *Fear reduction* (escaping psychological pain, not physical pain) was now reinforcing their running into the black compartment. (Take note: there no longer was an objective basis for escaping from the white compartment).

Then the conditions were changed again. Still no shock was delivered in the white compartment, but the experimenters shut the door between the two compartments, blocking the rats' exit. The animals frantically sought to escape from the white compartment. Their frenzied behavior made their fear obvious. Eventually, in the absence of any shock, they calmed down. It took a while, but with time their fear of the white compartment disappeared. How do we know this? After they had calmed down and the doorway was opened, they were no longer inclined to run into the black compartment. *Their fear extinguished because they were kept in contact with the conditions that they feared without the result they feared happening*. Thus, they had been "cured" of their irrational fear of the white compartment.

Dr. Miller demonstrated in the first instance how escape behavior was instigated by the physical pain of the electric shock. He then demonstrated how the fear (psychological pain) that had become *classically conditioned* to characteristics of the white room motivated escaping from it. By turning off the shock apparatus, he showed how *their escape behavior was motivated by fear and reinforced by fear reduction*. Lastly, he showed how *their conditioned fear could be extinguished by continued exposure to the white room without the painful shock occurring*.

In another experiment, Dr. Miller demonstrated how *a conditioned fear can lead to learning a new response*. The experiment began in the same way, but in the phase of the experiment where the shock was turned off and the door was closed, something new was added. When the animals, in their frenzy to escape, happened to press a bar projecting from the wall near the door, the door opened allowing them to escape. They learned to press the bar very quickly. Once having learned this escape response, they continued to run out of the white compartment into the black one.

This new experiment showed two important things: Because of the new response they learned of bar pressing, the rats were denied the opportunity to learn that they were no longer in danger in the white compartment, even as their fear instigated this new learning. This learning blocked extinction of a conditioned fear that was no longer realistic. *The response they learned of bar pressing is what behavioral psychologists refer to as avoidance behavior, which is governed by the principle of negative reinforcement and illustrates why avoidance behavior can be dysfunctional.*

Experiments such as this one (there have been many), elucidate *how fears are learned and maintained*. Many of the dysfunctional behaviors that characterize the mental disorders are learned and maintained because of avoidance behavior. The most effective treatments we have for phobias and generalized anxiety disorder, considered the basic anxiety disorders, have come from treatments derived directly from studies of avoidance behavior. This also is true for the successful treatment of obsessive-compulsive disorder. And it is true for depression. *As you shall see in the next chapter, addressing avoidance behavior is the key to treating depression.*

Research results demonstrate that the behaviors that characterize the mental disorders are governed by the same principles as ordinary behaviors. Once having identified the cause, it was a short step to pursuing remedies for dysfunctional behaviors. The treatment methods in behavior therapy originated in such research results that demonstrated how behaviors can be changed. A fundamental strength of behavior therapy is that each treatment was developed *empirically*, first in laboratory studies and then in clinical applications. Behavioral treatments for depression, as we shall see, grew out of this body of research.

Behavior therapy came into being in the early 1960s, during the height of psychiatry's wedding with psychoanalysis, when a new behaviorally based treatment challenged psychoanalytic theory and practice in the treatment of phobias. Back then, psychiatrists were unyielding in their adherence to Freudian theory and psychoanalytic treatment for mental disorders. Psychiatrists believed eliminating mental disorders required "uncovering unconscious" psychological forces they alleged underlay behavior. They rejected efforts directed at "symptoms," viewing the behaviors that characterized the mental disorders as trivial and mostly irrelevant to the hidden causes of these disorders. It is critical to point out that the psychoanalysts were operating on the basis of their theory, not on the basis of objective analyses of data.

Phobias, for example, were interpreted according to psychoanalytic theory as merely symbolic representations of an "intrapsychic conflict." Elimination of a phobia was deemed to require ferreting out the "repressed, underlying causes" of the disorder. Few phobic patients got better; the disorder was regarded as largely intractable. Although psychoanalytic theory recognized the need to specify the cause of phobias, they invoked anecdotal evidence as proof (case histories). Psychoanalytic theory regarding causation had no scientific foundation. Yet for several decades psychoanalytic theory and treatment were highly regarded. Even today some brought up during the heyday of psychoanalysis still believe that unless they have excavated an "unconscious representation" of a childhood trauma they cannot really understand or eliminate a long-standing psychological problem.

Joseph Wolpe, a South African psychiatrist, later at Temple University Medical School in Philadelphia, challenged Freudian theory and practice related to phobias. Following his psychiatric training he sought training in experimental psychology laboratories where studies were being conducted on fear conditioning and extinction. He learned how psychological researchers had shown that fear reactions were governed by the same principles as other behaviors. Research results, such as Dr. Miller's studies of avoidance behavior, showed Dr. Wolpe how to condition and how to extinguish fear responses. Dr. Wolpe concluded he now had a better explanation for mental disorder than he had been taught in his psychiatric training. Based on this research on the conditioning of fears he developed a straightforward behavioral treatment method designed to extinguish phobias in humans according to the learning principles Dr. Miller had demonstrated. Dr. Wolpe stated that phobias should be construed simply as *conditioned fears, not as unconscious processes or representations of hidden childhood traumas.*

Psychiatrists were horrified and warned that focusing on the phobia itself would not work and would deprive the patient of "psychological defenses" and precipitate a psychosis. A heated controversy erupted in psychiatric and psychological journals that lasted several years until outcome research results confirmed that Dr. Wolpe's method was highly effective. Patients did not become psychotic, they got better, and maintained their improvement even when followed up for as long as 7 years. The success of Dr. Wolpe's treatment stimulated considerable applied research and was a major contributor to the development of behavior therapy.

Dr. Wolpe's challenge to the widely accepted psychoanalytic diagnosis, theory, and treatment, which began in the mid-1960s, applies equally to today's medicalization of psychiatry. *One empty system has been substituted for another.* Knowledge of science eventually led to the downfall of psychoanalysis as a respected scientific basis for health care. The same absence of science lies behind psychiatry's medicalization of mental disorder and it should meet the same fate.

By contrast, behavioral theory and treatment both derive directly from science, beginning with studies of how learning determined the behavior of animals, then verified successfully on humans. Why is it a stretch to accept a learning theory explanation for mental disorder derived in this way? We are animals, products of evolution. Our most fundamental defining feature is our learning ability and behavioral research has been well verified.

Based on results of experiments such as Dr. Miller's laboratory rat studies, as well as on the many clinical studies that followed, a common procedure in behavior therapy is to devise a treatment method that extinguishes avoidance behavior. The therapist arranges for the patient to come in contact with the feared situation to extinguish (unlearn) unrealistic fears. Someone who is afraid of heights is helped to progressively approach the edge of a roof top rather than avoid doing so. Just as the rats learned that they would not be shocked in the white room when they were kept in it, the patient learns that approaching and standing at a roof's edge does not mean that he will fall to his death. A therapist eases the pain of doing so. Similar treatment is directed at social anxiety and generalized anxiety disorder. Patients diagnosed with obsessive-compulsive disorder provide another illustration of this principle. After touching a doorknob, hand washing (the immediately reinforced response) terminates a fear of contamination. For a short time, the person feels relieved that he has rid himself of contaminants, reinforcing the escape behavior. As we shall see, these results also apply to the treatment of depression because *avoidance behavior is a basic cause of depression.*

In accounting for mental disorder, a number of other behavioral mechanisms aside from avoidance behavior have received empirical support. Some disorders appear to result from a failure to learn good social coping skills (a *behavioral deficit*), which leads to problems in social situations. Studies of aggression reveal the presence of a related and somewhat opposite problem: the *learning of inappropriate aggressive responses* to stress, frustration, and failure. Both kinds of disorders may be related to defective role models in childhood, but we need to make a greater investment in research to discover the behavioral/environmental causes for these dysfunctional reactions. There is great reason to believe finding these answers is crucial to our understanding and treatment of many mental disorders.

Not uncommonly, deviant behaviors are attributed to genetics or disease (mental illness). A famous study by Drs. Teodoro Ayllon and Edward Haughton illustrate the relevance of an alternative behavioral explanation. Hospitalized patients, diagnosed as schizophrenic, engaged in bizarre behavior when they were called for meals, greatly complicating patient care. The staff assumed these psychotic behaviors were uncontrollable expressions of their illness. Drs. Ayllon and Haughton had a different theory. They believed that the well-intended coaxing of patients by the nurses at dinner time (increased attention) was reinforcing these deviant behaviors. They persuaded the psychiatrists in charge to adopt a procedure whereby patients who responded within 30 minutes were fed and all the others were then locked out of the dining room. Applying this reinforcement contingency to the meal soon led to marked improvement. The time frame was successively adjusted incrementally to 20 minutes, 15 minutes, and finally to 5 minutes, as the patients gave up being bizarre in favor of getting fed. When we understand the reinforcers governing behavior in a given situation, we are able to intervene effectively.

Schizophrenia is one of the few mental disorders that may require a medical as well as a behavioral explanation. Yet, in all likelihood, behavioral issues are critically important to an understanding of schizophrenic psychotic behavior. We need to study this, not foreclose it.

****

This brings us back to the issue of diagnosis. Diagnosis of mental disorders pertains to deviant behaviors, their causes, and their consequences. Again, a behavioral model addresses the conditions that govern normal behavior as well as abnormal behavior. For example, sadness is the normal response to loss. The fact that it is normal does not detract from its painfulness. A person in pain needs and deserves understanding and support, which in today's world may not be as readily available.

Because normality is not covered by health insurance, eligibility for professional help is contingent on calling normality, abnormality (recall the discussion in Chapter 1). Thus, although sadness in reaction to loss is normal and can sometimes be a reason to seek professional help, insurance reimbursement requires casting distress as a mental disorder. The conflation of sadness and depression legitimizes health insurance reimbursement, but when normality is confused with abnormality, it comes at high cost. It miscasts a normal response, and it can lead to prescriptions of potentially harmful antidepressant drugs.

A validated, reliable behaviorally based understanding of the distinction between normality and abnormality should replace the DSM. A new diagnostic system needs to be developed to address insurance coverage rationally, a system that specifies how toxic environments and dysfunctional coping behaviors are responsible for mental disorders. The behavioral diagnostic systems that have been developed so far are rudimentary. They aim to identify the behavioral mechanisms governing classes of dysfunctional behaviors. Such a system needs to specify, for example, how sadness (normality) can be transformed into depression (abnormality). The current behavioral systems are incomplete and much more research is needed. Devising a complete behavioral diagnostic system will require substantial NIMH funding.

An impartial NIMH that made decisions based on scientific evidence would prioritize replacing the DSM with such a behaviorally based, empirically derived system for diagnosing mental disorders. We know that some of the deviant behaviors that characterize mental disorders have been learned by means of a combination of positive and negative reinforcement; for example, alcoholism and drug addiction. Alcohol and street drugs immediately yield pleasure and temporarily relieve misery. An abundance of research indicates that central to a behavioral system would be the adverse effects of avoidance behavior. The great majority of those currently being diagnosed with phobias, social anxiety, obsessive-compulsive disorder, and depression would be explained in these terms. As I have indicated, other disorders likely arise for different reasons. Some mental disorders probably are the result of behavioral deficits with regard to coping skills and others to problems with emotional regulation. There probably are other causes as well. More research is needed.

Importantly, a behaviorally based diagnostic system will specify cause and effect, and it will provide valid and reliable relationships and distinctions. The

DSM fails to meet these basic requirements. A behavioral diagnostic system *constructed empirically* will not be based on the opinions of a panel of "experts," riddled with conflicts of interest. It will point to treatments that are *functionally related to the diagnoses*. The relationship between diagnosis and treatment is a prime element in diagnostic manuals for physical illnesses, but not mental disorders. Fixing this travesty is long overdue.

****

Behavior therapists aim to identify the learned dysfunctional behaviors that govern the problems their patients bring to them. Sometimes the conditioning that underlies these dysfunctional behaviors is easy to trace and to recognize. This is often true of phobias. In other cases, the crucial behavioral/environmental contingencies take time to identify. Once identified, helping the patient requires the therapist's guidance and support. A behavior therapist focuses on the basis for the problem in the patient's life circumstances and how he or she is responding to them and guides the process of problem solving.

It is not unusual for a patient to be mistaken in his formulation of his problem's origin. This is why the brief questionnaires used by some doctors to diagnose various mental disorders are not trustworthy. In a sense, the difficulty a behavior therapist faces with making a diagnosis is like the problem discussed with fMRI imagery because the instrument is unable to fully measure prior reactions. The therapist is presented with a later version of the problem somewhere down the pike. The patient may offer explanations that appear credible but often are invalid because they are based on conjecture (anecdotal evidence), not objective observation of the problem's actual basis.

However, unlike fMRI imagery, where no access is possible to what has come before, a well-trained behavior therapist can come to identify the important behavioral/environmental relationships by careful listening and testing out of hypotheses. The problem is occurring in the present so the behaviors that support the problem also must be occurring in the present. This makes them available for identification and study. Rarely do dysfunctional behaviors depend upon some seminal childhood experience, as favored in psychoanalytic theory. The therapist works with the patient to discover the details of how the problem is being played out, and *together* they arrive at an identification of the dysfunctional learning that has taken place and how the patient can behave to rectify it.

This last point is worth reiterating. When it comes to treating physical illnesses and physical injuries a doctor, on her own, can administer a treatment that cures the problem. An internist prescribes an antibiotic that cures a bacterial infection; a surgeon removes an infected appendix; an orthopedist puts a cast on a fractured arm enabling the arm to heal properly. Doctors, by dint of their medical expertise, can fix many physical problems with minimal patient participation. But when it comes to psychological problems, *problems in living*, the healing process is different. It takes two to tango and the most important factor in effecting change is not the behavior of the doctor. The treatment process is collaborative, but its success hinges on the patient engaging in new, corrective behavior.

No doctor treating a mental disorder can correct dysfunctional behaviors by prescribing a pill. No pill can do that. Sometimes the placebo effect enables a patient to make corrections on his own, but it is the ensuing behavior, not the pill that is responsible for the help, and some problems are too difficult for such a resolution. A therapist's help often is necessary for an effective, lasting remedy.

An interesting example related to this issue in physical medicine is found in a report of the treatment of phantom pain after an amputation of a limb. Quite commonly following an amputation, the nerves that send signals from the brain continue to send impulses as pain, as if the missing limb is still there. The body part that has been lost was directly involved in contacting the environment, the fundamental ability pointed to by Drs. Darwin and Dawkins evolved because it enhanced survival of our species. Dr. Terrence Sheehan at the Adventist Health Care Center in Maryland treats many diabetic patients who have lost a leg because of damage to their blood vessels. Dr. Sheehan wrote,

> The whole person hurts, which worsens pain. We have trained peer visitors and therapists to work with people on their varied needs. But the patients do most of the work. They must acknowledge their loss, work through body-image changes and overall life changes. Then the pain often starts to dissipate.

There is, however, a fundamental difference between the treatment of physical illness and mental disorder. While the cooperation and attitude of a physically ill patient may facilitate a cure, the fact remains that many physical illnesses can be cured without any or with little patient participation. Diagnosis and successful treatment of a physical illness is different because for the most part it is based upon the results of laboratory tests and a physical examination, followed by administering a well-established physiological treatment. Alleviating mental disorder, on the other hand, *depends upon active patient participation* in the therapy, a psychological process.

Behavior therapy is a form of psychotherapy, but psychotherapies differ, being organized around several different theories. A fundamental requirement of all psychotherapies is the development of a warm, trusting relationship to facilitate psychological changes. In fact, that is the sum total of some peoples' experience with their therapist, and they are satisfied.

Behavioral diagnosis and treatment is aimed at behavioral change and has a prerequisite. It is dependent upon what the therapist gleans from a patient's speech and behavior that relates to a body of scientific evidence bearing on the origins of learned behavior. The therapist sifts subjective information, aiming toward eventually forming hypotheses about dysfunctional learning. This takes some time and careful, active, supportive listening. The early sessions are devoted to developing a behavioral accounting of the problem. Only when this has happened is the therapist in a position to clarify for the patient what the remedy requires.

When a treatment plan has been formulated, the therapist outlines for the patient what the therapist believes is problematic, clarifying what the patient must do to accomplish what is necessary for a lasting remedy. This always includes a discussion of how the patient must face her fears. The therapist is not a bystander in the therapeutic process. She helps the patient to follow the plan. Admittedly, this can be hard work for the patient, although often not as difficult as expected, and hard work that is rewarded is especially satisfying. This is one of those instances in life when the easy way often is unsatisfactory. Evolution has gifted us with problem solving ability. It is an ability that we should not squander.

Behavior therapy is distinguishable from other psychotherapies on the basis of having a verified scientific basis. Its basis in science should not be misconstrued as cold. A good relationship between a patient and a therapist is essential in behavior therapy because commonly the patient is directed to do things that are feared and have been avoided. It can feel as if the quality of the person's life is at issue, making belief in the process essential. Trust in the therapist is therefore a prerequisite for successful treatment. The objective basis for behavior therapy is scientific and we think of science as impartial and cold, so it is easy to assume that behavior therapy must be a cold or heartless process. That is mistaken. Behavior therapy is a collaboration, and the therapist engages in the treatment compassionately, not mechanically.

12

Behavior Therapy for Depression

Tell me and I forget, teach me and I may remember, involve me and I learn.
—Benjamin Franklin

Part One

Charles Ferster was a founder of the *Journal of the Experimental Analysis of Behavior*, a highly regarded psychological journal reporting basic behavioral research. A year after my arrival at American University he, too, joined the Psychology Department at AU and later came to serve as its chairman. Earlier in his career he collaborated with B. F. Skinner in the research that led to the publication in 1957 of "Schedules of Reinforcement," which is a technical, detailed exploration of the ways in which reinforcement can be delivered according to different ratios and frequencies. We saw that this book was a resource used in the design of smartphones and computer video games.

Dr. Ferster became interested in the cause of mental disorders. In particular, he sought the cause of depression and his analyses led him to conclude that *a prime determinant of depression is the loss of positive reinforcers, often as the result of avoidance behavior.* This finding is consistent with what other researchers have reported for depression and for anxiety disorders. Dr. Ferster's work, which well predated the publication of DSM-III, makes clear what is wrong with the DSM's definition of depression.

Causation is the key to understanding mental disorders as well as physical illnesses. Like many others, Dr. Ferster spoke to the centrality of specifying the *causation* of a disorder or illness when arriving at a diagnosis and a treatment plan. In the absence of physiological data that related the great majority of mental disorders to physical causation, he pointed to the explanatory value of behavioral observations. He emphasized the necessity of doing a *functional analysis* of the behaviors that characterize a mental disorder to identify its causation. A functional analysis requires identifying the *antecedent and current conditions* supporting a behavior. He wrote,

> (. . .)Whether a man who moves and acts slowly is 'depressed' or merely moving slowly is not easily or reliably determined by observing his behavior alone. The relation of his behavior to events in the past or present environment is a critical element in the description(. . ..) (Take the example of a man running down a corridor). The man could be running because someone is chasing him. The man could be running because the train will leave in ten minutes from a distant station. The man could be running because he has just won a sweepstake prize(. . ..) (These) are examples of extremely diverse kinds of behavioral control.
>
> In the first instance it may be termed avoidance behavior because it increases the distance from an aversive stimulus. We could describe the second example as behavior reinforced by (the schedule of the train). In the third example, the sweepstake winner is running because of an emotional state. A child's crying is an example of (. . .)even more diverse behavioral control. Crying could occur as a reflex effect of a loud noise(. . .)or a temperature change(. . .)or food deprivation; or it could result from a parental reaction providing consequences to the child(. . ..)The form of the child's crying will depend on the reactivity of the parent, just as the (. . .) rat's bar pressing response was determined (by the lever).

Dr. Ferster is making a distinction between the *topography*, the external pattern of a behavior, and how the behavior is *functionally* related to the circumstances of its occurrence. A functional analysis asks why the man is running so that we can understand the man's behavior. We need to ask why the man is running. *Valid diagnoses and treatments of mental disorders, like physical illnesses, should be the outcome of functional analyses that identify causation.* We will understand the man's behavior when we know *why* he is running. DSM diagnoses are an example of a topographical description; they focus on the act itself without considering the function of the behavior. Making a diagnosis based on lowered mood, feelings of worthlessness, difficulty maintaining concentration, and sleep and appetite problems, are topographical descriptions. They do not tell us much about the cause of depression because many obvious behaviors may not have anything to do with causation.

As I have indicated, behavioral treatments evolved from studies of how the behaviors that characterize different mental disorders are *learned*, *maintained*, and *eliminated*. These factors are explanations; the first two explain causation, the last one explains the cure. Arriving at answers to these three factors came from functional analyses of behavior in psychology laboratories. You have seen examples of several disorders caused by avoidance behavior. In each of these cases use of the scientific method in psychology laboratories led to the discovery of avoidance behavior as the explanation for the disordered behavior. I referenced Dr. Wolpe's work on phobias, Dr. Foa's work on obsessive-compulsive disorder, and Dr. Barlow's work on social anxiety. Once the causation has been identified, functional analyses also inform researchers and clinicians how to remedy the dysfunctional learning that is supporting the deviant behaviors, constituting a cure. Patients learn to approach their irrational fears, not to avoid them. We will see that the concept of avoidance behavior is critically important as the cause of depression.

Dr. Ferster wrote that in a functional analysis of behavior, the main indicator of which behaviors are the important ones is their behavioral frequency:

> Depression appears to be an especially appropriate fit for the behavioral psychologist because of the missing items of behavior that are so prominent (. . ..) The most obvious characteristic of a depressed person is a loss of certain kinds of activity coupled with an increase in avoidance and escape activity (. . ..).

Rather than being based on anecdotal evidence as is the case with the DSM, the diagnostic process in behavior therapy is a product of a functional analysis. The behaviors that are characteristic of depression are behaviors that have fallen in frequency, such as reduced attention and productivity, social withdrawal, and a reduced response to praise or reward. The loss of such previously positively reinforced behaviors is common in depression. *Behavior therapy directs attention to eliminating avoidance behaviors that block reinstatement of positive behaviors that were lost and that are likely to be positively reinforced when they recur.* Thus, the goal of treatment is to extinguish avoidance behaviors by replacing them with approach behaviors that are positively reinforcing.

****

In Chapter 11, the dysfunctional behaviors that characterize mental disorder were traced to two forms of behavior: *overt* behaviors and *covert* behaviors. Covert behaviors are cognitions (mental representations). *Cognitions take on importance because of their relationship to overt behaviors.* How we think, our beliefs and expectations, often dictate how we act. The behaviors that characterize the mental disorders, including depression, originate as disturbances of both kinds.

In the 1940s and 1950s, Dr. O. Hobart Mowrer, professor of psychology at the University of Illinois and Dr. Fred Kanfer, professor of psychology at Purdue University began studying cognitions as a source of mental disorder. They recognized that *unobservable behaviors*, cognitions, were related to mistaken and disordered behavior. Researchers began looking into how thoughts were affected by experience and vice versa, with reference to distortions. They studied different kinds of cognitions: *assumptions, expectations, and beliefs* as they affect behavior. They came to what at the time seemed like an extraordinary conclusion that now strikes many as obvious: namely, that human behavior is highly influenced by cognitions.

From a cognitive-behavioral perspective, sadness and depression are the emotions associated with *loss of a positive reinforcer*; that is, the loss of a valued relationship, object, or condition in life. In Chapter 1, I reviewed the research that showed that negative experiences, chiefly *losses*, lead to sadness and depression. Other studies indicate that central to mental disorder is *the adoption of a dysfunctional response to loss.*

All of us, from our everyday experience, are familiar with how our behavior is mediated by thoughts. *What we believe contributes directly to how we act.* This is attested daily by the consumer behaviors discussed in Chapter 10 and by many of the learned behaviors cited in Chapter 11.

Michael Mahoney reviewed the research in cognitive psychology to provide a framework for how cognitions lead to dysfunctional behavior. Dr. Mahoney wrote,

> Suffice it to say that the adult human being thinks a lot(. . ..) As with many evolutionary developments, mediation carries both adaptive and unadaptive features. In some ways, the thinking organism may be its own worst enemy. Our symbolic representations of reality are frequently naive and inaccurate.

Let's examine this a bit more closely. In Dr. Mahoney's book, "Cognition and Behavior Modification," he gives examples of how cognitions influence behavior, such as how we estimate probabilities before making choices. He concludes that knowledge of cognitive causation, of a person's thoughts, is indispensable in therapy. To back this up, he reviews cognitively based procedures directed at behavioral change that have been devised on the basis of cognitive research.

Perhaps, the best-known example is Walter Mischel's marshmallow test. Dr. Mischel was a professor of psychology at Stanford and Columbia. His study concerned what is referred to often as "delay of gratification." In his experiment, children were given the choice between an immediate small reward versus a delayed larger reward. Although they preferred the larger reward, when the smaller reward was present few of the children could resist it. The children were able to overcome this problem when they were taught cognitive strategies to distract themselves. Dr. Mischel demonstrated that self-control need not be construed as an innate strength known as "will-power," but as a skill, *a learned behavior*. Later, in an interview published in the New Yorker magazine, he described how he had used cognitive methods to overcome his addiction to cigarettes.

Other cognitive research has studied *problems with focus*. The research literature on *impulsivity* suggests that attending to distracting stimuli is common in impulsive and hyperactive children. Rather than attending to the teacher, a child may be listening to and reacting to other sounds and noises, such as people talking in the hall, airplanes passing overhead, or dwelling on disturbing experiences in his home life. *Once the behavioral/environmental cause is understood, effective strategies can correct the problem.* A behavioral orientation, unlike a chemical imbalance explanation, enables the solution by being informed by data.

The placebo effect falls under a category of cognitions referred to as *"expectancies."* As we have indicated, the placebo effect occurs because of positive expectancies associated with a treatment. But once again, there is another side to this. If your expectations are negative, if you are expecting things to go wrong, you may cancel your plans, a response that can have undesirable consequences. A person who believes he does not belong may behave in ways to make this belief a self-fulfilling prophecy, avoiding potentially helpful situations.

Misperceptions, another kind of cognitive distortion, have been studied because they can have formidable effects. For example, in friendships and romantic relationships, many have to wrestle with misperceptions. Or a more dire example, it is not uncommon for emaciated anorexic patients to perceive themselves as obese, even leading to fatal self-starvation.

These are some categories of *cognitive errors* that involve assumptions or conclusions that lead to behaviors that are implicated in mental disorder. *Cognitive behavior therapy (CBT) is directed at identifying and correcting such dysfunctional expectations and beliefs and the behaviors that are governed by them.* A cognitive behavior therapist initiates a conversation with the patient that is aimed at assessing the circumstances–actual and imagined–surrounding the problematic behaviors. In arriving at a treatment plan, behavior therapists focus first on identifying the conditioned behaviors and negative beliefs that characterize the patient's behavior. Because rarely is a patient able to formulate these problems to herself with any clarity, this diagnostic grounding in false beliefs often is revealing to patients and sets the stage for efforts to change. The next step is to design and implement strategies that help the patient to remedy these dysfunctional cognitions and overt behaviors. The aim is to replace passivity and avoidance with goal-directed behavior that increases successful and pleasurable experiences. Skills training is provided when there are deficits in the behaviors required for success.

Throughout the treatment, the therapist and the patient make assessments to measure progress and to determine when the treatment has been completed satisfactorily. The process is one of identifying the cognitions and behaviors that are hypothesized to be responsible for the patient's problems, at the same time enhancing more realistic, positive cognitions and useful behaviors that aid in problem-solving. Opportunities are found to promote the learning of more functional behaviors. For example, a patient with social anxiety may believe if he approaches someone of the opposite sex he will automatically be rejected. The patient may be asked to identify someone of interest and to initiate a conversation, which is practiced with the therapist in advance to increase the patient's capability and self-confidence in carrying out the assignment. Activities such as these promote problem solving and positive changes.

Like most things that we value in life because they have lasting benefits, behavior therapy requires effort. That's what it took for each of us to learn to walk, to tell time, to do addition and subtraction, and how to make a living. All of these valued activities, and so many more, required effort to learn how to do them successfully. No one learned these lessons by taking a pill.

****

Part Two

There are several versions of behavior therapy that are in use to treat depression, each with considerable research behind them, and all of them have been demonstrated to be effective. Yet, as is the case with all treatment regimens, there are differences between them, and questions remain as to the most effective and efficient way of delivering behavior therapy. With more research funding these treatments will get even better.

The two most common approaches are cognitive behavior therapy (CBT) and behavioral activation (BA). CBT is a behaviorally based treatment that places more of an emphasis on *cognitive causation* of the disorder. It developed soon after researchers recognized the importance of thoughts and beliefs as determinants of human behavior. CBT originated with two pioneers in this field: the psychologist, Albert Ellis, and the psychiatrist, Aaron Beck.

The earliest version of cognitive behavior therapy was that of Dr. Ellis. He devised Rational Emotive Psychotherapy in the late 1950s. Dr. Ellis believed that for a psychotherapy to be successful it must eliminate the *self-defeating beliefs and the behaviors related to them* that are the basis for mental disorder. He established the Institute for Rational Living in New York, a treatment facility that has been offering this form of treatment ever since.

Dr. Beck is professor emeritus of psychiatry at the University of Pennsylvania. Like Dr. Ellis, he stated that *mental disorder is the product of faulty cognitions.* He devised Cognitive Behavior Therapy in the 1960s and later established the Beck Institute for Cognitive Behavior Therapy Research in Philadelphia, which also continues to be active. These two cognitive-behavioral treatments are based on very similar conceptualizations of depression and other mental disorders, and they make use of similar therapeutic procedures.

In Rational Emotive Therapy, Dr. Ellis came up with a list of twelve core irrational ideas he saw as commonly responsible for mental disorder and how they needed to be changed. Here are a few of them: the idea that it is a dire necessity for an adult to be loved by everyone for everything one does—instead of concentrating on one's own self-respect, and on loving rather than being loved; the idea that it is easier to avoid than to face life's responsibilities—instead of the idea that the so-called easy way is invariably the much harder in the long run; the idea that one should be thoroughly competent, intelligent, and achieving in all possible respects—instead of accepting oneself as an imperfect creature; the idea that because something once strongly affected one's life, it will indefinitely affect it—instead of the idea that one can learn from one's past experiences but not be overly-attached to or prejudiced by them; the idea that one has virtually no control over one's emotions and that one cannot help feeling certain things—instead of the idea that one has enormous control over one's destructive emotions if one chooses to work at it. Dr. Ellis called these counter arguments, "restructuring." They are central to his therapy.

Dr. Beck's Cognitive Behavior Therapy conceptualizes depression as resulting from the same kind of faulty perceptions, beliefs, and appraisals identified by Dr. Ellis. Dr. Beck specifies these cognitions as including low self-esteem, self-blame, and feeling overwhelmed by responsibilities. These negative cognitions lead to expectations of rejection, and an attitude of general hopelessness. He believes they become organized into "core schema," leading the person to develop negative views of himself, the world, and the future. He calls the distortions in these three viewpoints a "negative triad" that is common in patients who are depressed.

Rather than ascribing depression to be of physical origin, the CBT therapies of Dr. Ellis and Dr. Beck *view depression as caused by psychological processes.* CBT attributes depression to negative learning experiences shaped by significant losses in life which are followed by failure to overcome loss and the development of negative self-descriptions. As I have indicated, loss is integral to life and not limited to the death of a loved one, occurring from such common events as the impairment of a valued relationship and many other experiences of loss that lead to the loss of self-esteem.

Their treatment is based on an *educational model* rather than a *medical model.* CBT is designed to correct mistaken ideas following negative experiences and the behaviors they spawn, which are deemed to be central to depression. Conceptualizing mental disorder in terms of faulty learning has distinct advantages over a medical model because the patient's own problem solving is central to the treatment. A learning model is directed at teaching independence rather than entailing dependency on a doctor. Learning such behavioral lessons is valuable after treatment has ended, when new problems arise.

Another form of behavior therapy for depression is called *Behavioral Activation* (BA), which was first formulated in the mid-1970s by Peter Lewinsohn, professor of psychology at the University of Oregon. Dr. Lewinsohn's early version of behavior therapy was derived from behavioral research, not from cognitive research. He was particularly influenced by Dr. Ferster's conceptualization of depression. He sought to identify the reduced frequency of positively reinforced behaviors in people who are depressed as compared with what had been the frequency of these behaviors prior to their depression.

Dr. Lewinsohn's treatment (BA) emphasizes reinstatement of lost positive behaviors. He does so by means of the patient's answers to a self-administered questionnaire, called the Pleasant Events Schedule. His questionnaire is more apt than those some doctors use to diagnose depression which are based on DSM criteria because Dr. Lewinsohn's questionnaire focuses on charting the frequency of behaviors that have a known relationship to the cause of depression.

An improved version of BA was described in 2001 by Dr. Christopher Martell, Dr. Michael Addis, and Dr. Neil Jacobson in their book, "Depression in Context." Rather than basing their treatment on questionnaire responses, they work from the patient's behavior in various life situations that relate to the problem, collecting more reliable data. Attention is directed at gathering data from the patient's actual experiences, collecting information about the context and cause of the dysfunctional behaviors. Because it is more objective, their approach is a better application of Dr. Ferster's ideas relating to functional analyses.

Behavioral activation (BA) has an important distinction from *cognitive behavior therapy* (CBT). Whereas CBT therapists view the problem as primarily *cognitively induced*, BA therapists view the problem as primarily *behavioral.* There is another important difference, although therapists differ on this in practice. CBT therapies, like medical approaches, tend to locate the problem as *internal* to the person, not in physiological terms, but mentally in the form of cognitions. A Behavioral Activation therapist does not view the problem as located inside the person. The problem is conceptualized as being in the connection between the behavior and the environmental conditions that are its context. Thus, the problem is viewed as "contextual," meaning it is not assumed to be somewhere in the individual, but in the context of a behavioral/environmental interaction. This is counter to our usual language and theory. Often, disordered behavior is attributed to a person's feelings. An explanation based on negative feelings directs attention to an internal state rather than the behavioral/environmental connections that account for the behavior.

In my book with Christopher Martell, "The Myth of Depression as Disease," I described a somewhat different, although related behavioral treatment for depression. The procedure is primarily behavioral in that the treatment targets the elimination of avoidance behavior as fundamental to remedying depression, but it includes attention to cognitions as a useful means of communicating with the patient about what is governing the problem and as a guide in implementing the treatment.

An article I published in the journal Behavior Modification in 2008, "Sadness, Depression, and Avoidance Behavior," provides the theoretical and research background for the procedure, and explains how a normal state of sadness can be transformed into the disorder of depression as a result of avoidance behavior:

> . . . the most important factor determining depression is avoidance behavior in response to opportunities to restore positive reinforcers that have been lost. Sadness, like anxiety, can become attached to avoidance responses whose long-term consequence is the prolonging of pain and interference with functioning. Depression is the outcome. Sadness is a function of loss; depression is a function of sadness and avoidance behavior. Stated most succinctly, sadness becomes depression as a consequence of the avoidance of those behaviors required to regain what has been lost.

This therapeutic approach aims directly at elimination of the avoidance behaviors that are deemed to be responsible for depression, accompanied by the reinstatement or learning of behaviors that are likely to be positively reinforced. Rarely does a patient understand the problem in these terms. It is the therapist's job to do a functional analysis to identify the behavioral/environmental relationships that are governing the patient's problem. As I have indicated, such functional relationships can be subtle. Their identification requires good collaboration between the patient and the therapist to get it right.

In this form of behavior therapy for depression, attention is directed at the *choice point that acts as a trigger for the avoidance behavior.* Let's look at some simple examples. The most obvious illustrations are the anxiety disorders. Take an elevator phobia, a mental disorder that is driven by anxiety-reducing avoidance behavior. This problem can be diagrammed as follows:

1. A negative experience (actual or modeled, for example, by a parent) led the person to learn to fear elevators and to avoid taking them.
2. Facing an elevator ➢ anxiety ➤ decision against taking the elevator ➢ relief from anxiety
3. Because avoidance behavior is negatively reinforced, the problem is established and maintained.

The darker arrow indicates the choice point which leads to avoidance behavior. The therapy is focused on helping the patient to recognize this choice point as critically important and to use this knowledge to overcome this choice to avoid.

The patient is encouraged to choose to place himself in the problematic situation. The therapist provides the help that is necessary for the patient to contend with the fears this provokes. He provides a mainstay of support. The therapy succeeds because the approach behaviors are positively reinforced.

A similar diagram can illustrate the onset and maintenance of depression. As I have reviewed above, most cases of depression also occur as the outcome of avoidance behavior. Depression occurs following loss when there is avoidance of the behaviors necessary to overcome the loss. Take, as a simple example, a man who has become depressed after losing his job:

1. Man loses his job in a bad economy
2. He engages in a number of behaviors aimed at finding a new job; scans the want ads in newspapers, networks with others, contacts potential employers, and goes for interviews.
3. Has repeated experiences of contacting potential employers and going for interviews without a job offer.
4. Thinks about continuing his job-seeking activities ➢ anticipates rejection ➤ stays home instead ➢ relief from anxiety.
5. Remains unemployed, concludes he is unemployable, experiences loss of income, loses self-esteem.
6. Depression.

Or take the case of a lonely man:

1. Man goes out on dates ➢ has unsuccessful experiences.
2. Finds himself attracted to another woman ➢ anticipates rejection ➤ avoids approaching her ➢ relief from anxiety.
3. Repetitions of above ➢ growth of belief he is undesirable to women.
4. Absence of a relationship with a woman is taken as confirmation of a negative view of himself as undesirable to women.
5. Depression.

Again, the therapy is directed at enabling the patient to change his behavior at the choice point identified by the darker arrow, to approach rather than to avoid. Cognitive strategies often are of help, but improvement always rests on abandoning avoidance behavior.

When I was in practice, with regularity I was contacted by patients who were dissatisfied with the drug treatment they were receiving from their psychiatrists or primary care doctors. Many had been diagnosed as depressed or as bipolar. I questioned the validity of many of these diagnoses, although not the patient's distress. In our first meeting, I told these prospective patients that I believed I could help them, but first they must first return to their doctor and get off their meds under medical supervision. When they did so and returned to see me (just about all of them did), without exception they told me their doctors had warned them their condition would worsen when they went off the drugs they were taking. That never happened. All of them improved substantially because of the treatment I provided as in the simple cases above. I know of only one patient who, although there was considerable improvement and she was outspoken about the benefit she derived, she believed she also benefited from taking a drug (Ritalin, which is a stimulant, not an antidepressant).

I have not generalized from my experience to assume that every case of depression can be successfully treated this way. However, I was in practice for several decades and over the course of that time I successfully treated many patients who had been diagnosed by psychiatrists and other doctors as depressed. The results did not give me reason to doubt my analysis of the cause of the problems my patients presented or the value of the treatment I offered them.

Nevertheless, *empirical substantiation is necessary to validate this treatment of depression*. As I have indicated, the theoretical basis for this procedure came from a solid research base. It was derived from a very substantial body of behavioral studies that has chronicled avoidance behavior as causative of depression. The article I published on avoidance behavior as it relates to depression outlines the design of a study to test the theory and the treatment experimentally (see Notes). There are recent studies that give some support for this treatment of depression, but more research is needed for this treatment to be corroborated empirically.

Are there people who are depressed on some basis other than avoidance behavior? Very likely. Life can be hard and harmful, and depressing, without avoidance behavior. And there may very well be some people—I believe a small number—who have been correctly diagnosed as depressed and whose depression cannot be explained in behavioral terms. But the success of behavior therapy gives strong evidence that the great majority of people diagnosed as depressed and prescribed antidepressant drugs would be better served if they received behavioral of treatment.

The basic premise behind behavior therapy is that alleviating depression does not result from prescribing drugs aimed at muting painful feelings. *Real help entails identifying the behaviors and often the cognitions that are related to loss and creating a treatment program designed to overcome that loss, most often by eliminating avoidance behavior.* Behavioral treatments are eminently sensible and straightforward. The treatment fits naturally with so much that we know about our functioning and the world we live in. Although it fits with common sense, behavior therapy is the product of painstaking empirical research on the variables that control behavior and are the causes of depression. It did not come from a committee of doctors voting on a treatment that just happened to be in their financial interest, and to correct a chemical imbalance explanation for depression that has failed scientific testing.

****

Part Three

I have discussed behavior therapy and its superiority to drug treatment. Now we have come to the most critical aspect of everything I have written. On what is this assessment based? *How effective is behavior therapy compared with antidepressant drugs in the treatment of depression?*

Remember, since antidepressant drugs function as placebos, studies comparing these drugs with behavior therapy are not comparing the effectiveness of a chemical treatment versus a psychological treatment but are comparing one psychological treatment with another. Unfortunately, antidepressants expose the patient to powerful chemicals that can be harmful. In addition, these studies are based on patients with diagnoses of depression of dubious validity, which raises questions about what exactly is being treated. There are very good reasons to believe most of these patients had been misdiagnosed as depressed.

It is true also that the deck has been stacked against psychological treatments in some of the prominent comparative treatment studies. Some of these studies have conditions that bias the results in favor of drug treatments. Just as was true for the outcome of antidepressant drugs, two of the NIMH treatment outcome studies found no difference in the effectiveness of behavior therapy and placebo. However, in the 1989 NIMH depression study (Elkin et al), one of the three sites offering behavior therapy was staffed by trainees, not by fully trained and experienced behavior therapists. This raises questions about the quality of the behavioral treatment that was tested. In the STAR*D study (Chapter 5), midway through the study, patients who were unimproved were given the option of behavior therapy or switching to another drug. Not many signed up for behavior therapy. Those who did, fared as well as the patients treated with drugs, meaning that they, too, showed a rate of improvement equivalent to that found in other studies using placebo. But these patients knew that they were in a drug study, and they had been heavily indoctrinated to believe in drug treatment. In addition, if they chose behavior therapy they had to go elsewhere and they had to pay for it, rather than the treatment being in a familiar setting and free. These are conditions that may have biased patients against the behavioral treatment. Moreover, the conditions of the 2006 STAR*D study were designed to test the effectiveness of antidepressant drugs. The study was not designed to test the effectiveness of behavior therapy. Even more importantly, Shea's NIMH study (Shea, et al, 1992) provided a measure of treatment effectiveness in a different way: *by follow-up* of the 1989 Depression Collaboration study's results. The study examined relapse, comparing each treatment's effectiveness after that treatment had ended. The researchers found that patients treated with antidepressants *did worse after the treatment had ended than those on placebo.* This was not true of patients treated with behavior therapy, *which was found to be the best treatment.* I will examine this better measure of treatment effectiveness shortly.

These issues aside, some placebo-controlled studies suggest antidepressant drugs are more effective than placebo; others show no drug/placebo difference. The same is true for behavior therapy. However, the great majority of studies favoring the effectiveness of antidepressant drugs are flawed because they are conducted on treatments that lasted only a few months. As discussed previously, basing conclusions on *short-term effects* enhances the apparent value of antidepressants. When assessments are made after 9 months or a year, results show that many patients treated with antidepressants reject them, and the results are no better than placebo, or worse, as noted above. Short-term studies are not good measures of the effectiveness of antidepressants. When studies are carried out longer, as Shea's study above, the results clearly favor behavior therapy.

Given the various sources of bias built into so many placebo-controlled depression treatment studies, the better method for comparing the effectiveness of alternative treatments is *relapse prevention.* Are the positive results reported for a treatment temporary or do they last? How many patients relapsed after treatment ended? Studies that report on relapse provide a better measure of the value of the treatment. *These studies report the number of patients who, after a treatment was deemed to be successful, had relapsed and returned to treatment.*

This is not to suggest that psychiatric relapse studies are free of bias. Although psychiatrists claim research results show that antidepressant drugs prevent relapse, their studies are designed in a way that invalidates them.

In 2020, Dr. Michael Hengartner, at Zurich University of Applied Sciences reviewed the basic problem with these studies, which are called "*discontinuation trials*." These studies are the basis for psychiatry's claim that antidepressants work and that they provide compelling evidence for the value of treating depression *long-term* with antidepressant drugs.

In these studies, all patients are prescribed an antidepressant. After a period of treatment, those who are considered in remission (as having benefited from the drugs) are then divided into two groups: those who will continue on the drugs versus those who are switched to placebo. The switch to placebo is abrupt. The resulting difference in the relapse rates of these two groups is interpreted as a measurement of treatment effectiveness. However, you have seen the evidence showing that antidepressant drugs are addictive and their prescription carries the warning that sudden abandonment of the drugs will lead to serious *withdrawal effects*. I have reviewed how these withdrawal effects often are misinterpreted (by the patient and by the doctor) as a recurrence of depression. *The design of these discontinuation trial studies is an embodiment of this mistake.* Given the standard psychiatric admonition against going off antidepressant drugs abruptly, this research design clearly stacks the deck in favor of the prescription of these drugs.

When relapse is assessed by studies that do not involve sudden withdrawal of the drug, the results for the drug treatments are poor. Indeed, results show that *long-term treatment with antidepressants, compared to short term treatment, is associated with higher relapse rates.* As you will recall from Chapter 5's analysis of the STAR*D study, remission was less than 10% after 12 months. Similar results (11% remission at 12 months) were found in another real-world effectiveness trial.

The results of outcome studies measuring relapse that have been conducted over the last several decades show that *behavior therapy has a significantly lower relapse rate than that which is found for antidepressant drugs.* The benefits derived from behavior therapy hold up, whereas when relapse rates for antidepressants are measured appropriately the results are that *the damage wrought by these drugs increases with time.*

As early as 1977, a study by Augustus Rush and others showed that behavior therapy not only outperformed psychiatric drugs in effectiveness (80% vs. 23%), six months after treatment ended, 68% of patients treated with drugs had relapsed and re-entered treatment versus 16% of patients treated behaviorally.

More recently, in Italy in 2004, Dr. Giovanni Fava found that even brief behavior therapy more effectively reduced relapse than did drugs. Following what was judged to be "successful" treatment with antidepressant drugs, continuing the treatment with behavior therapy led to a significantly lower relapse rate of 40%, versus 90% for those continuing in clinical management who did not receive behavioral treatment.

In 2005, Dr. Claudi Bochting and his Dutch associates found that for patients with multiple bouts of depression, behavior therapy significantly reduced the rate of relapse. Another study published in 2005 by Dr. Steven Hollon and others found a relapse rate of 31% following behavior therapy vs. 76% for patients who had been treated with antidepressants.

Many other studies have shown that medical treatment of depression significantly increases the likelihood of relapse (the opposite of what psychiatrists claim) whereas psychological treatment decreases relapse. Here is a snapshot of the evidence favoring the greater effectiveness of psychological treatment over drug treatment and of the harmful effects of antidepressant drug treatment, as viewed in several recent studies published in 2019.

The National Institute for Health Care Excellence (NICE) is an arm of the Department of Health in Great Britain. NICE provides analyses of the effectiveness and safety of drugs, and it is highly respected worldwide for its recommendations regarding clinical guidelines. In 2019, NICE reviewed 124 treatment outcome studies of depression, comparing the relapse rates of antidepressant drug treatment with psychological treatment. Results consistently showed that psychological treatment was superior to antidepressants in protecting against relapse. They investigated short-term versus long-term outcomes, finding that psychological treatments became *more effective* with time and antidepressants *less effective.* A third of patients on antidepressants relapsed within six months and recurrence of depression was more likely the longer antidepressants were taken. Only 10% of patients taking antidepressants achieved sustained remission. Underlining the negative results for antidepressants was the finding that *recurrence of depression was more likely for patients taking antidepressants than for those on placebo.* Patients taking antidepressant drugs long-term reported feeling addicted and long-term use of antidepressants was associated with serious health risks. These results not only strikingly favor behavior therapy for depression, they constitute a stark warning against choosing drug treatment.

These results pertain to the issue of safety in addition to effectiveness, reporting the potential *adverse effects of these drugs.* In Chapter 7 I reviewed the safety concerns that have been raised about antidepressant drugs by Drs. Glenmullen and Fava, and Robert Whitaker. As I indicated, they are not alone in their concerns. Other researchers and reviewers of research echo their conclusions. One has stated, "there is emerging evidence that (. . .) persistent use of antidepressants may be pro-depressants." Another has warned that "antidepressants probably should be avoided in bipolar depression, mixed manic-depressive states, and in neurotic depression."

You have read in this book multiple factors that pertain to these adverse results: These diagnoses and the distinctions between them are neither valid nor reliable causing rampant misdiagnosis; the chemicals in antidepressant drugs have not been shown to be effective, but they are powerful; these chemicals are addictive and known to be physically harmful.

Drs. Amsterdam and Kim at the University of Pennsylvania were interested in examining this possibility of an *adverse* relationship between taking antidepressant drugs and relapse in patients diagnosed as depressed. They studied 148 patients diagnosed with bipolar depression who were treated with antidepressant drugs. Rather than reducing the likelihood of relapse, they found that both previous use of antidepressants and continued use of antidepressants *increased* the risk of relapse and *shortened* the time to relapse. The risk of relapse was three times higher for these patients than for patients who had been prescribed a placebo.

Dr. Michael Hengartner, whom I cited above, examined whether taking antidepressant drugs was associated with an increased risk of hospitalization. He focused on relapses that led to hospitalization, studying 151 hospitalized patients. To control for severity and disability, he assigned patients into pairs by matching them for severity on 14 clinically relevant impairments. The results were that 36% of those prescribed antidepressants were hospitalized at least once, as opposed to 22% of matched non-users. For those hospitalized two or more times, the rate of hospitalization for antidepressant users was 22%; for non-users it was 2%. In addition, those on antidepressants were hospitalized for 22 days compared to 8.5 days for their matched non-users. Taking antidepressants was significantly associated with a *greater risk of relapse into severe depression*, and a greater likelihood of hospitalization and the likelihood of longer hospitalization.

Another important criterion is suicide prevention. A study using the FDA database reported that the number of suicides among 19,000 patients treated by SSRIs did not differ significantly from placebo. However, Dr. David Healy, making use of more complete data from the FDA files, reanalyzed these data and found that the rates of suicides and attempted suicides were roughly 2.5 times greater for those prescribed SSRIs than for those on placebo. These results suggest that the SSRIs may induce suicidal behavior in some patients. Thus, the conventional wisdom that it is necessary and prudent to prescribe an antidepressant when there is a suicidal risk is not supported by an abundance of research results.

As an anecdotal example, during more than 40 years practicing behavior therapy no patient I treated committed suicide.

NICE found that patients are less likely to drop out of talk therapy than they are drug therapy. This was particularly the case for the most severely depressed patients. And a study conducted by the World Health Organization in Great Britain found that patients treated by means other than antidepressant drugs had "general health" and "milder" depressive symptoms and were less likely to be viewed any longer as "mentally ill."

In summary, the chemicals in antidepressant drugs have not been found effective, but they can induce harm and even grievous harm. Relapse is the common outcome. Behavior therapy poses no such risks and has been found to be more effective than drugs. *These results provide compelling evidence for choosing psychological treatment, not drug treatment, for depression.* Indeed, the data comparing the effectiveness of behavior therapy versus drug treatments show that behavior therapy is the best treatment we have not only for depression, but for phobias, social anxiety, obsessive-compulsive disorder, substance abuse, and many other forms of distress. These results are even more noteworthy given the comparatively miniscule investment the NIMH has made in research related to behavior therapy compared with drug treatments. There is little question that treating mental disorders effectively requires the NIMH to significantly increase funding for behavioral research.

****

This is a book that examines scientific evidence. You have seen that the evidence pertaining to the diagnosis of depression, the medical explanation given for depression, and the claims for the effectiveness of antidepressant drugs, all fail to meet scientific standards. As a good scientist, Dr. Hengartner, whom I referenced above in relation to outcome research findings, reminds his readers of the scientific dictum that absence of evidence does not automatically imply evidence of absence. It is an admonition deserving of respect, but the findings showing the superiority of behavior therapy over antidepressant drugs do not stand alone. A wide array of research results show that the medicalized care of depression has failed scientific testing in all of the crucial areas related to health care: diagnosis, explanation, and treatment outcome. There is more than enough evidence to take decisive action in favor of adopting a behavioral orientation to mental disorder.

We have been betting on a horse that keeps losing rather than the horse that keeps winning. It is essential that our scientific establishment, most notably the NIMH, prioritize behavioral research when there are such strong reasons the payoff will be great indeed. In summary, the standard of care for depression is a medicalized system that has failed. A psychological system has far greater promise for patients immediately and in the future. Scientific evidence directly challenges how mental health care for depression is being delivered. It is past time for the contrived evidence supporting the medicalization of mental health care to be examined for what it is and what it has wrought and for things to change.

A 2014 report by the World Health Organization of the United Nations makes the same argument. The WHO report takes aim at the medicalization of psychiatry, making the point that person/environment interactions (a psychological explanation) are basic to mental disorder and that medicalization has had seriously detrimental effects on mental health care:

> A growing research base has produced evidence that the status quo, preoccupied with biomedical interventions, including psychotropic medications and non-consensual measures, is no longer defenseless in the context of improving mental health(. . ..) Public policies continue to neglect the importance of pre-conditions of poor mental health, such as violence and the breakdown of communities, systematic socioeconomic disadvantage and harmful conditions at work and in schools(. . ..) Reductive biomedical approaches to treatment that do not adequately address contexts and relationships can no longer be considered congruent with the right to health.

The tragedy of psychiatry's false medicalization of mental health care is that it has prevented us from adequately recognizing and addressing the social and behavioral causes of psychological pain and mental disorder. Just as it would be a mistake to choose a psychological treatment for a medical problem, it is a mistake to choose a medical treatment for a psychological problem.

Notes

Introduction

1. *Longevity*:
   Johnson, S. (2021). *Extra Life: A Short History of Living Longer.* New York: Riverhead Books.

Chapter 1: Sadness and Depression

1. *Sadness vs. Depression:*
   Horwitz, A. and Wakefield, J. (2007). *The Loss of Sadness: How Psychiatry Transformed Normal Sorrow into Depressive Disorder.* New York: Oxford University Press.
2. *Book review of Horwitz and Wakefield*:
   McHugh, P. (August 30, 2007). *Book Review: The Loss of Sadness. New England Journal of Medicine.* DOI.10.1056/NEJMbkrev58551.
3. *DSM-III*:
   Diagnostic and Statistical Manual of Mental Disorders, Third Edition, (1980). American Psychiatric Association.

4. *Earlier editions of the DSM:*
   a. *Diagnostic and Statistical Manual of Mental Disorders*, 1952, American Psychiatric Association.
   b. *Diagnostic and Statistical Manual of Mental Disorders, Second Edition*, 1968, American Psychiatric Association.
5. *Sadness has value*:
   Lomas, T. (2018). The quiet virtues of sadness: A selective theoretical and interpretive appreciation of its potential to contribute to well-being. *New Ideas in Psychology*, 49, 18–26. DOI: 10.1016/j.newideapsych.2018.01.002
6. *Paul Ekman*:
   a. Ekman, P. and Friesen, W. (1971). Constants across cultures in the faces and emotion. *Journal of Personality and Social Psychology*, 17, 124–129.
   b. Ekman, P. (1992). Basic emotions. In T. Dalgleish and M. Power (Eds.), *Handbook of Cognition and Emotion*. Sussex, UK: John Wiley and Sons.
7. *Tegmark quotation on feelings:*
   Tegmark, M. (2017). *Life 3.0: Being Human in the Age of Artificial Intelligence*. New York: Alfred Knopf.
8. *R. E. M.:*

R. E. M. (1992). Album: *Automatic for the People.*

9. *Sadness vs. Depression in literature:*
   a. Homer (800 BC). *The Iliad.*
   b. Melville, H. (1853). Bartleby, the Scrivener: A story of wall street. *Putnam's Magazine.*
   c. Plath, S. (1963). *The Bell Jar.* New York: Harper Perennial.
   d. Styron, W. (1951). *Lie Down in Darkness.* Indianapolis: Bobbs-Merrtll.
   e. Wordsworth, W. Surprised by Joy-Impatient as the Wind. In W. Braithwaite (Ed.) (1909). *The Book of Georgian Verse.* New York: Brentano's.
   f. Miller, A. Death of a Salesman, in Horwitz, A. and Wakefield, J. (2007). *The Loss of Sadness: How Psychiatry Transformed Normal Sorrow into Depressive Disorder* (pp. 3–4).
   g. Hemingway, E. (1929). *A Farewell to Arms.* New York: Scribner.
   h. Stover, L. (2015). Melancholy's Sweet Allure. *New York Times*, November 8, 2015, 17.
   i. Goodwin, D. (2005). *Team of Rivals: The Political Genius of Abraham Lincoln.* New York: Simon and Schuster.

j. Wilson, E. (2008). *Against Happiness.* New York: Farrar, Straus and Giroux.

10. *Loss as precipitant of sadness and depression:*
    a. Paykel, E., Myers, J., Dienelt, M., Klerman, G., Lindenthal, J., and Pepper, M. (1969). Life events and depression: A controlled study. *Archives of General Psychiatry*, 21, 753–760.
    b. Paykel, E. (1978). Contribution of life events to causation of psychiatric illness. *Psychological Medicine*, 8, 245–253.
    c. Sethi, B. (1964). Relationship of separation to depression. *Archives of General Psychiatry*, 10, 486–496.
    d. Surtees, P., McC.Miller, P., Ingham, J., Kreitman, N., Rennie, D. and Sashidharan, S. (1986). Life events and the onset of affective disorder. *Journal of Affective Disorders*, 10, 37–50.
    e. Finlay-Jones, R. (1981). Types of stressful life events and the onset of anxiety and depressive disorder. *Psychological Medicine*, 11, 803–815.
    f. Myers, J., Lindenthal, J. and Pepper, M. (1971). Life events and psychiatric impairment. *Journal of Nervous and Mental Disease*, 152, 149–157.
    g. Levi, L., Fales, C., Stein, M. and Sharp, V. (1966). Separation and attempted suicide. *Archives of General Psychiatry*, 15, 158–165.
    h. Clayton, P. (1975). The effect of living alone on bereavement. *American Journal of Psychiatry*, 132, 133–137.
    i. Finlay-Jones, R. and Brown, G. (1981). Types of stressful life event and onset of anxiety and depressive disorders. *Psychological Medicine*, 11, 803–815.
    j. Brown, G., Sklair, F., Harris, T., and Birley, L. (1973). Life events and psychiatric disorders. Part 2: Nature of causal link. *Psychological Medicine*, 3, 159–176.
    k. Paykel, E. (1994). Life events, social support, and depression. *Acta Psychiatra Scanda Suppl*, 377, 50–58.
    l. Wakefield, J. (1992). The concept of mental disorder: On the boundary between biological facts and social values. *American Psychologist*, 47, 373–388.
    m. Kessler, R. (1997). The effects of stressful life events on depression. In J. Spence, et al. (Eds.), *Annual Review of Psychology* (pp. 191–214). Palo Alto, CA: Annual Reviews.

11. *Kendler on loss:*
    a. Kendler, K., Heath, A., Martin, N. and Eaves, L. (1987). Symptoms of anxiety and symptoms of depression. *Archives of General Psychiatry*, 44, 451–457.
    b. Kendler, K., Neale, M., Kessler, R., Heath, A. and Eaves, L. (1992). A population-based twin study of major depression in women. *Archives of General Psychiatry*, 49, 257–266.
    c. Kendler, K., Neale, M., Kessler, R., Heath, A. and Eaves, L. (1992). A population-based twin study of major depression in women: the impact of varying definitions of illness. *Archives of General Psychiatry*, 49, 257–266.
    d. Kendler, K. (2005). "A gene for . . ." The nature of gene action in psychiatric disorders. *American Journal of Psychiatry*, 162(7), 1243–1251.
    e. Kendler, K., Neale, M., Kessler, R., Heath, A. and Eaves, L. (1993). A twin study of recent life events and difficulties. *Archives of General Psychiatry*, 50, 789–796.
    f. Kessler, R. (1997). The effects of stressful life events on depression. In J. Spence, J. Darley and D. Foss (Eds.), *Annual Review of Psychology* (pp. 191–214). Palo Alto, CA: Annual Reviews.
    g. Brown, G. and Harris, T. (1989). *Life Events and Illness.* New York: Guilford.
12. *Theories of loss:*
    a. Freud, S. (1959). Mourning and melancholia. In E. Jones (Ed.), *Collected Papers* (pp. 152–170). New York: Basic Books. (Original work published in 1917).
    b. Harlow, H. (1958). The nature of love. *American Psychologist*, 13, 573–585.
    c. Bryan, D. and Strachey, A. (1927). *Selected Papers of Karl Abraham.* New York: Basic Books.
    d. Bowlby, J. (1980). *Attachment and Loss: Volume III: Loss, Sadness, and Depression.* New York: Basic Books.
    e. Skinner, B. (1953). *Science and Human Behavior.* New York: Macmillan.
13. *Angell quotation:*
    Angell, M. (July 14, 2011). The illusions of psychiatry. *New York Review of Books*, LVIII(121), 20.

14. *deGrasse Tyson and Goldsmith quotation:*
deGrasse Tyson, N. and Goldsmith, D. (2004). *Fourteen Billion Years of Cosmic Evolution*. New York: W. W. Norton and Company.
15. *Spitzer quotation:*
Spitzer, R. (2007). Forward. In A. Horwitz and J. Wakefield (Eds.), *The Loss of Sadness: How Psychiatry Transformed Normal Sorrow into Depressive Disorder* (pp. viii). New York: Oxford University Press.
16. *DSM and Grief:*
    a. J. Wolfe, S. (2013). Grief and antidepressant use. *Health Letter, Public Citizen*, 29, May 2013.
    b. Whoriskey, P. (2012). Antidepressants to treat grief? Psychiatrists with ties to drug industry say yes. *Washington Post*, December 20, 2002.
    c. Frances, A. (2010). Good grief. *New York Times*, April 15, 2010, WK9.
    d. Friedman, R. (2012). Grief, depression, and the DSM-V. *New England Journal of Medicine*, 366, 1855–1857.
    e. Spence, D. (2012). The psychiatric oligarchs who medicalize normality. *British Medical Journal*, 344, May 2012.
    f. Casey, B. (2005). Snake phobias, moodiness, and a battle in psychiatry. *New York Times*, June 14, 2005, F1.
17. *Changed frequencies of diagnoses of depression*:
    a. Hasin, D. (2005). Epidemiology of major depressive disorder: Results from the National Epidemiological Survey on Alcoholism and Related Conditions. *Archives of General Psychiatry*, 62, 1097–1106.
    b. Wing, J. and Babbington, P. (1985). Epidemiology of Depression. In E. Beckham and W. Leber (Eds.), *Handbook of Depression* (pp. 765–794). New York: Guilford Press.
    c. Kessler, R. (2002). Epidemiology of depression. In I. Gottlieb and C. Hamman (Eds.), *Handbook of Depression* (pp. 23–42). New York: Guilford Press.
    d. Kessler, R., Berglund, P., Demler, O., Jin, R., Merikangas, K. and Walters, E. (2005). Lifetime prevalence and age-of-onset distributions of DSM-IV disorders in the National Comorbidity Survey Replication. *Archives of General Psychiatry*, 62, 593–602.
    e. Pratt, L. and Brody, D. (2011). Antidepressant use in persons aged 12 and over: US, 2005–2008. *NCHS data brief*, no. 76. Hyattsville, MD: National Center for Health Statistics, Centers for Disease Control.

f. Winerman, L. (2017). By the numbers: Antidepressant use on the rise. *Monitor on Psychology*, 11.

g. Nielsen, M. and Gotzsche, P. (2011). An analysis of psychotropic drug sales. Increasing sales of selective serotonin reuptake inhibitors are closely related to number of products. *International Journal of Risk and Safety in Medicine*, 23(2), 125–132. DOI: 10.3233/JRS-2011-0526.

18. *CDC*:
Pratt, L., Brody, D. and Gu, Q. (2011). Antidepressant use in persons aged 12 and over: United States, 2005–2008. National Center for Health Statistics, Brief No. 76, October 2011.

19. *Quotation from Horowitz and Wakefield:*
Horwitz, A. and Wakefield, J. (2007). *The Loss of Sadness: How Psychiatry Transformed Normal Sorrow into Depressive Disorder* (pp. 6).

20. *What qualifies for a diagnosis*:
    a. Mojtabai, R. and Olfson, M. (2011). Proportion of antidepressants prescribed without a psychiatric diagnosis. *Health Affairs*, 30, 1434–1442.
    b. Rosenberg, R. (2013). Abnormal is the new normal. *Slate*, April 12, 2013.

21. *Case and Deaton*:
    a. Case, A. and Deaton, A. (2020). *Deaths of Despair and the Future of Capitalism*. Princeton, NJ: Princeton University Press.
    b. Epstein, H. (2020). Left Behind. *New York Review of Books*, March 26, 2020, pp. 28–30.

Chapter 2: The Medicalizing of Psychiatry

1. *Lapouse:*
Lapouse, R. (1967). Problems in studying the prevalence of psychiatric disorder. *American Journal of Public Health and the Nation's Health*, 57(6), 947–954.

2. *George Washington:*
Knox, J. (1933). The medical history of George Washington, his friends, physicians, and advisers. *Bulletin of the Institute of the History of Medicine*, 1, 174–191.

3. *History of Medicine*:
   a. Wootton, D. (2006). *Bad Medicine.* USA: Oxford University Press.
   b. Rosenberg, C. (1979). *The Therapeutic Revolution: Medicine, Meaning, and Social Change in Nineteenth Century America*, in Vogel, M. and Rosenberg, C. (Eds.). University of Pennsylvania Press.
   c. Wood, G. (2014). The bleeding founders. *New York Review of Books*, July 10, 2014.
4. *Pasteur*:
   Walker, J. (2004). *Discovery of the Gene.* London: Icon Books.
5. *Biological treatments:*
   a. Singleton, M. (2014). The "science" of eugenics: America's Moral Detour. *Journal of American Physicians and Surgeons*, 19(4), 122–125.
   b. Rikoff, J. (2016). Neuroscience and the law: Don't rush in. *New York Review of Books*, LXIII, 30–32.
6. *Eugenics:*
   a. Dowbiggin, A. (1992). An exodus of enthusiasm: G. Alder Blumer, eugenics, and US psychiatry. *Medical History*, 36, 379–402.
   b. Sfera, A. (2013). Can psychiatry be misused again? *Frontiers in Psychiatry.* DOI: 10.3389/fpsyt.2013.00101.
   c. Sicherman, B. (1980). *The Quest for Mental Health in America: 1880–1917.* Arno Press.
   d. Fuller, T. and Miller, J. (2001). *The Invisible Plague: The Rise of Mental Illness from 1750 to the Present.* New Brunswick, NJ: Rutgers University Press (pp. 280–285).
7. *Lobotomy*:
   a. Acharya, H. (2004). The rise and fall of frontal leukotomy. In W. Whitelaw (Ed.), *The Proceedings of the 13th Annual History of Medicine Proceedings.* Calgary (pp. 32—41).
   b. Braslow, J. (1997). *Mental Ills and Bodily Cures: Psychiatric Treatment in the First Half of the Twentieth Century.* Oakland: University of California Press.
   c. Goldbecker-Wood, S. (September 21, 1996). Norway compensates lobotomy victims. *British Medical Journal*, 313(7059), 708–709. DOI: 10.1136/bmj/.313.7059.708a.PMD 11644825.
8. *Freud, 1909:*
   a. Freud, along with Carl Jung, was invited by G. Stanley Hall, President of Clark University and first President of the American Psychological

Association, to deliver a series of talks at Clark University in 1909 on his theory of psychoanalysis. The talks were controversial. A prime criticism of Freud's theories was that they were non-scientific. However, the publicity the talks received brought Freud's ideas into the limelight.

b. Jones, E. (1953). *The Life and Work of Sigmund Freud, Volumes 1–3.* New York: Basic Books.

9. *Kirk and Kutchins quotation:*
Kirk, S. and Kutchins, H. (1992). *The Selling of the DSM: The Rhetoric of Science in Psychiatry.* New York: Aldine De Gruyer. (p. 19).

10. *Reliability studies:*
    a. Ash, P. (1949). The reliability of psychiatric diagnosis. *Journal of Abnormal and Social Psychology*, 44, 272–276.
    b. Rosenhan, D. (1973). On being sane in insane places. *Science*, 114, 316–322.

11. *Decline in medical students choosing psychiatry:*
    a. Nelson, B. (1982). Psychiatry's anxious years: Decline in allure as a career leads to self-examination. *New York Times*, November 2, Section C, 1, Science Desk.

    See also:
    b. Spingarn, N. (1974). Psychiatrists: an endangered species? Review of E. Torrey, "The Death of Psychiatry." *Chronicle of Higher Education*, November 23, 1974, 10.
    c. Wyatt, W. (2003). Biological causation in the professional and popular cultures: Tactics for dealing with an oversold model. Presented at the Association for Behavior Analysis, May 24, 2003, San Francisco, CA.

12. *Behavioral Psychology:*
    a. Ferster, C. and Perrott, M. (1968). *Behavior Principles.* New York: Appleton-Century-Crofts.
    b. Krasner, L. and Ullman, L. (Eds.) (1966). *Research in Behavior Modification.* New York: Holt, Rinehart, and Winston.
    c. Rimm, D. and Masters, J. (1974). *Behavior Therapy: Techniques and Empirical Findings.* New York: Academic Press.

13. *Wolpe and Beck:*
    a. Wolpe, J. (1958). *Psychotherapy by Reciprocal Inhibition.* Stanford, CA: Stanford University Press.

b. Beck, A. (1967). *Depression: Causes and Treatment.* Philadelphia: University of Pennsylvania Press.
c. Beck, A. (1976). *Cognitive Therapy and the Emotional Disorders.* New York: International University Press.
d. Rush, A., Beck, A., Kovacs, M. and Hollon, S. (1977). Comparative efficacy of cognitive therapy and pharmacotherapy in the treatment of depressed outpatients. *Cognitive Therapy and Research*, 1, 17–37.

14. *The DSM:*
    a. Diagnostic and Statistical Manual of Mental Disorders, 1952, American Psychiatric Association.
    b. *Diagnostic and Statistical Manual of Mental Disorders, Second Edition*, 1968, American Psychiatric Association.
    c. *Diagnostic and Statistical Manual of Mental Disorders, Third Edition*, 1980, American Psychiatric Association.
15. *Falsifiability:*

Popper, K. (1959). *The Logic of Scientific Discovery.* New York: Basic Books (pp. 95).

16. *Horwitz and Wakefield*:
    a. Horwitz, A. and Wakefield, J. (2007). *The Loss of Sadness: How Psychiatry Transformed Normal Sorrow into Depressive Disorder.* New York: Oxford University Press.
    b. Kirk, S. and Kutchins, H. (1992). *The Selling of the DSM: The Rhetoric of Science in Psychiatry.* New York: Aldine De Gruyer.
17. *De Grasse Tyson quotation*:
    De Grasse Tyson, N. (2017). *Astrophysics for People in a Hurry.* New York: W. W. Norton & Co.
18. *Boswell quotation:*
    Boswell, T. (2016). Small sample size skews the numbers for Nats, Cubs. *Washington Post*, June 10, 2016, D1.

Chapter 3: The DSM-III Data: Truth vs. Truthiness

1. *Klerman quotation:*
   Klerman, G. (1982). Statement made at the *1982 Annual Meeting of the American Psychiatric Association.* See Kirk, S. and Kutchins, H., The Selling of the DSM. (pp. 6).

2. *Klerman on reliability:*
   a. Kirk, S. and Kutchins, H. (1992). *The Selling of the DSM: The Rhetoric of Science in Psychiatry.* New York: Aldine de Gruyer (pp. 133).
   b. Klerman, G. (1986). *Historical Perspectives on Contemporary Directions in Psychopathology.* New York: Guilford Press (pp. 3–28).
   c. Klerman, G. (1986). Historical perspectives on contemporary schools of psychopathology. In T. Millon and G. Klerman (Eds.), *Contemporary Directions in Psychopathology: Toward the DSM-IV.* New York: Guilford Press (p. 25).
   d. Maxmen, J. (1986). *The New Psychiatry.* New York: Signet.
3. *NIMH*:
   Parloff, M. (2004). Personal communication with Dr. Morris Parloff, the former NIMH branch chief for Psychological Research, 1/05/04.
4. *Spitzer on committee:*
   Angell, M. (July 2011). The illusions of psychiatry. *New York Review of Books*, LVIII(12).
5. *Kirk and Kutchens on Task Force:*
   Kirk, S. and Kutchins, H. (1992). *The Selling of the DSM: The Rhetoric of Science in Psychiatry.* New York: Aldine De Gruyer (pp. 14).
6. *Davies interview with Spitzer:*
   Davies, J. (2014). *Cracked: Why Psychiatry Is Doing More Harm Than Good.* London: Icon Books Ltd.
7. *DSM-III diagnoses established by vote:*
   a. Johnston, L., Johnstone, L. and Boyle, M. (2018). The power threat meaning framework: Towards the identification of patterns in emotional distress, experiences and troubled or troubling behavior, as an alternative to functional psychiatric diagnosis. *Leister: British Psychological Society.*
   b. Davies, J. (2016). How voting and consensus created the Diagnostic and Statistical Manual of Mental Disorders (DSM-III). *Anthropology and Medicine,* 1–15. DOI: 10.1080/13648470.2016.1226684.
8. *Spitzer on reliability:*
   Spitzer, R., Forman, J. and Nee, J. (1979). DSM-III field trials: I. Initial interrater diagnostic reliability. *American Journal of Psychiatry,* 136, 815–817.
9. *Kirk and Kutchins on Kappa:*
   Kirk, S. and Kutchins, H. (1992). *The Selling of the DSM* (pp. 38–45; 60–750).

10. *Kirk and Kutchins on reliability comparisons with previous editions of the DSM:*
    Kirk, S. and Kutchins, H. (1992). *The Selling of the DSM* (pp. 121, 139).
11. *Kirk and Kutchins on Axis I, Axis II, and specific diagnoses:*
    Kirk, S. and Kutchins, H. (1992). *The Selling of the DSM* (pp. 143–151).
12. *No physiological tests for mental disorder:*
    a. Timini, S. (2014). No more psychiatric labels: Why formal psychiatric diagnostic systems should be abolished. *International Journal of Clinical and Health Psychology*, 14, 208–215.
    b. Lakeman, R. and Cutcliffe, J. (2016). Diagnostic sedition: Re-Considering the ascension and hegemony of contemporary psychiatric diagnoses. *Issues in Mental Health Nursing*, 37(2).
13. *Spitzer quote to Spiegel*:
    Spiegel, A. (2005). The dictionary of disorder: How one man revolutionized psychiatry. *The New Yorker*, January 3, 2005.
14. *DSM-V:*
    Freedman, R., Lewis, D., Michels, R., Pine, D., Schultz, S., Tamminga, C., Gabbard, G., Gau, S., Javitt, D., Oquendo, M. and Shrout, P. (2013). The initial field trials of DSM-V: New blooms and old thorns. *American Journal of Psychiatry*, 170, 1–5.
15. *Tyrer quotations:*
    Tyrer, P. (2012). DSM—In 100 words. *British Journal of Psychiatry*, 200, 67.

Chapter 4: Psychiatry's Brain Disease Theory

1. *Neurobollocks and Biobabble*:
   a. Poole, S. (2012). Your brain on pseudoscience: The rise of popular neurobollocks. *New Statesman*, September 6, 2012.
   b. Healy, D. (2006). *Let Them Eat Prozac: The Unhealthy Relationship between the Pharmaceutical Industry and Depression*. New York: New York University Press.
2. *Koch*:
   Brock, T. (1999). *Robert Koch: A Life in Medicine and Bacteriology*. Washington, DC: ASM Press.
3. *Identifying Feelings in animals?*
   Feldman, R. (2018). Do animals feel love? Why we might never know. *Washington Post*, February 18, 2018.

4. *Tests of chemical imbalance theory:*
   a. Stittleburg Restorative Health Care. (March 2005). Let's talk depression and antidepressants. *National Review of Neuroscience*, 6(3), 241–246.
   b. Belmaker, R. and Agam, M. (January 3, 2008). Major depressive disorder. *New England Journal of Medicine*, 358, 55–68. DOI: 10.1056/NEJMra 073090.
   c. Moncrieff, J. (2018). What does the latest meta-analysis really tell us about antidepressants? *Epidemiology and Psychiatric Sciences*, 27(5).
5. *Any mental disorder*:
   Lacasse, J. and Leo, J. (2005). Serotonin and depression: A disconnect between the advertisements and the scientific literature. *PLoS Medicine*, 2(12), published November 8, 2005: e392. DOI: 10.1371/journal.pmed.0020392
6. *Origins of the chemical imbalance theory:*
   a. The next several pages are summaries of discussions in several chapters of: Valenstein, E. (1998). *Blaming the Brain: The Truth about Drugs and Mental Health*. New York: The Free Press.
   b. Schildkraut, J. (1967). Biogenic amines and emotion. *Science*, 156, 21–30.
   c. Goldhill, O. (2017). 30 years after Prozac arrived, we still buy the lie that chemical imbalances cause depression. *Quartz*, December 29, 2017.
7. *Kirsch quotation:*
   a. Kirsch, I. (2009). *The Emperor's New Drugs: Exploding the Antidepressant Myth*. London: The Bodley Head (p. 99).
   b. Kirsch, I. (2004). Antidepressants and the placebo effect. *Z. Psychol.*, 222(3), 128–134. DOI: 10.1027/2151-2604/a000176
8. *Angell quotation:*
   Angell, M. (2011). The epidemic of mental illness: Why? *New York Review of Books*, June 23, 2011.
9. *Genetic vulnerability studies:*
   a. Caspi, A., Sugden, K., Moffitt, T., Taylor, A., Craig, I., Harrington, H., McClay, J., Mill, J., Martin, J., Braithwaite, A., and Poulton, R. (July 18, 2003). Influence of life stress on depression: Moderation by a polymorphism in the 5-HTT gene. *Science*, 386–389.
   b. Risch, N., Herrell, R., Lehner, T., Liang, K., Eaves, L., Hoh, J., Griem, A., Kovacs, M., Ott, J. and Merikangas, K. (2009). Interaction

between the serotonin transporter gene (5-HTTLPR), stressful life events, and risk of depression: A meta-analysis. *Journal of the American Medical Association*, 301, 2462–2471.

c. Valenstein, E. (1998). *Blaming the Brain: The Truth about Drugs and Mental Health.* New York: The Free Press (pp. 126 and 140).

10. *Fava quotation:*
Fava, G. (December 2008). Psychosocial determinants of recovery in depression. *Dialogues in Clinical Neuroscience*, , 10(4), 461–472.

11. *Science article:*
Caspi, A., Sugden, K., Moffitt, T., Taylor, A., Craig, I., Harrington, H., McClay, J., Mill, J., Martin, J., Braithwaite, A. and Poulton, R. (July 18, 2003). Influence of life stress on depression: Moderation by a polymorphism in the 5-HTT gene, *Science*, 386–389.

12. *JAMA article:*
Rieckmann, N., Rapp, M., and Nordhorn, J. (2009). Gene-environment interactions and depression. *Journal of the American Medical Association*, 302(17), 1859–1862. DOI: 10.1001.jama.2009.1578.

13. *2019 genetic test*:
Border, R., Johnson, E., Evans, L., Smolen, A., Berley, N., Sullivan, P. and Keller, M. (March 2019). No support for historical candidate gene or candidate-by-gene interaction hypotheses for major depression across multiple large samples. *American Journal of Psychiatry.*

14. *Joseph books and articles:*
    a. Joseph, J. (2003). *The Gene Illusion: Genetic Research in Psychiatry and Psychology under the Microscope.* UK: PCCS Books.
    b. Joseph, J. (2015). *The Trouble with Twin Studies: A Reassessment of Twin Research in Social and Behavioral Sciences.* Oxford, New York: Rutledge.
    c. Joseph, J. and Leo, J. (2006). Genetic relatedness and the lifetime risk for being diagnosed with schizophrenia: Gottesman's 1991 Figure 10 reconsidered. *The Journal of Mind and Behavior*, 27, 73–90.
    d. Joseph, J. (2001). Separated twins and genetics of personality differences: A critique. *American Journal of Psychology*, 114, 1–30.

15. *Bouchard study:*
Bouchard, T., Lykken, D., McGue, M., Segal, N. and Tellegen, A. (1990). Sources of psychological differences: The Minnesota study of twins reared apart. *Science*, 250, 223–228.

16. *Shields study:*
    a. Shields, J. (1962). *Monozygotic Twins Brought Up Apart and Brought Up Together.* London: Oxford University Press.
    b. Winerman, L. (2004). A second look at twin studies. *The Monitor,* 35, 46.
17. *Bentall quotations:*
    Bentall, R. (2009). *Doctoring the Mind: Is Our Current Treatment of Mental Illness Really Any Good?* New York: New York University Press (p. 123, 127).
18. *Related research:*
    a. Kendler, K. (2005). "A gene for . . . .": The nature of gene actions in psychiatric disorders. *American Journal of Psychiatry,* 162, 1243–1252.
    b. Joseph, J. (2004). The fruitless search for schizophrenia genes. *Ethical Human Psychology and Psychiatry,* 6, 167–181.
19. *Environmental effects on health:*
    a. Ustun, A., Wolf, J., Covalan, C., Neville, T., Bos, R., and Neira, M. (2016). Diseases due to unhealthy environments: an updated estimate of the global burden of disease attributable to environmental determinants of health. *Journal of Public Health,* 39, September 2017.
    b. Remoundu, K. and Koundouri, P. (August 2009). Environmental effects of public health: An economic perspective. *International Journal of Environmental Research and Public Health,* 6.
20. *Exercise and the brain*:
    Godman, H. (2018). Regular exercise changes the brain to improve memory, thinking skills. *Harvard Health Publishing,* April 9, 2014.
21. *Epigenetics:*
    a. Russo, V., Martienssen, R., and Riggs, A. (1996). *Epigenetic Mechanisms of Gene Regulation.* Plainview, NY: Cold Spring Harbor Laboratory Press.
    b. Bind, A. (2007). Perceptions of epigenetic. *Nature,* 447, 396–398.
    c. Rutherford, A. (2015). Beware the pseudo gene genies. *The Guardian,* 19 July 2015.
22. *Twin study of Parkinson Disease*:
    Tanner, C., O'Henary, R., Goldman, S., Ellenberg, J., Chan, P., Mayeux, R., and Langston, W. (January 27, 1999). Parkinson disease in twins: An etiologic study. JAMA, 281(4), 341–346. DOI: 10.1 001/jama.281.4.341.
23. *Orr quotation:*
    Orr, H. (2014). Stretch genes. *New York Review of Books,* June 5, 2014.

24. *Nature Neuroscience:*
Noble, K., Houston, S., and Brito, N. (2015). *Nature Neuroscience.* http://dx.doi.org/10.1038/nn.3983.
25. *National Academy of Science:*
Mitchell, C., Hobcraft, J., McLanahan, S., Siegel, S., Berg, A., Gunn, J., Garfinkel, I., and Notterman (2014). *Proceedings of the National Academy of Science.* http://dx.doi.org/10.1073/pnas.1404293111.
26. *2008 study:*
Fernald, L., Gertier, P., and Neufeld, L. (2008). Role of cash in conditional cash transfer for programs of child health, growth, and development: An analysis of Mexico's opportunidades. *Lancet*, 371, 828–837.
27. *Book on fMRI research:*
Satel, S. and Lillienfeld, S. (2013). *Brainwashed: The Seductive Appeal of Mindless Neuroscience.* New York: Basic Books.
28. *Satel and Lillienfeld quotation:*
Satel, S. and Lillienfeld, S. (2013). *Brainwashed: The Seductive Appeal of Mindless Neuroscience.* New York: Basic Books. (Introduction).
29. *fMRI overinterpretation:*
Eklund, A., Nichols, T. and Knuttson, H. (2016). Cluster failure: Why fMRI inferences for spacial extent have inflated false-positive rates. *Proceedings of the National Academy of Sciences of the United States of America*, 113, 7900–7905. DOI: 10.1073/pnas.1602413113.
30. *Dead salmon study:*
Bennet, C., Wolford, G. and Miller, M. (2009). The principled control of false positives in neuroimaging. *Social Cognitive and Affective Science*, 4, 417–422.
31. *Quotations from fMRI scientists:*
Zimmer, C. (2014). The new science of the brain. *National Geographic*, February 2014, 36–43.
32. *Frances quotation:*
Frances, A. (2014). *Saving Normal: An Insider's Revolt against Out-of-Control Psychiatric Diagnosis, DSM-V, Big Pharma and the Medicalization of Ordinary Life.* New York: William Morrow (p. 19).
33. *Satel and Lilienfeld quotation:*
Satel, S. and Lilienfeld, S. (2013). *Brainwashed: The Seductive Appeal of Mindless Neuroscience.* New York: Basic Books (pp. xix).

Chapter 5: Measuring Antidepressant Effectiveness: STAR*D

1. *Antidepressants/placebos:*
   a. Elkin, I., Shea, T., Watkins, J., Imber, S., Sotsky, S., Collins, J., Glass, D., Pilkonis, P., Leber, W., Docherty, J., Fiester, S. and Parloff, M. (1989). NIMH treatment of depression collaborative research program: I. General effectiveness of treatments. *Archives of General Psychiatry*, 46, 971–982.
   b. Shea, M., Elkin, I., Imber, S., Sotsky, S., Watkins, J., Collins, J., Pilkonis, P., Beckham, E., Glass, D., Dolan, R. and Parloff, M. (1992). Course of depressive symptoms over follow-up: Findings from the National Institute of Health treatment of depression collaborative research program. *Archives of General Psychiatry*, 49, 782—787.
   c. Antonuccio, D., Danton, W., DeNelsky, G., Greenberg, R. and Gordon, J. (1999). Raising questions about antidepressants. *Psychotherapy and Psychosomatics*, 68, 3–14.
   d. Antonuccio, D. and Kirsch, I. (2000). The rumble in Reno: The psychosocial perspective in depression. *Psychiatric Times*, 17, 24–28. http://www.mhsource.com/pt/p000824.html.
   e. Kirsch, I., Scoboria, A. and Moore, T. (2002). Antidepressants and placebos: Secrets, revelations, and unanswered questions. *Prevention and Treatment*, 5, 2002b. http://journals.apa.org/prevention/volume5/pre0050033r.html.
   f. Kirsch, I., Moore, T., Scoboria, A., and Nicholls, S. (2002). The emperor's new drugs: An analysis of antidepressant medication data submitted to the U. S. Food and Drug Administration. *Prevention and Treatment*, 23, (2002a). http://journals.apa.org/prevention/volume5.
   g. Antonuccio, D., Danton, W., DeNelsky, G., Greenberg, R. and Gordon, J. (1999). Raising questions about antidepressants. *Psychotherapy and Psychosomatics*, 68, 3–14.
   h. Kirsch, I., Scoboria, A. and Moore, T. (2002). Antidepressants and placebos: Secrets, revelations, and unanswered questions. *Prevention and Treatment*, 5, 2002b.
   i. Moncrieff, J., Wessely, S. and Hardy, R. (2001). Antidepressants using active placebos. (Cochrane Review). *Cochrane Data Base Systematic Review*, 2, CD 003012.

j. Bockting, C., Schene, A., Spinhoven, P., Koeter, M., Wouters, L., Huyser, J. Kamphuis, J., and The DELTA Study Group. (2005). Preventing relapse/recurrence in recurrent depression with cognitive therapy: A randomized controlled trial. *Journal of Consulting and Clinical Psychology*, 73, 647–657.
k. Krystal, J., Rosenheck, R., Cramer, J., Vessicchio, J. and Jones, K. (2011). Adjunctive risperidone treatment for antidepressant-resistant symptoms of chronic military servicerelated PTSD: A randomized trial. *Journal of the American Medical Association*, 306(5), 493–502. DOI: 10.1001/jama.2011.1080.
l. Moore, T. (1999). It's what's in your head. *Washingtonian*, October 1999, 45–49.
m. Wolfe, S. (2014). How effective are antidepressants for depression? *Worst Pills, Best Pills News*, 20, February 2014.
n. Lacasse, J. and Leo, J. (November 8, 2005). Serotonin and depression: A disconnect between the advertisements and the scientific literature. *PLOS Medicine*, 2.

2. Antonuccio:

a. Antonuccio, D., Danton, W., DeNelsky, W., Greenberg, R. and Gordon, J. (1999). Raising questions about antidepressants, *Psychotherapy and Psychosomatics*, 68, 3–14.
b. Walsh, B., Seidman, S., Sysko, R. and Gould, M. (2002). Placebo response in studies of major depression. *Journal of the American Medical Association*, 287, 1840–1847.
c. Turner, E., Matthews, A., Linardatos, E., Tell, R. and Rosenthal, R. (2008). Selective publication of antidepressant trials and its influence on apparent efficacy. *New England Journal of Medicine*, 358, 252–260.
d. Mengartner, M. (2017). Methodological flaws, conflicts of interest, and Scientific fallacies: Implications for evaluation of antidepressants' efficacy and harm. *Frontiers in Psychiatry*, 8, 275.

3. *Supportive studies*:

a. Dwan, K., Deculier, E., Easterbrook, P., Elm, E., Gamble, C., Ghersi, D., Ioannidis, J., Simes, J. and Williamson, P. (2008). Systematic review of the empirical evidence of study publication bias and outcome reporting bias. *PLOS One*, 3, e3081. DOI: 10.1371/journal.pone.0003081.

b. Ebrahim, S., Bance, S., Athale, A., Malachowski, C. and Ioannidis, J. (2016). Meta-analyses with industry involvement are massively published and report no caveats for antidepressants. *Journal of Clinical Epidemiology*, 70, 155–163.
c. Moncrieff, J. and Kirsch, I. (2015). Empirically derived criteria cast doubt on the clinical significance of antidepressant-placebo differences. *Contemporary Clinical Trials*, 43, 60–62.
d. Ionnidis, J. (2008). Effectiveness of antidepressants: An evidence myth constructed from a thousand randomized trials? *Philosophy, Ethics, and Humanities in Medicine*, 3, 14. DOI: 10.1186/1747-5341-3-14.
e. Moncrieff, J. (2007). Are antidepressants as effective as claimed? No, they are not effective at all. *Canadian Journal of Psychiatry*, 52, 96–97.
f. Hrobjartsson, A., Thomsen, A., Emanuelsson, F., Tendal, B., Hilden, J., Boutron, I., Ravaud, P. and Brorson, S. (2013). Observer bias in randomized clinical trials with measurement scale outcomes: A systematic review of trials with both blinded and nonblinded assessors. *Canadian Medical Association Journal*, 185, 201–211.
g. Moncrieff, J. and Kirsch I. (2005). Efficacy of antidepressants in adults. *British Medical Journal*, 331, 155–157.
h. Melander, H., Rastad, J., Meijer, G. and Beermann, B. (2003). Evidence b(i)ased medicine—Selective reporting from studies sponsored by the pharmaceutical industry. *British Medical Journal*, 326, 1171–1173.
i. Spielman, S. and Kirsch, I. (2014). Drug approval and drug effectiveness. *Annual Review of Psychology*, 10, 741–766.
j. Every-Palmer, S. (2014). How evidence-based medicine is failing due to biased trials and selective publication. *Journal of Evaluation in Clinical Practice*. http://doi.org/101111/jep.12147.
k. Friedman, D. (2010). Lies, damned lies, and medical science. *The Atlantic*, November 2010.

4. *Lancet study:*
   a. Cipriani, A., Furukawa, T., Salanti, G., Chaimani, A., Atkinson, L. and Ogama, Y. (2018). Comparative efficacy and acceptability of 21 antidepressant drugs for the acute treatment of adults with major depressive disorder; a systematic review and network meta-analysis. *The Lancet*. DOI: https://doi.org/10.1016/S0140-6736(17)32802-7.
   b. Sifferlin, S. (2018). These antidepressants are most effective, study says. *Time*, February 21, 2018.

c. Neuroskeptic. (2018). About that new antidepressant study. *Discover Magazine*, February 24, 2018.

5. *NIMH, 1989:*
   Elkin, I., Shea, T., Watkins, J., Imber, S., Sotsky, S., Collins, J., Glass, D., Pilkonis, P., Leber, W., Docherty, J., Fiester, S. and Parloff, M. (1989). NIMH treatment of depression collaborative research program: I. General effectiveness of treatments. *Archives of General Psychiatry*, 46, 971–982.
6. *NIMH follow-up study, 1992*:
   a. Shea, M., Elkin, I., Imber, S., Sotsky, S., Watkins, J., Collins, J., Pilkonis, P., Beckham, E., Glass, D., Dolan, R. and Parloff, M. (1992). Course of depressive symptoms over follow-up: Findings from the National Institute of Health treatment of depression collaborative research program. *Archives of General Psychiatry*, 49, 782–787.
   b. Leventhal, A. and Antonuccio, D. (2009). On chemical imbalances, antidepressants, and the diagnosis of depression. *Ethical Human Psychology and Psychiatry*, 11, 199–214.
   c. Fournier, J., deRubeis, R., Hollon, S., Dimidjian, S., Amsterdam, J., Shelton, R. and Fawcett, J. (2010). Antidepressant drug effects and depression severity: A patient level meta-analysis. *JAMA*, 303, 47–53.
7. *2018 JAMA study*:
   Qato, D., Ozenberger, K. and Olfson, M. (2018). Prevalence of prescription medications with depression as a potential adverse effect among adults in the United States. *Journal of the American Medical Association*, 319, 2289–2298.
8. *Active placebo studies:*
   a. Greenberg, R. and Fisher, S. (1989). Examining antidepressant effectiveness: findings, ambiguities, and some vexing puzzles. In S. Fisher and R. Greenberg (Eds.), *The Limits of Biological Treatments for Psychological Distress.* Hillside, NJ: Lawrence Erlbaum Associates.
   b. White, K., Kando, J., Park, T., Waternaux, C. and Brown, W. (1992). Side effects and the "blindability" of clinical drug trials. *American Journal of Psychiatry*, 149, 173.
   c. Kirsch, I. (2014). Antidepressants and the placebo effect. *Z. Psychology*, 222(3), 128–134. DOI: 10.1027/2151-2604/a000176.
   d. Moncrieff, J. (2003). A comparison of antidepressant trials using active and inert placebos. *International Journal of Methods in Psychiatric Research*, 12, 117–127.

9. *Harvard Mental Health Letter:*
MacDonald, A. (2010). New Insights into treatment-resistant depression. Harvard Mental Health Letter, (2008). Finding the right depression medication. December 9, 2010.
10. *DSM protocol:*
Rush, A., Fava, M., Wisnewski, S., Lavori, P., Trivedi, M., Sackeim, H., Thase, M., Nierenberg, A., Quitkin, F., Kashner, T., Kupfer, D., Rosenbaum, J., Alpert, J., Stewart, J., McGrath, P., Biggs, M., Wilson, K. and Lebowitz, B. (2004). Sequenced treatment alternatives to relieve depression (STAR*D); Rationale and design. *Controlled Clinical Trials*, 25, 119–142.
11. *STAR*D Study publications:*
   a. Trivedi, M., Rush, A., Wisnewski, S., Nierenberg, A., Warden, D., Ritz, L., Norquist, G., Howland, R., Lebowitz, B., McGrath, P., Wilson, K., Biggs, M., Balasubramani, G. and Fava, M. (2006). Evaluation of outcomes with citalopram for depression using measurement-based care in STAR*D: implications for clinical practice. *American Journal of Psychiatry*, 163, 28–40.
   b. Rush, A., Trivedi, M., Wisnewski, S., Stewart, J., Nierenberg, A., Thase, M., Ritz, L., Biggs, M., Warden, D., Luther, J., Wilson, K. and Niederehe, G. (2006). Bupropion-SR, sertraline, or venlafaxine-XR after failure of SSRIs for depression. *New England Journal of Medicine*, 354, 1232–1242.
   c. Trivedi, M., Fava, M., Wisnewski, S., Thase, M., Quitkin, F., Warden, D., Ritz, L., Nierenberg, A., Lebowitz, B., Biggs, M., Luther, J. and Wilson K. (2006). Medication augmentation after the failure of SSRIs for depression. *New England Journal of Medicine*, 354, 1243–1252.
   d. Fava, M., Rush, J., Wisnewski, S., Nierenberg, A., Alpert, J., McGrath, P., Thase, M., Warden, D., Biggs, M., Luther, J., Niederehe, G. and Ritz, L. (2006). A comparison of mirtazapine and nortriptyline following two consecutive failed medication treatments for depressed outpatients: A STAR*D report. *American Journal of Psychiatry*, 163, 1161–1172.
   e. Nierenberg, A., Fava, M., Trivedi, M., Wisnewski, S., Thase, M., McGrath, P., Alpert, J., Warden, D., Luther, J., Niederehe, G., Lebowitz, B., Wilson, K. and Rush, A. (2006). A comparison of lithium and T3 augmentation following two failed medication

treatments for depression: A STAR*D report. *American Journal of Psychiatry*, 163, 1519–1530.

f. McGrath, P., Stewart, J., Fava, M., Trivedi, M., Wisnewski, S., Nierenberg, A., Thase, M., Davis, L., Biggs, M., Wilson, K., Luther, J., Niederehe, G., Warden, D. and Rush, A. (2006). Tranylcypromine versus venflaxaline plus mirtazapine following three failed antidepressant medication trials for depression: A STAR*D report. *American Journal of Psychiatry*, 163, 1531–1541.

g. Rush, A., Trivedi, M., Wisnewski, S., Nierenberg, A., Stewart, J., Warden, D., Niederehe, G., Thase, M., Lavori, P., Lebowitz, B., McGrath, P., Rosenbaum, J., Sackeim, H., Kupfer, D., Luther, J. and Fava, M. (2006). Acute and longer-term outcomes in depressed patients requiring one or several treatment steps: A STAR*D report. *American Journal of Psychiatry*, 163, 1905–1917.

12. *Kirsch's 2018 reanalysis of STAR*D data*:
Kirsch, I., Medina, T., Pigott, H. and Johnson, B. (2018). Do outcomes of clinical trials resemble those "real world" patients? A reanalysis of the STAR*D antidepressant set. *Psychology of Consciousness: Theory, Research, and Practice*, 5, 339–345.

13. *Our critiques of the STAR*D study:*
   a. Boren, J., Leventhal, A. and Pigott, H. (2009). Just how effective are antidepressant medications? Results of a major new study. *Journal of Contemporary Psychotherapy*, 39, 93–100.
   b. Pigott, H., Leventhal, A., Alter, G. and Boren, J. (2010). Efficacy and effectiveness of antidepressants: Current status of research. *Psychotherapy and Psychosomatics*, 79, 267–279.
   c. Pigott, H. (2011). STAR*D: A tale and trail of bias. *Ethical Human Psychology and Psychiatry*, 13, 6–28.

14. *Pigott on NIMH STAR*D authors*:
Pigott, H. (2011). A tale and trail of bias. *Ethical Human Psychology and Psychiatry*, 13, 6–28.

15. *Moncrieff quotation*:
Moncrieff, J. (2018). Results of world's largest antidepressant study look dismal. October 12, 2018.

16. *Planck quotation:*
Planck, M. (1909). *Eight Lectures on Theoretical Physics*. Columbia University.

17. *Ioannidis quotation:*
Jacobson, R. (2015). Many antidepressant studies found tainted by pharma company influence. *Scientific American*, October 21, 2015.
18. *Gabrieli*:
Gabrieli, J. (2018). Brain scans may predict optimal mental health treatments. *Scientific American*, March 2018.
19. *Friedman in NY Times*:
Friedman, R. (2017). LSD to cure depression? not so fast. *The New York Times*, February 13, 2017.
20. *Aviv in New Yorker*:
Aviv, R. (2019). Bitter pill. *The New Yorker*. April 8, 2019.
21. *Insel to researchers:*
Insel, T. (2009). Disruptive insights in psychiatry: Transforming a clinical discipline. *Journal of Clinical Investigation*, 119 (4), 700–705.
22. *Journal of Clinical Epidemiology:*
Ebrahim, S. (2016). Meta-analyses with industry involvement are massively published and report no caveats for antidepressants. *Journal of Clinical Epidemiology*, 70, 155–163.
23. *Antonuccio and Healy*:
Antonuccio, D. and Healy, D. (2112). Relabeling the medications we call antidepressants. *Scientifica*, 2012, Article ID 965908. DOI: 10.6064/2012/965908.

Chapter 6: Drug Effects and Placebo Effects

1. *Placebos and hypnosis:*
Kirsch, I. (1999). Hypnosis and placebos: Response expectancy as a mediator of suggestion effects. *Ankles de psicologia*, 15, 99–110.
2. *Kirsch's book:*
Kirsch, I. (2011). *The Emperor's New Drugs: Exploding the Antidepressant Myth*. New York: Basic Books.
3. *Kirsch's first study:*
Kirsch, I. and Sapirstein, G. (1998). Listening to Prozac by hearing placebo: A meta-analysis of antidepressant medication. *Prevention and Treatment*, Article 0002a; (1998). http://www.journals.apa.org/prevention/volumeIpre0010002a.html

4. *Very small drug effect;*
   Kirsch, I. (2002). Yes, there *is* a placebo effect, but is there a powerful antidepressant drug effect? *Prevention and Treatment*, 5. http://journals.apa.org/prevention/volume5/pre0050022i.html
5. *Kirsch's Analysis of SSRI Clinical Trials:*
   a. Kirsch, I., Moore, T., Scoboria, A. and Nicholls, S. (2002). The emperor's new drugs: an analysis of antidepressant medication data submitted to the U. S. Food and Drug Administration. *Prevention and Treatment*, 23 (2002a). http://www.journals.apa.org/prevention/volume5/pre0050023a.html.
   b. Kirsch, I., Scoboria, A. and Moore, T. (2002). Antidepressants and placebos: Secrets, revelations, and unanswered questions. *Prevention and Treatment*, 5, 2002b. http://journals.apa.org/prevention/volume5/pre0050033r.html.
   c. Antonuccio, D., Burns, D. and Danton, W. (2002). Antidepressants: A triumph of marketing over science? *Prevention and Treatment*, 5. http://journals.apa.org/prevention/volume 5/pre0050025c.html.
   d. Wolfe, S. (2014). How effective are antidepressants for depression? *Worst Pills, Best Pills*, 20; www.worstpills.org. February 2014.
6. *Moore quotation:*
   Moore, T. (1999). It's what's in your head. *The Washingtonian*, October 1999, 45–49.
7. *"Dirty little secret:"*
   Hollon, S., DeRubeis, R., Shelton, R. and Weiss, B. (2002). The emperor's new drugs: Effect size and moderation effects. *Prevention and Treatment*, 5, posted July 15, 2002. http://journals.apa.org/prevention/volume5/pre0050028c.html.
8. *Kirsch, 2008:*
   Kirsch, I., Deacon, B., Medina, T., Scoboria, A., Moore, T. and Johnson, B. (2008). Initial severity and antidepressant benefits: A meta-analysis of data submitted to the food and drug administration. *PLOS Medicine*, February 26, 2008: DOI: 10.137/journal.pmed.0050045.
9. *Supportive research:*
   a. Ioannidis, J. (2008). Effectiveness of antidepressants: An evidence myth constructed from a thousand randomized trials? *Philosophy, Ethics, and Humanities in Medicine*, 14. https://doi.org/10.1186/1747-5341-3-14.

b. Carroll, A. (2018). New study tilts the debate over antidepressants. *New York Times*, March 13, 2018, A 15.

c. Moncrieff, J. and Kirsch, I. (2015). Empirically derived criteria cast doubt on the clinical significance of antidepressant-placebo differences. *Contemporary Clinical Trials*, 43, 60–62.

d. Moncrieff, J. (2007). Are antidepressants effective? No, they are not effective at all. *Canadian Journal of Psychiatry*, 52, 96–97.

e. Hengartner, M. (2017). Methodological flaws, conflicts of interest, and Scientific fallacies: Implications for evaluation of antidepressants' effectiveness and harm. *Frontiers in Psychiatry*, 8, 275.

f. Moncrieff, J. and Kirsch, I. (2005). Efficacy of antidepressants in adults. *British Medical Journal*, 331, 155–157.

g. Kirsch, I. and Moncrieff, J. (2007). Clinical trials and the response rate illusion. *Contemporary Clinical Trials*, 28, 348–351.

h. Jacobsen, J., Katakam, K., Schou, A., Hellmuth, S., Stallknecht, S., Moller, K., Iversen, M., Banke, M., Petersen, I., Klingenberg, L., Krogh, J., Ebert, S., Timm, A., Lindschou, J. and Gluud, C. (2017). Selective serotonin reuptake inhibitors versus placebo in patients with major depressive disorder. A systematic review with meta-analysis and Trial Sequential Analysis. *BMC Psychiatry*, 17, 58.

10. *The Hamilton Scale:*

a. Hamilton, M. (1967). Development of a rating scale for primary depressive illness. *British Journal of Social and Clinical Psychology*, 6, 278–296.

b. Hamilton, M. (1980). Rating depressive patients. *Journal of Clinical Psychiatry*, 41, 21–24.

11. *NICE Guidelines:*

National Institute for Health and Care Excellence: *Clinical Guidelines*, 2003.

12. *Absence of drug/placebo difference:*

a. Moncrieff, J. and Kirsch, I. (2015). Empirically derived criteria cast doubt on the clinical significance of antidepressant-placebo differences. *Contemporary Clinical Trials*. http://dx.doi.org/10.1016/j.cct.2015.05.005

b. Moncrieff, J. (July 16, 2005). Efficacy of antidepressants in adults. *British Medical Journal*, 155–157.

c. Hengartner, M. and Ploderl, M. (October 2018). Statistically significant antidepressant-placebo differences on subjective symptom-rating scales do not prove that the drugs work: Effect size and method bias matter!, *Frontiers in Psychiatry*. https://doi.org/10.3389/fpsyt.2018.00517

13. *Lancet study*:
    a. Cipriani, A., Furukawa, T., Salanti, G., Chaimani, A., Atkinson, L. and Ogawa, Y. (2018). Comparative efficacy and acceptability of 21 antidepressant drugs for the acute treatment of adults with major depressive disorder; a systematic review and network meta-analysis. *The Lancet*. DOI: https://doi.org/10.1016/S0140-6736(17)32802-7.
    b. Sifferlin, S. (2018). These antidepressants are most effective, study says. *Time*, February 21, 2018.
    c. Neuroskeptic. (2018). About that new antidepressant study. *Discover Magazine*, February 24, 2018.
    d. Kirsch, I. and Moncrieff, J. (2007). Clinical trials and the response rate illusion. *Contemporary Clinical Trials*, 28, 348–351. http://dx.doi.org/10.1016/j.cct.2006.10.012
    e. Hengartner, M. (2017). Methodological flaws, conflicts of interest, and scientific fallacies. *Frontiers in Psychiatry*, 8, Mini Review. December 2017. doi:10.3389/fpsyt.2017.00275.
14. *Severity*:
    a. Shea, M., Elkin, I., Imber, S., Sotsky, S., Watkins, J., Collins, J., Pilkonis, P., Beckham, E., Glass, D., Dolan, R. and Parloff, M. (1992). Course of depressive symptoms over follow-up: Findings from the National Institute of Health treatment of depression collaborative research program. *Archives of General Psychiatry*, 49, 782–787.
    b. Fournier, J, DeRubeis, R., Hollon, S., Dimidjian, S., Amsterdam, J., Shelton. R., Fawcett, J. (January 6, 2010). *JAMA*, 303(1), 47–53. DOI: 10.1001/jama 2009.1943.
15. *Psilocybin:*
    Klein, E. (2021). Can mushrooms heal us? *New York Times*, Sunday Review, March 21, 2021.
16. *Groopman quotation*:
    Groopman, J. (2018). The elusive artificial heart. *New York Review of Books, LXV*, September 28, 2018.
17. *Sharon Begley:*
    Begley, S. (2010). The depressing news about antidepressants. *Newsweek*, February 8, 2010, 35–41.
18. *Margaret Heffernan book:*

Heffernan, M. (2011). *Willful Blindness: Why We Ignore the Obvious at Our Peril.* New York: Walker.

19. *Carey:*
    Carey, B. (2017). England's mental health experiment: No-cost talk therapy. *New York Times*, July 24, 2017.

Chapter 7: Antidepressant Drug Safety

1. *Liver toxicity, movement disorders, and hospitalizations for induced psychoses:*
   a. Volcan, C., Corruble, E., Naveau, S. and Perlemuter, G. (2014). Antidepressant-induced liver injury: A review for clinicians. *American Journal of Psychiatry*, 171, 404–415.
   b. Gerber, P. and Lind, L. (1998). Movement disorders, such as akathisia, Parkinson's Disease, dystonia (acute rigidity) dyskinesia (abnormal involuntary movements) and tradeoff dyskinesia. *American Pharmacotherapy*, 32, 692–698.
   c. Preda, A. (2001). Antidepressant-associated mania and psychoses resulting in psychiatric admissions. *Journal of Clinical Psychiatry*, 62, 30–33.
   d. Frances, A. (2011). Antidepressant use has gone crazy: Bad news from the CDC. *Psychiatric Times*, October 28, 2011.
   e. De Vries, Y., Roest, A., Beijers, L., Turner, E. and DeJonge, P. (2016). Bias in the reporting of harms in clinical trials of second generation antidepressants for depression and anxiety: A meta-analysis. *European Neuropharmacology*, 26, 1752–1759.
2. *Adverse effects of antidepressants:*
   a. Moncrieff, J. and Cohen, D. (2006). Do antidepressants cure or create abnormal brain states? *PLOS Medicine*, 3, 961–965.
   b. Horgan, J. (2016). Psychiatrists must face possibility that medications hurt more than they help. *Scientific American*, December 13, 2016.
   c. Whitaker, R. (2005). Anatomy of an epidemic: Psychiatric drugs and the astonishing rise of mental illness in America. *Ethical Human Psychology and Psychiatry*, 7, Spring 2005.
   d. Fava, G. (2003). Can long-term treatment with antidepressant drugs worsen the course of depression? *Clinical Psychiatry*, 64, 123–133.
3. *Sexual dysfunction:*

Montego, A., Llorca, G., Izquierdo, J. and Villademoros, F. (2001). Incidence of sexual dysfunction associated with antidepressant agents: A prospective multi-center study of 1022 outpatients. *Journal of Clinical Psychiatry*, 62(Suppl 3), 5–9.

4. *Serotonin syndrome:*
   Brody, J. (2007). Personal health: A mix of medicines that can be lethal. *New York Times*, February 27, 2007.
5. *SSRIs, Bone Density, Falls:*
   a. Diem, S., Blackwell, T., Stone, K., Yaffe, K., Haney, E., Bliziotes, M. and Ensrud, K. (2007). Use of antidepressants and rates of hip bone loss in older women. *Archives of Internal Medicine*, 167, 188–194.
   b. Carome, M. (2017). Drugs that increase the risk of falling. *Worst Pills, Best Pills News*, January 2017.
   c. Johnell, K., Bergman, J. and Salmi, P. (2017). Psychotropic drugs and the risk of fall injuries, hospitalizations, and mortality among older adults. *International Journal of Geriatric Psychiatry*, 32, 414–420.
6. *SSRIs and first-time seizures:*
   Keller, D. (2015). Antidepressants linked to first-time seizures. *European Psychiatric Association, 23rd Congress*, Vienna, Austria, April 6, 2015.
7. *Direct to consumer advertising:*
   a. Kravitz, R., Epstein, R., Feldman, M., Franz, C., Azari, R., Wilkes, M., Hinton, L. and Franks, P. (2005). Influence of patient's requests for direct-to-consumer advertised antidepressants: A randomized clinical trial. *Journal of the American Medical Association*, 293, 1995–2002, 1.
   b. Greene, J. A. and Herzberg, D. (2010). Hidden in plain sight: 2010. *American Journal of Public Health*, 100(5), 793–803.
   c. Ventola, C. (October 2011). Direct-to-consumer pharmaceutical advertising: Therapeutic or toxic? *Pharmacy and Therapeutics*, 669–674, 681–684.*d.* Shaw, A. (2008). Direct-to-consumer advertising of pharmaceuticals: DTC regulation. *Pro Quest*, March 2008.
   e. Kravitz, R. L., Epstein, R., Feldman, M., Franz, C., Azari, R., Wilkes, M., Hinton, L. and Franks, P. (2005). Influence of patient's requests for direct-to-consumer advertised antidepressants: A randomized controlled trial. *Journal of the American Medical Association*, 293, 1995–2002.
8. *Babies in utero:*

a. Carey, B. (2005). Treatment of depression in pregnancy affects babies. *New York Times*, February 4, 2005, A5.
b. Rabin, R. (2014). Pills may put babies at risk. *New York Times*, September 2, 2014, D4.
c. Domar, A., Moragianni, V., Ryley, D. and Urato, A. (2012). The risks of selective serotonin reuptake inhibitor use in infertile women: A review of the impact on fertility, pregnancy, neonatal health, and beyond. *Human Reproduction*, 28, 160–171.
d. Mortensen, J., Olsen, J., Larsen, H., Bendsen, J., Obel, C. and Sorensen, H. (2003). Psychomotor development in children exposed in utero to benzodiazepines, antidepressants, and anti-epileptics. *European Journal of Epidemiology*, 18, 769–771.
e. Eke, A.C., Saccone, G. and Berghella V. (2016). Selective serotonin reuptake inhibitor (SSRI) use during pregnancy and risk of preterm birth: A systematic review and meta-analysis. *Journal of Gynecology*, 123, 12. DOI: 10.1111/1471-0528.14144.
f. Stolzer, J. (2010). The risks associated with maternal antidepressant use during prenatal and postnatal stages of development. *Ethical Human Psychology and Psychiatry*, 12, 86–98.
g. Huybrechts, K., Sanghani, R., Avorn, J. and Urato, A. (March 26, 2014). Preterm birth and antidepressant medication use during pregnancy: A systematic review and meta-analysis. *PLOS One*. DOI.org/10.1371/journal.pone.0092778.
h. Hanley, G. (July 22, 2014). Patterns of psychotropic medicine use in pregnancy in the United States from 2006 to 2011 among women with private insurance. *BMC Pregnancy Childbirth*, 14(242). DOI: 10.1186/1471-2393-14-242.
i. Clements, C., Castro, V., Blementhal, S., Rosenfield, H., Murphy, S., Fava, M., Erb, J., Churchill, S., Kaimal, A., Doyle, A., Robinson, E., Smoller, J., Kohane, I. and Perlis, R. (June 2015). Prenatal antidepressant exposure is associated with risk of attention-deficit hyperactivity disorder but not autism spectrum disorder in a large health system. *Moi Psychiatry*, 20(6), 727–304. DOI: 10.1038/mp. 2014.90 Epub 2014 August 26.
j. Berard, A, Zhao, J. and Odile, S. (January 12, 2017). Antidepressant use during pregnancy and risk of major congenital malformations in a cohort of depressed pregnant women: An updated analysis of the

Quebec Pregnancy Cohort. *British Medical Journal, 7*(1), e013372. DOI: 10.1136/bmjopen-2016-0013372.

k. Anderson, K., Lind, J. and Simeone, M. (2020). Maternal use of specific antidepressant medications during early pregnancy and the risk of selected birth defects. *JAMA Psychiatry*, 77(12), 1246–1255. Doi:10.10.1001/jamapsychiatry.2020.2453.

l. Dubovsky, S. (2020). We still don't know which antidepressants are riskiest during pregnancy. *New England Journal of Medicine Journal Watch*. Review of JAMA Psychiatry 2020, August 5.

9. *Autism and Antidepressants during pregnancy*:
   a. Boukhris, T., Sheehy, O., Mottron, L. and Berard, A. (2015). Antidepressant use during pregnancy and the risk of autism spectrum disorder in children. *JAMA Pediatrics*, do:10.1001/jamapediatrics.2015.3356. Published online December 14, 2015.
   b. Harrington, R. (2014). Use and offspring with autism spectrum disorder or developmental delay. *Pediatrics*, www.pediatrics.org/cg/doi/10.1542/peds.2013-3406.
   c. Rabin, R. (2014). Pills may put babies at risk. *Science Times: New York Times*, September 2, 2014, D4. *British Medical Journal Open*, 4(4), e006135. DOI: 10.1136/bmjopen-2014-006135.
10. *Women and antidepressants; post-partum depression:*
    a. Wehrein, P. (2011). Astounding increase in antidepressant use by Americans. *Harvard Health Publishing*, October 20, 2011.
    b. Pratt, L., Brody, D. and Gu, Q. (2011). Antidepressant use in persons aged 12 and over: United States, 2005–2008. *National Center for Health Statistics*, Brief No 76. October 2011.
    c. Robertson, E., Grace, T., Wallington, T. and Stewart, D. (2004). Antenatal risk factors for postpartum depression: Synthesis of recent literature. *General Hospital Psychiatry*, 26, 289–295.
11. *Off-label prescribing of antidepressants and anti-psychotic drugs:*
    a. Comparative efficacy and tolerability of antidepressants for major depressive disorder in children and adolescents: a network meta-analysis, *The Lancet*, (2016). http://dx.doi.org/10.1016/50140-6736(16)30385-3.
    b. Davenport, L. (2014). More than 50% of antipsychotics prescribed off label. *Medscape*, December 30, 2014.
    c. Vedantam, S. (2004). Antidepressant use in children soars despite efficacy doubts. *Washington Post*, April 18, 2004, A10, Col. 1.

   d. Carey, B. (2006). Use of antipsychotics by young people in U. S. rose fivefold in decade, researchers report. *New York Times*, June 6, 2006, A18.
   e. Schwarz, A. (2015). Still in a crib, yet being given antipsychotics, *New York Times*, December 11, 2015, A1.
   f. Marston, L., Nazareth, I., Petersen, I., Walters, K. and Osborn, D. (2014). Prescribing of antipsychotics in UK primary care: A cohort study. *British Medical Journal*. http://dx.doi.org/10.1136/bmjopen-2014-006135.
   g. Roberts, E. (2006). A rush to medicate young minds. *Washington Post*, October 8, 2006, B7.
   h. Wolfe, S. (2013). Youth stimulant abuse at record high. *Public Citizen Health Letter*, 29, August 2013.
   i. Critser, G. (2005). *Generation Rx*. Boston: Houghton Mifflin (pp. 46—48).
   j. Flamm, H. (2018). Why are nursing homes drugging dementia patients? *Washington Post*, jOutlook, August 12, 2018, B3.
   k. Roberts, J. (2006). A rush to medicate young minds. *Washington Post*, October 8, 2006, B7.

12. *Negative side effects of antidepressants:*
   a. Preda, A., MacLean, R., Mazure, C. and Bowers, M. (January 2001). Antidepressant associated mania and psychoses resulting in psychiatric admissions. *Journal of Clinical Psychiatry*, 6 (1), 30–33.
   b. Brumbilla, P., Cipriani, A., Hotopf, M. and Barbui, C. (2005). Side-effect profiles of fluoxetine in comparison with other SSRIs, tricyclic and newer antidepressants: A meta-analysis of clinical trial data. *Pharmacopsychiatry*, 38(2), 69–77.
   c. Horgan, J. (2016). Psychiatrists must face possibility that medications hurt more than they help. *Scientific American*. December 13, 2016.
   d. Toni. (2005). Psychiatric drugs: Chemical warfare on humans. Interview with Robert Whitaker, August 31, 2005.
   e. Hoehn, S., Harris, G., Pearlson, G., Cox, C., Machlin, S. and Camargo, E. (1991). A fluoxetine (prozac) induced frontal lobe syndrome (apathy and indifference) in an obsessive-compulsive patient. *Journal of Clinical Psychiatry*, 52, 131–133.
   f. Fava, G. (2003). Can long-term treatment with antidepressant drugs worsen the course of depression? *Journal of Clinical Psychiatry*, 64, 123–133.

13. *Atypical antipsychotics:*
    a. Carey, B. (2006). Use of antipsychotics by young people in U.S. Rose Fivefold in Decade, researchers report. *New York Times*, June 6, 2006, A18.
    b. Carome, M. (2015). Dangerous atypical antipsychotics minimally effective for depression. *Worst Pills, Best Pills News*, 21, December 2015.
    c. Davenport, L. (2015). Antipsychotics over-prescribed in intellectually disabled? *Medscape Medical News: Psychiatry*, September 16, 2015.
    d. Sheehan, R., Hassiotis, A., Walters, K., Osborn, D., Strydom, A. and Horsfall, L. (2015). Mental illness, challenging behavior, and psychotropic drug prescribing in people with intellectual disability: UK population-based cohort study.
    e. *BMJ* 2015, 351. DOI: http://dx.doi.org/10.1136/bmj.h4326. Published September 1, 2015.
    f. *British Medical Journal Open* 2014, 4, e 006135. DOI: 10.1136 bmjopen-2014-006135.
    g. Whitaker, R. (2005). Psychiatric drugs: Chemical warfare on humans. Interview, August 31, 2005. http://www.newstarget.com/011353.html.
    h. Valenstein, E. (1998). *Blaming the Brain: The Truth about Drugs and Mental Health*. New York: The Free Press.
14. *Negative side effects of anti-psychotic drugs:*
    a. Wolfe, S. (2013). Use of atypical antipsychotics in children at all-time high. *Health Letter, Public Citizen Research Group*, April 2013.
    b. Vedantam. S. (2009). A silenced drug study creates an uproar. *Washington Post*, March 18, 2009, A6.
15. *Antidepressants, violence, and suicide:*
    a. Moore, T., Glenmullen, J. and Fuberg, C. (2010). Prescription drugs associated with violence towards others. *PLOS One*, www.plosone.org/article/info%3Adoi%2F10.137%Fjou.
    b. Healy, D. (2004). *Let Them Eat Prozac: The Unhealthy Relationship Between the Pharmaceutical Industry and Depression*. New York: New York University Press (see pp. 238–243).
    c. Miller, M., Swanson, S., Azrael, D., Pate, V. and Sturmer, T. (June 2014). Antidepressant dose, age, and risk of deliberate self-harm. *Journal of Internal Medicine*, 174(6), 899—909. DOI: 10.1001/jamainternmed.2014.1053.

d. Wolfe, S. (2007). Research as public relations: Antidepressants and suicide in youth. *Health Letter, Public Citizen Research Group*, 23, October 2007.
e. Harris, G. (2004). Antidepressant study seen to back expert. *New York Times*, August 20, 2004, A18.
f. Wise, J. (2016). Suicidality and aggression during antidepressant treatment: Systematic review and data analysis based on clinical study reports. *British Medical Journal.* BMJ, 352, 545.
g. Peng Xie. (2016). Comparative efficacy and tolerability of antidepressants for major depressive disorder: A network meta-analysis. *Lancet.* DOI: 10.1016/50140-6736(16)30385-3.
h. Brogan, K. and Loberg, K. (2016). *A Mind of Your Own.* New York: Harper Wave.
i. Whitaker, R. (2005). Psychiatric drugs: Chemical warfare on humans. Interview, August 31, 2005. http://www.newstarget.com/011353.html.
j. Yasmina Molero, Lichtenstein, P., Zetterqvist, J., Gumpert, C. and Fazel, S. (2015). Selective serotonin reuptake inhibitors and violent crime. *PLOS Medicine*, September 15, 2015.

16. *AJP and black box warnings*:
    a. Gibbons, R., Brown, H., Hur, K., Marcus, S., Bhaumik, D., Erkens, J., Herings, R. and Mann, J. (2007). Early evidence on the effects of regulators' suicidality warnings on SSRI prescriptions and suicide in children and adolescents. *American Journal of Psychiatry*, 1 September 2007. https://doi.org/10.1176/appl.ajp.2007.07030454.
    b. Gibbons, R., Brown, C., Hur, K., Marcus, S., Bhaumik, D. and Mann, J. (July 1, 2007). Relationship between antidepressants and suicide attempts: An analysis of the veterans administration data sets. *American Journal of Psychiatry*, 164.
    c. Leon, A. (2007). The revised warning for antidepressants and suicidality: Unveiling the black boxed statistical analysis. *American Journal of Psychiatry.* http://doi.org/10.1176/appl.ajp.2007.07050775.
17. *Sidney Wolfe*:
    a. Public Citizen Foundation. (2016). *Public Citizen: The Sentinel of Democracy.* Washington, DC: Doyle Printing.
    b. Juredin, J. (December 2007). The black box warning: Decreased prescriptions and increased youth suicide? *American Journal of Psychiatry.* https://doi.Org/10.1176/appi.ajp.2007.07091463.

18. *Public Citizen warning re: SSRIs and suicide*:
    Carome, M. (2020). Do not use paroxetine (Brisdelle) for treatment of hot flashes. *Worst Pills, Best Pills News*, 3, 26, March 2020.
19. *Nader quotation on Wolfe*:
    Public Citizen Foundation. (2016). *Public Citizen: The Sentinel of Democracy* (p. 45). Washington, DC: Doyle Printing.
20. *SSRIs and suicide:*
    a. Fergusson, D., Doucette, S., Glass, K., Shapiro, S., Healy, D., Hebert, P. and Hutton, B. (2005). Association between suicide attempts and selective serotonin repute inhibitors: Systematic review of randomized controlled trials. *British Medical Journal*, 330, 396.
    b. Ault, A. (1991). Health care watchdog. *Health Watch*, July/August 1991.
    c. Donovan, S., Clayton, A., Beeharry, M. and Jones, S. (2000). Deliberate self-harm and antidepressant drugs. Investigation of a possible link. *British Journal of Psychiatry*, 177, 551–556.
    d. Jick, H. and Jick, S. (2004). Antidepressants and the risk of suicidal behaviors. *Journal of the American Medical Association*, 292, 338–343.
    e. Aursnes, I., Tvete, I., Gaasemyr, J. and Natvig, B. (2005). Suicide attempts in clinical trials with Paxil randomized against placebo. *BMC Medicine*, 3, 14.
    f. Sharma, T., Guski, L., Freund, N. and Gotzsche, P. (2016). Suicidality and aggression during antidepressant treatment: systematic review and meta-analyses based on clinical study reports. *British Medical Journal*, 352. doi:10.1136/bmj.165.
    g. Healy, D. (2004). *Let Them Eat Prozac: The Unhealthy Relationship between the Pharmaceutical Industry and Depression.* New York: New York University Press (pp. 238–243).
    h. Miller, M. (June 2014). Antidepressant dose, age, and the risk of deliberate self-harm. *JAMA Internal Medicine*, 174(6), 899–909. DOI: 10.1001/jamainternmed.2014.1053.
21. *In the military:*
    a. Rosenberg, R. (2010). Army and suicides: www.dissidentvoice.org, August 3, 2010.
    b. Somashekhar, S. and Nakashima, E. (2014). Military's mental health system struggles to meet demands, needs. *Washington Post*, April 6, 2014, A3.

22. *Incomplete reporting of side effects:*
    a. Whoriskey, P. (2012). Can drug research still be trusted? *Washington Post*, November 25, 2012, A1.
    b. Vedantam, S. (2009). Silenced drug study creates an uproar. *Washington Post*, March 18, 2009.
    c. Thomas, K. (2015). Drug makers' data on side effects is called lacking in a report. *New York Times*, February 3, 2015, B3.
    d. Medscape Psychiatry. (2007). Medication errors and patient safety in mental health. September 26, 2007. (Updates can be found under *Medwatch Psychiatry*).
    e. Medscape Psychiatry. (2019). Medication errors and patient safety in mental health. March 15, 2019.
    f. Grasso, B. and Bates, D. (2003). Medication errors in psychiatry: Are patients being harmed? *Psychiatric Services*, 4, 599.
    g. Grasso, B., Shore, M., Clary, C., Eng, B., Huckshorn, K., Parks, J., Minkoff, K., Evans, S. and Golash, T. (2007). Medication errors in psychiatric care: Incidence and reduction strategies. *Medscape*, June 29, 2007.
    h. Grasso, B. (2003). Use of chart and record reviews to detect medication errors in state psychiatric hospitals. *Psychiatric Serv.*,29(8), 391–401.
    i. Thomas, K. (2015). Drug makers' data on side effects is called lacking in a report. *New York Times*, February 2, 2015.
    j. Preda, A, MacLean, R., Mazure, C. and Bowers, M. (January 2001). Antidepressant associated mania and psychoses resulting in psychiatric admissions. *Journal of Clinical Psychiatry*, 62(1), 30–33.
23. *Addictive effects of antidepressants:*
    a. Read, J., Cartwright, C. and Gibson, K. (2018). How many of 1809 antidepressant users report withdrawal effects or addiction? *International Journal of Mental Health Nursing*, 6, 1805–1815.
    b. Carey, B. and Gebeloff, R. (2016). Many people taking antidepressants discover they cannot quit. *New York Times*, April 7, 2018.
    c. Goetzsche, P. (2016). Antidepressants are addictive and increase the risk of relapse. *British Medical Journal*, 352. https:/doi.org/10.1136/bmj.i1574.
    d. Andrews, P., Kornstein, S., Halberstadt, L., Gardner, C. and Neale, M. (2011). Blue again: Perturbational effects of antidepressants, suggest monoaminergic homeostasis in major depression. *Frontiers in Psychology*, 2, 159. DOI: 10.3389/fpsy9.2011.00159

e. Healy, D. (2004). *Let Them Eat Prozac: The Unhealthy Relationship between the Pharmaceutical Industry and Depression.* New York: New York University Press.
f. Rosenbaum, J., Fava, M., Hoog, S., Ascroft, R. and Krebs, W. (1998). Selective serotonin reuptake inhibitor discontinuation syndrome: A randomized trial. *Biological Psychiatry*, 44, 77–87.
g. Fava, G., Gatti, A., Belaise, C., Guidi, J. and Offidani, E. (2015). Withdrawal symptoms after selective serotonin inhibitor discontinuation: A systematic review. *Psychotherapy and Psychosomatics*, 84, 72–81.
h. Baldessarini, R., Tondo, L. and Ghiani, C. (2010). Illness risk following rapid versus gradual discontinuation of antidepressants. *American Journal of Psychiatry*, 167, 934–941.
i. Baldessarini, R. (2014). Risks in discontinuation trials with antidepressants. *Journal of Clinical Psychiatry*, 75, 1443.
j. Gardarsdottir, H., Egberts, T., Stolker, J. and Heerdink, E. (2009). Duration of antidepressant drug treatment and its influence on risk of relapse/recurrence: Immortal and neglected time bias. *American Journal of Epidemiology*, 170, 280–285.
k. Vijapura, S., Laferton, J., Mintz, D., Kaptchuk, T. and Wolfe, D. (2016). Psychiatrists attitudes toward non-pharmacologic factors within the context of antidepressant pharmacotherapy. *Academic Psychiatry*, 40, 783–789.
l. Hengartner, M. and Ploderl, M. (2018). False beliefs in academic psychiatry: The case of antidepressant drugs. *Ethical Human Psychology and Psychiatry*, 20, 6–16.
m. Siem, B. (2020). I took antidepressants for years. Getting off them was horrific. *Washington Post*, Health Section, January 7, 2020, E5.

24. *Heather Ashton on benzodiazepines*:
    a. Ashton, H. (2002). *Benzodiazepines: How They Work and How to Withdraw*. Newcastle University. Benzo.org.uk/manual.
    b. Sheik, K. (2020). Heather Ashton, 90; Helped people quit drugs. *New York Times*, January 5, 2020, 22.
25. *JAMA on adverse main effects of antidepressants*:
    a. Qato, D., Ozenberger, K. and Olfson, M. Prevalence of prescription medications with depression as a potential adverse effect among adults in the United States. *Journal of the American Medical Association*, 319, 2289–2298.

   b. Carome, M. (2018). New research shows drugs associated with a risk of depression are widely used. *Worst Pills, Best Pills News*, October 2018, 24.

26. *Increased suicide rate*:
    Hedegard, H., Curtin, S. and Warner, M. (2017). Suicide mortality in the United States, 1999–2017. *NCHS Data Brief* No. 330, November 2018.
27. *Robert Whitaker on Medwatch*:
    Whitaker, R. (2005). *Psychiatric Drugs: Chemical Warfare in Humans.* Interview, August 3, 2005. http: //www.newstarget.com/011353.html.
28. *Glenmullen:*
    Glenmullen, J. (2000). *Prozac Backlash: Overcoming the Dangers of Prozac, Zoloft, Paxil, and Other Antidepressants with Safe, Effective, Alternatives.* New York: Simon and Schuster.
29. *Whitaker:*
    Whitaker, R. (2010). *Anatomy of an Epidemic: Magic Bullets, Psychiatric Drugs, and the Astonishing Rise of Mental Illness in America.* New York: Crown Publishers.
30. *Silverman:*
    Silverman, C. (1968). The epidemiology of depression. *American Journal of Psychiatry*, 124, 883–891.
31. *Schuyler:*
    Schuyler, D. (1974). *The Depressive Spectrum.* New York: Aronson.
32. *Hyman quotations:*
    Whitaker, R. (2005). Anatomy of an epidemic: Psychiatric drugs and the astonishing rise of mental illness in America. *Ethical Human Psychology and Psychiatry*, 7, 23–35.
33. *Long-term effects of antidepressants:*
    a. Fava, G. (1994). Can long-term treatment with antidepressant drugs worsen the outcome of depression? *Psychotherapy and Psychosomatics*, 61, 125–131.
    b. Fava, G. (2003). Do antidepressant drugs increase chronicity in affective disorders? *Journal of Clinical Psychiatry*, 64, 123–133.
    c. Moncrief, J. and Cohen, D. (2006). Do antidepressants cure or create abnormal brain states? *PLOS Medicine.* http://www.plosmedicine.org/articles/info:doi/10.1371/journal.pmed.0030240.
    d. Carome, M. (2018). New research shows drugs associated with a risk of depression are widely used. *Worst Pills, Best Pills News*, October 2018, 24.

34. *Klein quotation; Fava and STAR*D:*
Fava, G., Tomba, E. and Grandi, S. (2007). The road to recovery from depression–don't drive today with yesterday's map. *Psychotherapy and Psychosomatics*, 76, 260–265.
35. *Tobacco smoking:*
   a. US Department of Health and Human Services. (2014). *The Health Consequences of Smoking–50 Years of Progress. A Report of the Surgeon General.* Atlanta: US Department of Health and Human Services, CDC, *National Center for Chronic Disease Prevention and Health Promotion, Office of Smoking and Health.*
   b. Jha, P., Ramasundarahettige, C., Landsman, V., Rostron, B., Thun, M., Anderson, R., McAfee, T. and Peto, R. (2013). 21st century hazards of smoking and benefits of cessation in the US. *New England Journal of Medicine*, 368, 341–350.
36. *Wolfe quotation on FDA drug testing*:
Public Citizen Foundation. (2016). *Public Citizen: The Sentinel of Democracy.* Washington, DC: Doyle Printing (p. 50).
37. *Joanna Moncrief:*
Moncrief, J. and Cohen, D. (2006). Do antidepressants cure or create abnormal brain states? *PLOS Medicine.* http://www.plosmedicine.org/articles/info:doi/10.1371/journal.pmed.0030240.
38. *Robert Berezin:*
Berezin, R. (2013). *Psychotherapy of Character: The Place of Consciousness in the Theater of the Brain.* Tucson: Wheatmark.
39. *Anti-anxiety drugs:*
Bacchumber, M., Hennessy, S., Cunningham, C. and Starrels, J. (February 18, 2016). Increasing benzodiazepine prescriptions and overdose mortality in the United States, 1996–2013. *American Journal of Public Health*, e1–e3.

Chapter 8: Conflict of Interest

1. *Drug companies fund research*:
   a. Llamas, M. (2018). Big pharma's role in clinical trials. *Drugwatch*, April 19, 2018.
   b. Lexchin, J. (2003). Pharmaceutical industry sponsorship and research outcome and quality: Systematic review. *British Medical Journal*, May 31, 2003. DOI: 10.1136/bmj.326.7400.1167.

c. Flacco, M., Manzoli, L., Boccia, S., Capasso, L., Alekovska, K., Rosso, A., Scaioli, G., DeVito, C., Siliquini, R., Villari, P. and Ioannidis, J. (2015). Head-to-head randomized trials are mostly industry sponsored and almost always favor the industry sponsor. *Journal of Clinical Epidemiology*, 68, 81–820.
d. Lexchin, J., Bero, L, Djulbergovic, B. and Clark, O. (2003). Pharmaceutical industry sponsorship and research outcome and quality: Systematic review. *British Medical Journal*, 326, 1167–1170.
e. Lundh, A., Sismondo, S., Lexchin, J., Busuioc, O. and Bero, L. (2012). Industry sponsorship and research outcome. *Cochrane Database Systematic Review*, 12, MR000033. DOI: 10.1002/14651858. MR000033.pub2.
f. Melander, H., Rastad, J., Meijer, G. and Beermann, B. (2003). Evidence b(i)ased medicine—selective reporting from studies sponsored by pharmaceutical industry: Review of studies in new drug applications. *British Medical Journal*, 326, 1171–1173.
g. Bekelman, J. and Gross, C. (2003). Scope and impact of financial conflicts of interest in biomedical research: A systematic review. *Journal of the American Medical Association*, 289, 454–465.
h. Friedman, I. and Richter, E. (2004). Relationship between conflicts of interest and research results. *Journal of General Internal Medicine*, 19, 51–56.
i. Perlis, R., Perlis, C., Wu, Y., Hwang, C., Joseph, M. and Nierenberg, A. (2005). Industry sponsorship and financial conflicts of interest in the reporting of clinical trials in psychiatry. *American Journal of Psychiatry*, 162, 1957–1960.
j. Ebrahim, S., Bance, S., Athale, A., Malachowski, C. and Ioannidis, J. (2016). Meta-analyses with industry involvement are massively published and report no caveats for antidepressants. *Journal of Clinical Epidemiology*, 70, 155–163.
k. Editorial. (2018). Medicine's financial contamination. *New York Times*, September 16, 2018, 8.

2. *Petersen quotation:*
Petersen, M. (2008). *Our Daily Meds*. New York: Farrar, Straus and Giroux., pp. 192.
3. *Conflicts of interest in drug prescribing:*
a. Wolfe, S. (2007). Conflicts of interest: The hidden side of science. *Health Letter, Public Citizen Research Group*, 23, January 2007.

b. Wolfe, S. (2007). Conflicts of interest: An issue that will not go away. *Health Letter, Public Citizen*, February 2007.
c. Bazell, R. (2006). Risky Rx: Drug maker's secret strategies: Disturbing glimpse into how marketing dupe's doctors–and patients. *NBC News*, August 15, 2006.
d. Carey, B. (2006). Study cites links to firms by psychiatrists. *New York Times*, April 20, 2006, A20.
e. Editorial. (2006). Our conflicted medical journals. *New York Times*, July 23, 2006.
f. Abelson, R. (2008). Doctors show their hand: Cleveland Clinic takes steps to disclose conflicts of interest. *New York Times*, December 3, 2008, B1.
g. Editorial. (2009). Not what we call due diligence. *New York Times*, January 13, 2009, A20.
h. Couchon, D. (2000). FDA advisers tied to industry. *USA Today*, September 25, 2000. http://www.commondreamer.org/headlines/09%500.01.html.
i. Collier, R. (2009). Medical literature made to order. *Canadian Medical Association Journal*, 181, 254–256.
j. Healy, D. and Cattel, D. (2003). Interface between authorship, industry, and science in the domain of therapeutics. *British Journal of Psychiatry*, 183, 22–27.

4. *Gotzsche:*
Gotzsche, P. (2013). *Deadly Medicines and Organized Crime: How Big Pharma Has Corrupted Health Care.* London: Radcliffe Publishing Ltd.
5. *Angell quotation:*
a. Angell, M. (2011). The illusions of psychiatry: An exchange. *New York Review of Books*, August 18, 2011.
b. Angell, M. (2009). Drug companies and doctors: A story of corruption. *New York Review of Books, 56*, 8–12.
6. *Harris quotation:*
Harris, G., Carey, B., and Roberts, J. (2007). Psychiatrists, children, and drug industry's role. *New York Times*, May 10, 2007, A1.
7. *Sunshine Laws:*
Carome, M. (2014). Sunshine law exposes vast industry payments to physicians. *Worst Pills, Best Pills News, 20*, December 2014.

8. *Moynihan quotation:*
   Moynihan, R. and Cassel, A. (2005). *Selling Sickness: How the World's Biggest Pharmaceutical Companies Are Turning Us All into Patients.* Vancouver, BC: Greystone Books.
9. *British Medical Journal article:*
   Spence, D. (2011). Bad medicine: Adult attention-deficit/hyperactivity disorder. *British Medical Journal, 343*, d7244.
10. *Conflicts of interest in setting psychiatric clinical guidelines:*
    a. Cosgrove, L., Bursztajn, H., Krimsky, S., Araya, M. and Walker, J. (2009). Conflicts of interest and disclosure in the American Psychiatric Association's clinical practice guidelines, *Psychotherapy and Psychosomatics, 78*, 228–232.
    b. Elliott, C. (2015). Minnesota's medical mess. *New York Times*, May 26, 2015, A17.
    c. Costrove, L. and Krimsky, S. (2012). A comparison of DSM-IV and DSM 5 panel members' financial associations with industry: a pernicious problem persists. *PLOS Medicine* (2012), *9*, e1001190. DOI: 10.1371/ournal.pmed.1001190
11. *New York Times Editorial:*
    Pregnant women and antidepressant drugs. *New York Times*, July 23, 2006.
12. *Smith quotation:*
    a. Smith, R. (2006). The trouble with medical journals. *Journal of the Royal Society of Medicine*, 99, 115–119.
    b. Smith, R. (2005). Medical journals are an extension of the marketing arm of pharmaceutical companies. *Health Letter, Public Citizen Research Group*, 21, July 2005.
    c. Smith, R. (2005). Curbing the influence of the drug industry: A British view. *Health Letter, Public Citizen Research Group*, 21, November 2005.
13. *Rising study:*
    a. Rising, K., Bacchetti, P. and Bero, L. (2008). Reporting bias in drug trials submitted to the Food and Drug Administration: A review of publication and presentation. *PLOS Medicine*, 5, e217.
    b. Piller, C. (2021). Researchers who flout the rules. *New York Times*, April 9, 2021, A23.

14. *Turner study:*
    a. Turner, E., Matthew, A., Linardatos, E., Tell, R. and Rosenthal, R. (2008). Selective publication of antidepressant trials and its influence on apparent efficacy. *New England Journal of Medicine*, 358, 252–260.
    b. Driessen, E., Hollon, S., Bockting, C., Cuijpers, P. and Turner, E. (September 30, 2015). Does publication bias inflate the apparent efficacy of psychological treatment for major depressive disorder? A systematic review and meta-analysis of US National Institutes of Health Funded Trials. *PLOS One*. DOI: 10.1371/journal.pone. 0137864.
15. *Horton quotation:*
    Horton, R. (March 25, 2004). The dawn of McScience. *New York Review of Books*, 51, 7–9.
16. *Disease Mongering*:
    a. Heath, I. (April 2006). Combating disease mongering: Daunting but nonetheless essential. *PLOS Medicine*, 3. 10.1371/journal.pmed.0030146.
    b. Wolfe, S. (2006). The fight against disease mongering. *Health Letter, Public Citizen Health Research Group*, 22, May 2006.
    c. Rosenberg, M. (2011). Fourteen years of deceptive television drug advertising. *Health Letter, Public Citizen Health Research Group*, May 2011.
    d. Rosenberg, M. (2010). Thirteen dirty big pharma tricks that rip you off and risk your health for profit. *Public Citizen Health Research Group*, December 2010.
    e. Wolfe, S. (2005). New "diseases:" Often invented by drug industry marketing departments sell you drugs. *Health Letter, Public Citizen Health Research Group*, 21, September 2005.
    f. PLOS Medicine Editors. (May 28, 2013). The paradox of mental health: Over-treatment and under-recognition. *PLOS Medicine*. https://doi.org/10.1371/journal.pmed.1001456.
17. *Gadsden quotation*:
    Moynihan, R. and Cassels, A. (2005). *Selling Sickness: How the World's Biggest Pharmaceutical Companies Are Turning Us All into Patients*. Vancouver, BC: Greystone Books. See Prologue.
18. *Francis quotation*:
    Francis, A. (2011). Antidepressant use has gone crazy: Bad News from the CDC. *Psychiatric Times*, October 28, 2011.

19. *Bipolar disorder in children:*
    a. Carey, B. (2007). Bipolar illness soars as a diagnosis for the young. *New York Times*, September 4, 2007.
    b. Healy, D. (April 11, 2006). The latest mania: Selling bipolar disorder. *PLOS Medicine*, 3: DOI: 10.1371/journal.pmed.0030185.
    c. Gellene, D. (2007). Science and medicine: Bipolar disorder in youths may be over-diagnosed. *Los Angeles Times*, September 4, 2007.
    d. Wolfe, S. (2013). Use of atypical antipsychotics in children at all-time high. *Health Letter, Public Citizen*, 29, April 2013.
20. *Biederman:*
    a. Harris, G. and Carey, B. (2008). Psychiatric researchers fail to reveal full drug pay. *New York Times*, June 8, 2008.
    b. Editorial. (2008). Expert or shill? *New York Times*, November 30, 2008.
21. *Angel on Biederman:*
    Angel, M. (2009). Drug companies & doctors: A story of corruption. *New York Review of Books*, January 15, 2009.
22. *Nemeroff:*
    Harris, G. (2008). Top psychiatrist didn't report drug maker's pay. *New York Times*, October 3, 2308.
23. *Goodwin:*
    Harris, G. (2008). Drug-makers paid radio host $1.3 million for lectures. *New York Times*, November 22, 2008.
24. *American Psychiatric Association:*
    a. Kaiser Health News. (2009). Senator Grassley Asks Psychiatry Association to Provide Information on Drug Industry Contributions. June 11, 2009.
    b. Carey, B. and Harris, G. (2008). Psychiatric group faces scrutiny over drug industry ties. *New York Times*, July 12, 2008.
    c. Couchon, D. (2000). FDA advisers tied to industry. *USA Today*, September 25, 2000. http://www.commondreams.org/headlines/092500-01, htm.
    d. Vedantam, S. (2002). Industry role in medical meeting decried: Symposium sponsored by pharmaceutical companies trouble more psychiatrists. *Washington Post*, A10.
    e. Pfeiffer, M. (June 10, 2001). Drug marketing is widespread. *Poughkeepsie Journal*, p. A2. https://www.cchrint.org/issues/the-corrupt-alliance-of-the-psychiatric-pharmaceutical-industry.

25. *NIMH:*
    a. Markowitz, J. (2016). There's such a thing as too much neuroscience. *New York Times*, October 15, 2016, A21.
    b. Wakefield quotation: Weir, K. (June 2012). The roots of mental illness: How much of mental illness can the biology of the brain explain? *Science Watch, American Psychological Association*, 43.
    c. Carey, B. (2021). While people languish, science plays the long game. *New York Times*, April 6, 2021, D8.
26. *Insel on $20 billion*:
    Rogers, A. (2017). Star neuroscientist Tom Insel leaves the Google-Spawned Verily for . . . a startup? Wired. May 11, 2017. https://www.wired.com

Chapter 9: Big Pharma and the FDA

1. Poor *FDA Oversight* :
    a. Critser, D. (2005). *Generation Rx*. New York: Houghton Mifflin Company.
    b. Petersen, M. (2008). *Our Daily Meds*. New York: Farrar, Strauss and Giroux.
    c. Bass, A. (2008). *Side Effects*. New York: Workman Publishing.
    d. Editorial. (2020). The FDA is in trouble: How to fix it. January 11, 2020.
2. *False Claims Act:*
    a. Wolfe, S. (2010). Pharmaceutical industry is biggest defrauder of the Federal Government under the False Claims Act, New Public Citizen Study Finds. *Public Citizen*, December 21, 2010. http://www.the pharmaletter.com/file/100780/public-citizen.
    b. Wikipedia, List of off-label promotion pharmaceutical settlements.
3. *Forest Pharmaceuticals:*
    Justice News. (2010). Drug maker forest pleads guilty; to pay more than $313 million to resolve criminal charges and false claims act allegations. *U. S. Department of Justice*, September 15, 2010.
4. *Vioxx:*
    Feeley, J. and Voreacos, D. (2011). Merck to pay $950 million, plead guilty in U. S. Vioxx Probe. *Bloomberg*, November 23, 2011.

5. *Paxil:*
   Carey, B. (2015). Antidepressant Paxil is unsafe for teen agers, new analysis says. *New York Times*, September 16, 2015.
6. *Avandia*:
   Harris, G. (2010). Research ties diabetes drug to heart woes. *New York Times*, February 19, 2010.
7. *Kristof on Risperdal:*
   Kristof, N. (2015). When crime pays: J & J's Drug Risperdal. *New York Times*, September 17.
8. *Xarelto:*
   a. Thomas, K. (2016). Document claims drug makers deceived a top medical journal. *New York Times*, March 2, 2016, B1.
   b. Rosenberg, Martha. (2011). Fourteen years of deceptive television drug advertising. *Public Citizen Health Letter*, 27, May 2011.
9. *CEO compensation:*
   Sabadish, N. and Mishel, L. (2013). CEO pay in 2012 was extraordinarily high relative to typical workers and other high earners. *Economic Policy Institute*, June 26, 2013.
10. *Smith:*
    a. Smith, R. (2005). Medical journals are an extension of the marketing arm of pharmaceutical companies. Health Letter: Public Citizen Research Group, 21, July 2005.
    b. Smith, R. (2005). Curbing the influence of the drug industry: A British view. *PLOS Medicine*, August 2, 2005.
11. *Hunter:*
    Hunter, L. (2013). *Crony Capitalism in America: 2008–2012*. AC2 Books.
12. *Ghost writing:*
    Goldacre, B. (2012). *Bad Pharma: How Drug Companies Mislead Doctors and Harm Patients*. New York: Faber and Faber (pp. 287, 298).
13. *Celexa Ghostwriting:*
    Carome, M. (2017). *Researchers Fight to Undo a Depression Drug's Dark History. Worst Pills, Best Pills News*, May 2017.
14. *New York Times Editorial*:
    Editorial. (2020). Politicizing Science will cost lives. *New York Times*, August 25, 2020, A22.
15. *Journal of Clinical Epidemiology*:
    Ebrahim, S. (2015). Meta-analyses with industry involvement are massively published and report no caveats for antidepressants. *Journal of Clinical Epidemiology*, 155–163. DOI: 10.1016/j.clinepi.2015.08.021

16. *Wolfe on systematic* bias:
    a. Wolfe, S. (2003). Sweetening the pill, health letter *Public Citizen Health Research Group*, 19, September 2003.
    b. Editorial. (1996). Drug companies and information about drugs: recommendations for doctors. *Journal of Internal Medicine*, 11, 642–644.
    c. Lorie, P., Almeida, C. and Stine, N. (2006). Financial conflict of interest disclosure and voting patterns at Food and Drug Advisory Committee meetings. *Journal of the American Medical Association*, 295, 1921–1928.
17. *Relman:*
    Wolfe, S. (2013). Sweetening the pill. *Public Citizen Research Group*, 19, September 2003.
18. *Angel:*
    a. Angel, M. (2004). The truth about the drug companies. *The New York Review of Books*, July 15, 2004, 51.
    b. Stiglitz, J. Scrooge and property rights. *British Medical Journal*, 333, 1279–1280.
19. *Marciniak:*
    Marciniak, T. (December 5, 2013). FDA official: "Clinical trial system is broken." *British Medical Journal*. https://doi.org/10.1136/bmj.f6980.
20. *Gotzsche on psychiatry*:
    Gotzsche, P. (2013). *Deadly Medicines and Organized Crime: How Big Pharma Has Corrupted Healthcare*. London: Radcliffe Publishing Ltd.
21. *New York/GlaxoSmithKline:*
    Thomas, K. and Schmidt, M. (2012). Glaxo agrees to pay $3 billion in fraud settlement. *New York Times*, July 31, 2012, A1.
22. *Peterson*:
    Peterson, M. (2008). *Our Daily Meds*. New York: Farrar, Strauss and Giroux.
23. *FDA survey*:
    Wolfe, S. (1998). FDA medical officers report lower standards permit dangerous drug approvals. *Public Citizen Health Research Group*, December 2, 1998.
24. *Safra Center quotation:*
    a. Light, D. (2015). Serious risks and few new benefits from FDA-approved drugs. *Health Affairs Blog, Health Policy Lab*, July 6, 2015.
    b. Vedantam, S. (2006). IN antipsychotics newer isn't better: Drug find shocks researchers. *Washington Post*, October 3, 2006, A1.

25. *Reilly:*
Al Faruque, F. (2014). Defending big pharma. *The Hill*, July 22, 2014.
26. *Stiglitz quotation:*
Stiglitz, J. (2015). Don't trade away our health. *New York Times*, January 31, 2015, A 19.
27. *Hamburg, RICCO:*
Sharav, V. (2016). Corrupt practices, FDA tainted approval, lawsuits. *Alliance for Human Research Practices*, April 23, 2016.
28. *Partnership of FDA and Drug Industry*:
    a. Carome, M. (2018). New report on big pharma settlements highlights need for tougher enforcement. *Worst Pills, Best Pills News*, July 2018, 24.
    b. Carome, M. (2018). Agency insiders recount FDA's Cozy relationship with industry. *Worst Pills, Best Pills News*, 24, September 2018.
    c. Editorial (2020). Here's how to fix the troubled FDA. *New York Times*, January 12, 2020. Sunday Review, 8.
29. *Harris on FDA follow up:*
Harris, G. (2006). New drugs hit the market, but promised trials go undone. *New York Times*, March 4, 2006, A8.
30. *CDC quotation:*
Kane, J. (2013). Prescription drug abuse: Top 10 things CDC says you should know. *PBS Newshour*, April 30, 2013.
31. *FDA guidance:*
    a. Carome, M. (2014). FDA "partnerships" incompatible with agency's regulatory role. *Worst Pills, Best Pills News*, June 2014, 20.
    b. Carome, M. (2015). Selling more drugs by misrepresenting their safety. *Worst Pills, Best Pills News*, September 2015, 21.
    c. Editorial (2020). The FDA is in trouble. Here's how to fix it. *New York Times*, January 11, 2020.
32. *Mathis homepage:*
    a. Carome, M. (2014). The FDA should not be promoting products it regulates. *Worst Pills, Best Pills News*, November 2014, 20.
    b. Vedantam, S. (2004). FDA withholding data on antidepressants. *Washington Post*, September 9, 2004.
33. *Gotzsche on Cymbalta:*
Gotzsche, P. (2013). *Deadly Medicines and Organized Crime: How Big Pharma Has Corrupted Healthcare* (p. 206). London: Radcliffe Publishing Ltd.

34. *Kessler:*
Glenmullen, J. (2000). *Prozac Backlash: Overcoming the Dangers of Prozac, Zoloft, Paxil, and Other Antidepressants with Safe, Effective, Alternatives* (p. 21). New York: Simon & Schuster.
35. *FDA and antidepressants:*
   a. Vedantam, S. (2004). FDA Urged withholding data on antidepressants. *Washington Post*, September 10, 2004, A02.
   b. Jacobson, R. (2015). Many antidepressant studies found tainted by pharma company influence. *Scientific American*, October 21, 2015.
36. *Lobbying congress:*
   a. Almashat, S. (2014). Pharmaceutical lobby reigns supreme in Washington. *Public Citizen Health Letter*, June 2014.
   b. Wolfe, S. (2003). Sweetening the pill. *Public Citizen Research Group*, September 2003, 119.
   c. Hancock, J. (2017). Big pharma can't lose. *New York Times*, September 24, 2017.

Chapter 10: Behavioral Science

1. *Menand quotation:*
   a. Menand, L. (2016). Show them the money. *The New Yorker*, May 16, 2016, 90.
   b. Menand, L. (2010). Can psychiatry be a science? *New Yorker*, March 2010.
2. *Dreifus in the New York Times:*
Dreifus, C. (2018). Rewiring her brain to win at poker. *New York Times*, Science Times, August 14, 2018, D5.
3. *Poole quotation:*
Poole, S. (2012). Your brain on pseudoscience: The rise of popular neurobollocks. *New Statesman*, September 6.
4. *Healy quotation:*
   a. Healy, D. (2006). *Let Them Eat Prozac: The Unhealthy Relationship between the Pharmaceutical Industry and Depression*. New York: New York University Press.
   b. Cooper, A. (2017). What is "brain hacking?" *60 Minutes*, April 9, 2017.

5. *Gladwell's book*:
Gladwell, M. (2008). *Outliers: The Story of Success*. New York: Little, Brown, and Company.
6. *Advertising and behavior principles:*
   a. Hawkins, D., Best, R. and Coney, K. (1998). *Consumer Behavior.* Boston, MA: McGraw-Hill.
   b. Miller, N. and Dollard, J. (1941). *Social Learning and Imitation*. New Haven, CT: Yale University Press.
7. *Brooks quotations:*
Brooks, D. (2017). How evil is tech?. *New York Times*, November 21, 2017, A25.
8. *Smart phones and behavior principles:*
   a. Fogg, B. J. (2003). *Persuasive Technology: Using Computers to Change What We Think and Do*. Boston, MA: Morgan Kaufman.
   b. Eyal, N. (2014). *Hooked: How to Build Habit-Forming Products.* London: Portfolio.
   c. Wu, T. (2020). Bigger brother. *New York Review of Books*, April 9, 2020, 18–19.
9. *Uber:*
   a. Scheiber, N. (2017). Uber pushes drivers' buttons. *New York Times*, April 3, 2017, 1.
   b. Madigan, J. (2015). *Getting Games: The Psychology of Video Games and Their Impact on People Who Play Them*. Langham, MD: Rowan & Littlefield.
   c. Hopson, J. Gamasutra: The art and business of making games. *Behavioral Game Design*, April 2001.
10. *Jaron Lanier*:
Lanier, J. (2018). *Ten Arguments for Deleting Your Social Media Accounts Right Now*. New York: Henry Holt & Co.
11. *New York Times on behavioral treatment of drug addiction*:
   a. Goodnough, A. (2020). The great read. *New York Times*, October 27, 2020.
   b. De Crescenzo, F., Ciabbittini, M., D'Alo, G., de Giorgi, R., Del Giovane, C., Cascar, C., Janiri, L., Clar, N., Ostacher, J. and Cipriani, A. (2008). Comparative efficacy and acceptability of psychosocial interventions for individuals with cocaine and amphetamine addiction: A systematic review and network meta-analysis. *PLOS Medicine*, December 26, 2018. https:/doi.org/10.1371/journal.pmed.1002715, December 26, 2018.

12. *Charles Darwin:*
    Darwin, C. (1859). *On the Origin of Species.* London: John Murray, Albemarle Street.
13. *Gregor Mendel:*
    Miko, I. (2008). Gregor Mendel's principles of inheritance form the cornerstone of modern genetics. *Nature Education*, 1(1), 134.
14. *Richard Dawkins:*
    Dawkins, R. (1976). *The Selfish Gene* (p. 52). London: Oxford University Press.
15. *John Colapinto*:
    Colapinto, J. (2021). *This Is the Voice.* New York: Simon & Schuster.
16. *Wrangham:*
    Wrangham, P. (2009). *Catching Fire: How Cooking Made Us Human.* New York: Basic Books.
17. *Hal Whitehead*:
    Angier, N. (2020). The other social influencers of the animal kingdom. *Science Times, New York Times*, May 11, 2021, D8.
18. *Pavlov:*
    Pavlov, I. (1897/1902). *The Work of the Digestive Glands.* London: Griffin.
19. *Thorndike:*
    Thorndike, E. (1898). Animal intelligence: An experimental study of the association processes in animals. *Psychology Monographs: General and Applied*, 2(4), i–109.
20. *Skinner:*
    Skinner, B. F. (1938). *The Behavior of Organisms.* New York: Appleton Century Crofts.
21. *Bandura:*
    Bandura, A. (1986). *Social Foundations of Thought and Action: A Social Cognitive Theory.* New Jersey: Prentice-Hall, Inc.
22. *Waldman quotation:*
    Waldman, K. (2015). Book review of "speak" by Louisa Hall. *New York Times*, August 30, 2015, 18.
23. *W. B. Cannon:*
    Cannon, W. B. (1929). *Bodily Changes in Pain, Hunger, Fear, and Rage.* New York: Appleton.
24. *Barlow:*
    a. Barlow, D. (1988). *Anxiety and Its Disorders: The Nature and Treatment of Anxiety and Panic.* New York: Guilford.

b. Barlow, D. and Durand, V. (1996). Fear, panic, anxiety, and disorders of emotion. In D. Hope (Ed.), *Perspectives in Anxiety, Panic, and Fear*, 43rd Edition, Nebraska Symposium on Motivation, pp. 251–328. Lincoln: University of Nebraska Press.

Chapter 11: Mental Disorder as Learned Behavior

1. *Torture:*
   a. Hoffman, D. (2015). Report to the Special Committee of the Board of Directors of the *American Psychological Association:* Independent Review Relating to APA Ethics Guidelines, National Security Interrogators, and Torture, July 2, 2015.
   b. Shaw, T., The Psychologists Take Over. (2016). *New York Review of Books*, February 25, 2016, 38–41.
   c. Haidt, J., Pinker, S. and Shaw, T. (2016). Moral psychology: An exchange. *New York Review of Books*, April 7, 2016, 82–85.
2. *Principles of learning:*
   a. Ferster, C. and Perrott, M (1968). *Principles of Behavior.* New York: Appleton-Century Crofts. (Much of this chapter is based on this book, which is a textbook for college students on behavior principles. I volunteered to be the interviewee of Dr. Ferster's final edit of the book).
   b. Krasner, L. and Ullman, L. (Eds.). (1966). *Research in Behavior Modification*. New York: Holt, Rinehart, and Winston.
   c. Eysenck, H. and Rachman, S. (1965). *The Causes and Cures of Neurosis.* San Diego: Robert R. Knapp.
   d. Mahoney, M. (1974). *Cognition and Behavior Modification.* Cambridge, MA: Ballinger.
   e. Ullman, L. and Krasner, L. Chapter Four in *Principles of Learning: A Psychological Approach to Abnormal Behavior.* Englewood Cliffs, NJ: Prentice-Hall (pp. 50–68).
   f. Staats, A. and Staats, C. (1963). *Complex Human Behavior: A Systematic Extension of Learning Principles.* New York: Holt, Rinehart, and Winston.
3. *We are animals*:
   a. De Waal, F. (2016). What i learned tickling apes. *New York Times, Sunday Review*, April 10, 2016.

b. Safina, C. (2015). *Beyond Words: What Animals Think and Feel*. New York: Henry Holt.

4. *Plasticity of the brain:*
   a. Diamond, M., Krech, D. and Rosenzweig, M. (1964). The effects of an enriched environment on the history of the rat cerebral cortex. *Journal of Comparative Neurology*, 123, 111–120.
   b. Bennett, E., Diamond, M., Krech, D. and Rosenzweig, M. (1964). Chemical and anatomical plasticity of the brain. *Science*, 146, 616–619.
   c. Lameira, A., FHardus, M., Bartlett, A., Shumaker, R., Wich, S. and Menken, S. (January 8, 2015). Speech-like rhythm in a voiced and voiceless orangutan call. *PLOS One*. http://dx.doi.org/10.1371/journal.pone.0116136.
5. *Pavlov:*
   Pavlov, I. (1897/1902). *The work of the digestive glands*. London: Griffin.
6. *Punishment:*
   Gershoff, E. (2002). Corporal punishment by parents and associated child behaviors and experiences. *Psychological Bulletin*, 128, 539–579.
7. *Phobias are learned:*
   a. Craske, M. and Barlow, D. (2000). *Mastery of Your Anxiety and Panic*. New York: Graywind Publications.
   b. Wolpe, J. (1958). *Psychotherapy by Reciprocal Inhibition*. Stanford, CA: Stanford University Press.
8. *Classically conditioned bodily responses:*
   Dworkin, B. (1993). *Learning and Physiological Regulation*. Chicago, IL: University of Chicago Press.
9. *Experiments by Miller:*
   Miller, N. (1948). Studies of fear as an acquirable drive: I. Fear as motivation and fear-reduction as reinforcement in the learning of new responses. *Journal of Experimental Psychology*, 38, 89–101.
10. *Research Basis for Behavior Therapy:*
    a. Staats, A. and Staats, C. (1963). *Complex Human Behavior*. New York: Holt, Rinehart, and Winston.
    b. Spielberger, C. (Ed.). (1966). *Anxiety and Behavior*. New York: Academic Press.
    c. Bandura, A. (1969). *Principles of Behavior Modification*. New York: Holt, Rinehart, and Winston.

d. Franks, C. (Ed.) (1969). *Behavior Therapy: Appraisal and Status.* New York: McGraw-Hill.
e. Rimm, D. and Masters, J. (1974). *Behavior Therapy: Techniques and Empirical Findings.* New York: Academic Press.

11. *Wolpe and phobias:*
Wolpe, J. (1979). *Psychotherapy by Reciprocal Inhibition.* Stanford, CA: Stanford University Press.
12. *Obsessive-compulsive disorder:*
Riggs, D. and Foa, E. (1993). Obsessive compulsive disorder. In D. H. Barlow (Ed.), *Clinical Handbook of Psychological Disorders: A Step-By-Step Treatment Manual* (pp. 189–239). New York: Guilford Press.
13. *Generalized Anxiety disorder*:
Newman, M., Llera, S., Erickson, T., Przeworski, A. and Castonguay, L. (2013). Worry and generalized anxiety disorder: A review and theoretical evidence of nature, etiology, mechanisms, and treatment. *Annual Review of Clinical Psychology*, 9, 275–297.
14. *Ayllon and Haughton experiment*:
Ayllon, T. and Haughton, F. (1962). Control of the behavior of schizophrenic patients by food. *Journal of the Experimental Analysis of Behavior*, 5, 343–352.
15. *Sheehan quotation on phantom pain:*
Karidis, A. (2015). Search to ease amputees' "phantom pain" continues. *Health and Science, Washington Post*, November 10, 2015, E2.

Chapter 12: Behavior Therapy for Depression

1. *Skinner:*
a. Skinner, B. F. (1948). *Walden Two.* Indianapolis: Hackett Publishing Company.
b. Ferster, C. and Skinner, B. (1957). *Schedules of Reinforcement.* New York: Appleton-Century-Crofts.
2. *Ferster quotation:*
Ferster, C. (1965). Classification of behavioral pathology. In L. Krasner and L. Ullman (Eds.), *Research in Behavior Modification.* New York: Holt, Rinehart, and Winston.
3. *Mowrer and Kanfer:*
a. Karoly, P. (2003). Kanfer, F. (1925–2002). *American Psychologist*, 58, 1095.

   b. Mowrer, O. (1960). *Learning Theory and Behavior.* New York: John Wiley & Sons.

4. *Mahoney quotation:*
   Mahoney, M. (1974). Cognition and behavior modification. Cambridge, MA: Balinger.

5. *Mischell's marshmallow test*:
   Konnikova, M. (2014). The struggle of a psychologist studying self-control. *The New Yorker*, October 9, 2014.

6. *Other disorders treated behaviorally:*
   a. Foa, E. (1978). Continuous imaginal exposure to feared disasters on obsessive-compulsive checkers. *Behavior Research and Therapy*, 9, 821–829.
   b. Barlow, D. (Ed). (2014). *Clinical Handbook of Psychological Disorders.* New York: Guilford Press.
   c. Linehan, M. (1993). *Cognitive-Behavioral Treatment of Borderline Personality Disorder.* New York: Guilford Press.
   d. Kar, N. (April 4, 2011). Cognitive behavioral therapy for the treatment of post-traumatic stress disorder: A review. *Neuropsychiatric Disease and Treatment*, 7.
   e. Benight, C. and Bandura, A. (2004). Social cognitive therapy of post-traumatic recovery: The role of perceived self-efficacy. *Behavior Research and Therapy*, 42, 1129–1148.

7. *Ellis:*
   Ellis, A. (1962). *Reason and Emotion in Psychotherapy.* New York: Lyle Stuart.

8. *Beck:*
   a. Beck, A. (1967). *Depression: Causes and Treatment.* Philadelphia: University of Pennsylvania Press.
   b. Beck, A. (1976). *Cognitive Therapy and the Emotional Disorders.* New York: International University Press.
   c. Beck, A., Rush, J., Shaw, B. and Emery, G. (1979). *Cognitive Therapy of Depression: A treatment Manual.* New York: Guilford Press.

9. *Ferster on behavioral analysis*:
   Ferster, C. (1966). Classification of behavioral pathology. In L. Krasner and L. Ullman (Eds.), *Research in Behavior Modification: New Developments and Implications.* New York: Holt, Rinehart, and Winston.

10. *Lewinshohn:*
    a. Lewinsohn, P. (1974). A behavioral approach to depression. In R. Friedman and M. Katz (Eds.), *The Psychology of Depression:*

Contemporary Theory and Research. New York: John Wiley (pp. 157–178).

b. Lewinsohn, P., Mischel, W., Chaplin, W. and Barton, R. (1980). Social competence and depression: The role of illusory self-perceptions. *Journal of Abnormal Psychology*, 89, 202–213.

11. *Martell, Addis, and Jacobson:*
    a. Martell, C., Addis, M. and Jacobson, N. (2001). *Depression in Context: Strategies for Guided Action*. New York: W. W. Norton & Company.
    b. Hopko, D., Lejussc, C., Ruggiero, K. and Eifert, G. (2003). Contemporary behavioral activation treatments for depression: Procedures, principles, and progress. *Clinical Psychology Review*, 23(5), 699–717; 23(5), 699–717. DOI: 10.1016150272-7358(03)00070-9.
12. *Leventhal and Martell:*
    Leventhal, A. and Martell, C. (2006). *The Myth of Depression as Disease: Limitations and Alternatives to Drug Treatment*. Westport, CT: Praeger.
13. *Leventhal quotation:*
    Leventhal, A. (2008). Sadness, depression, and avoidance behavior. *Behavior Modification*, 32, 759–779.
14. *Corroboration of Leventhal treatment:*
    Allen, M. (2018). A computer-based avatar task designed to assess behavioral inhibition extends to behavioral avoidance but not cognitive avoidance. *Peer J*. DOI: 10.7717/peerj.5330
15. *Khan in PLOS, 2012:*
    Khan, A., Faucett, J., Lichtenberg, P., Kirsch, I. and Brown, W. (2012). A systematic review of comparative efficacy of treatments and controls for depression. *PLOS One*. DOI: 10.1371/journal.pone. 0041778. July 30, 2012.
16. *Outcome*:
    This section, in the main, is a summary of references on the subject provided by: Kirsch, I. (2011). *The Emperor's New Drugs: Exploding the Antidepressant Myth*. New York: Basic Books.
17. *Comparative outcome research:*
    a. Rush, A. (1977). Comparative efficacy of cognitive therapy and pharmacotherapy in the treatment of depressed outpatients. *Cognitive Therapy and Research*, 1, 17–37.

b. Antonuccio, D., Danton, W. and DeNelsky, G. (1995). Psychotherapy versus medication for depression: Challenging the conventional wisdom with data. *Professional Psychology*, 26, 574–585.
c. Persons, J. (1996). The role of psychotherapy in the treatment of depression. *Archives of General Psychiatry*, 53, 283–290.
d. Hollon, S., DeRubeis, R., Evans, M., Wiemer, M., Garvey, M., Grove, W. and Tuason, V. (1992). Cognitive therapy and pharmacotherapy for depression: Singly and in combination. *Archives of General Psychiatry*, 49, 774–781.
e. Hollon, S., Thase, M. and Markowitz, J. (2005). Treating depression: Pills or talk. *Mind: Scientific American*, 14, 35–39.
f. De Rubeis, R. (2005). Cognitive therapy vs medications in the treatment of moderate to severe depression. *Archives of General Psychiatry*, 62, 409–416.
g. Kirsch, I. (2011). *The Emperor's New Drugs: Exploding the Antidepressant Myth.* New York: Basic Books.
h. Vittengl, J. and Jarrett, R. (August 1, 2015). Cognitive therapy to prevent depressive relapse in adults. *Current Opinion in Psychology*, 4, 26–31.
i. Barlow, D., Bullis, J., Comer, J. and Ametaj, A. (2013). Evidence-based psychological treatments: An update and a way forward. *Annual Review of Clinical Psychology*, 42, 191–237.
j. Biesheuvel-Leliefeld, K., Kok, G., Bockting, C., Cuijpers, P., Hollon, S., Marwijk, H. and jm it. F. (2015). Effectiveness of psychological interventions in preventing recurrence of depressive disorder: Meta-analysis and meta-regression. *Journal of Affective Disorders*, 174, 400–410.
k. Lewis, G. , Ades, A., Amos, R., Araya, R, and Brabyn, S. (2019). Antidepressants barely relieve symptoms of depression. *Lancet Psychiatry*, 654.

18. *Relapse:*
   a. Simons, A., Murphy, G., Levine, J. and Wetzel, R. (1986). Cognitive therapy and pharmacotherapy for depression. *Archives of General Psychiatry*, 43, 43–48.
   b. Evans, M., Hollon, S., DeRubeis, R., Piasecki, J., Grove, W., Garvey, M. and Tuason, V. Differential relapse following cognitive therapy and pharmacotherapy for depression. *Archives of General Psychiatry*, 49, 802–808.

c. Hollon, S., DeRubeis, R. and Shelton, R. (2005). Prevention of relapse following cognitive therapy vs. medications in moderate to severe depression. *Archives of General Psychiatry*, 62, 417–422.
d. Bochting, C., Schene, A., Spinhoven, P. and Kamphuis, J. (2005). The DELTA Study Group. Preventing relapse/recurrence in recurrent depression with cognitive therapy: A randomized controlled trial. *Journal of Consulting and Clinical Psychology*, 73, 647–657.
e. Fava, G., Ruini, C., Rafanelli, C., Finos, L., Conti, S. and Grandi, S. (2004). Six year outcome of cognitive therapy for prevention of recurrent depression. *American Journal of Psychiatry*, 161, 1872–1876.
f. NICE, Depression Management of Depression in Primary and Secondary Care. Clinical Practice Guideline No. 23, *National Institute for Clinical Excellence*: www.nice.org.uk/page.aspx?o=235213.
g. Goetzsche, P. (2020). Long-term use of benzodiazepines, stimulants and lithium is not evidence-based. *Clinical Neuropsychiatry*, 17(5), 281–283.

19. *Behavior therapy, antidepressants, and suicide:*
a. McLean, P. and Hakstian, A. (1979). Clinical depression: Comparative efficacy of outpatient treatments. *Journal of Consulting and Clinical Psychology*, 47, 818–836.
b. McLean, P. and Hakstian, A. (1990). Relative endurance of unipolar treatment effects: longitudinal follow-up. *Journal of Consulting and Clinical Psychology*, 58, 482–488.
c. Khan, A., Warner, H. and Brown, W. (2000). Symptom reduction and suicide risk in patients treated with placebo in antidepressant clinical trials. *Archives of General Psychiatry*, 57, 311–317.
d. Brown, G., Ten Have, T. and Henriques, G. (2005). Cognitive therapy for the prevention of suicide attempts. *Journal of the American Medical Association*, 294, 563–570.
e. Lippincott, W. (2015). No longer wanting to die. *New York Times, Sunday Review*, May 17, 2015, 2.
f. Carey, B. (2005). Talk therapy succeeds in reducing suicide risk. *New York Times*, April 9, 2006, D7.

20. *Exercise as a treatment for depression:*
a. Helegadottir, B., Forsell, Y., Hallgren, M., Moller, J. and Ekblom, O. (August 2017). Long-term effects of exercise at different intensity levels on depression. *Preventive Medicine*, 105. DOI: 10.1016/j.ypmed.2017.08.008.

b. Reynolds, G. (2015). A prescription for youth. *New York Times*, January 13, 2005, D4.

21. *Discontinuation studies of relapse*:
    a. Hengartner, M. (2020). How effective are antidepressants for depression over the long term? A critical review of relapse prevention trials and the issue of withdrawal confounding. *Sage Perspectives*. https://doi.org/10.1177/2045125320921694. May 8, 2020.
    b. Moncrieff, J. (2006). Why is it so difficult to stop psychiatric drug treatment? It may be nothing to do with the original problem. *Med Hypotheses*, 67, 517–523.
22. *Behavior therapy found superior in treatment of anxiety disorders:*
    a. Hollon, S., Stewart, M. and Strunk, D. (2006). Enduring effects for cognitive behavior therapy in the treatment of depression and anxiety. *Annual Review of Psychology*, 2006, 285–315.
    b. Zhang, Z., Zhang, L., Zhang, G., Jin, J., and Zheng, Z. (2018). The effect of CBT and its modifications for relapse prevention in major depressive disorder: A systematic review and meta-analysis. *BMC Psychiatry*, 18, 50.
    c. Rush, A., Trivedi, M., and Carmody, T. (2004). One-year clinical outcomes of depressed public sector outpatients: A benchmark for subsequent studies. *Biological Psychiatry*, 56, 46–53.
23. *NICE 2019 comparative outcome study*:
    McPherson, S. and Hengartner, M. (2019). Long-term outcomes of trials in the National Institute for Health Care Excellence depression guideline. *British Journal of Psychiatry Open*, 5. OI:10.1192/bjo.2019.65.
24. *Relapse greater with antidepressant use*:
    Amsterdam, J. and Kim, T. (July 2019). Prior antidepressant treatment trials may predict a greater risk of depressive relapse during antidepressant maintenance therapy. *Journal of Clinical Psychopharmacology*, 39, 344–350.
25. *Hospitalization risk with antidepressants*:
    Hengartner, M. (February 22, 2019). Antidepressant use during acute inpatient care is associated with an increased risk of psychiatric rehospitalization over a 12-month follow-up after discharge. *Frontiers in Psychiatry*. DOI.org/10.3389/fpsyt.2019.00079
26. *Another 2019 outcome study of antidepressants (Zoloft)*:
    Lewis, G., Duffy, L., Ades, A., Amos, R., Araya, R., Brabyn, S., Button, K., Churchill, R., Derrick, C., Dourick, C., Gilbody, S., Fawsitt, C.,

Hollingworth, W., Jones, V., Kendrick, T., Kessler, D., Kourali, D., Khan, N., Lanham, P., Pervin, J., Peters, T., Riozzie, D., Salaminios, G., Thomas, L., Welton, N., Wiles, N., Woodhouse, R. and Lewis, G. (2019). The clinical effectiveness of sertraline in primary care and the role of depression severity and duration (PARMA): A pragmatic, double-blind, placebo controlled randomized trial. *Lancet-Psychiatry*, DOI: https://doi.org/10.1016/S2215-0366(19)30366-9. September 19, 2019.

27. *FDA and Healy*:
    a. Khan, A., Warner, H., and Brown, W. (2000). Symptom reduction and suicide risk in patients treated with placebo in antidepressant chemical trials. *Archives of General Psychiatry*, 57, 311–317.
    b. Healy, D. (2004). *Let Them Eat Prozac: The Unhealthy Relationship between the Pharmaceutical Industry and Depression.* New York: New York University Press.
    c. Teicher, M., Glod, C. and Cole, J. (1990). Emergence of intense suicidal preoccupation during fluoxetine treatment. *American Journal of Psychiatry*, 47, 207–210.
    d. Glenmullen, J. (2000). *Prozac Backlash: Overcoming the Dangers of Prozac, Zoloft, Paxil, and Other Antidepressants with Safe, Effective, Alternatives.* New York: Simon and Schuster.
28. *Other outcome studies showing superiority of behavior therapy vs. psychiatric drugs:*
    a. (phobias): Thng, C. (2020). Recent developments in the intervention of specific phobia among adults: A rapid review. *F1000 Research.* DOI: 10.12.688/1000research.20082.1
    b. (phobias) Gujar, K., Van Wikj, A., Kumar, R. and de Jungh, A. (2018). Efficacy of virtual reality exposure therapy for the treatment of dental phobia in adults: A randomized controlled study. *Journal of Anxiety Disorders*, 62, 100–108.
    c. (phobias) Wolitzky-Taylor, K., Horowitz, and Powers, M. (2008). Psychological approaches in the treatment of specific phobias: a meta-analysis. *Clinical Psychology Revies*, 6, 1021–1037.
    d. (OCD) Hezel, D. and Simpson, H. (2019). Exposure and response prevention for obsessive-compulsive disorder: A review and new directions. *Indian Journal of Psychiatry.*
    e. DOI: 10.4 103/psychiatry.IndianJPsychiatry 516.18.
    f. (OCD) Jones, M., Wooton, B. and Vaccaro, L. (2012). The efficacy and response prevention for geriatric obsessive-compulsive disorder: A

clinical case illustration. *Case Report: Open Access*. Article ID 394603. https://doi.org/10.1155/2012/394603.

g. (OCD) Abramowitz, J. (2006). The psychological treatment of obsessive-compulsive disorder. *Canadian Journal of Psychiatry*, 7, 407–416.

h. (social anxiety) Heimberg, R. and Leibowitz, M. (1998). Cognitive behavioral group therapy versus phenylzene therapy. *Archives of General Psychiatry*, 55, 1133–1141.

i. (social anxiety) May-Wilson, E., Dias, S., Mavaranazelli, I., Kew, K., Clark, D. and Ades, A. (2014). Psychological and pharmacological interventions for social anxiety disorder in adults: A systematic review and network meta-analysis. *The Lancet Psychiatry*, 5, 368–376.

j. (substance abuse) DeCreszenzo, F., Ciabattini, M., D'Alo, G., de Giorgi, R., Del Giovane, M., P'Alo, G., Giorgi, R., Giovane, C., Cassar, C., Janiri, L., Clark, N., Ostacher, M. and Cipriani, A. (2018). Comparative efficacy and acceptability of psychosocial interventions for individuals with cocaine and amphetamine addictions: A systematic review and network meta-analysis. *PLOS Medicine*. https:/doi.org/10.1371/journal.pmed.1002715.

k. (borderline personality disorder) Linehan, M., Comtois, K., Murray, A., Brown, M., Gallop, R., Heard, H., Korslund, K., Tutek, D., Reynolds, S. and Lindenbolm, N. (2006). Two year randomized controlled trial and follow-up of dialectical behavior therapy by experts for suicidal behaviors and borderline personality disorder. *Archives of General Psychiatry*, 63, 757–766.

29. *United Nations WHO report:*
World Health Organization. (2014). *Summary Report*: *Promoting Mental Health: Concepts, Emerging Evidence, Practice.*

Index

B

C

D

E

F

G

H

I

J

K

L

M

R

S

T

U

V

W

Y

Z

Printed by
CPI books GmbH, Leck